N.ORR.N.Y.

BEAUTIES

AND

ACHIEVEMENTS

OF

THE BLIND.

BY WM. ARTMAN AND L. V. HALL

"E'en he who, sightless, wants his visual ray
May by his touch alone award the day."

AUBURN:
PUBLISHED FOR THE AUTHORS
1864.

WM. J. MOSES, STEREOTYPER AND PRINTER, AUBURN, N. Y.

To the American Public,

WHOSE PHILANTHROPIC HEART

EVER MOVES AT HUMANITY'S CALL

This Volume

IS RESPECTFULLY INSCRIBED

CONTENTS.

PAGE

Introduction, ... 9
Memoirs of Eminent blind Authors, ... 15
Homer, ... 17
Ossian, ... 29
Milton, ... 43
Rev. Richard Lucas, D. D., ... 52
T. Carolan, ... 63
Thomas Blacklock, D. D., ... 70
Huber, ... 84
Holman, ... 102
Wilson, ... 115
Beauties from a Blind Man's Offering, . . . 128
Mrs. S. H. DeKroyft, ... 142
Miss Frances Brown, ... 152
Miss Frances Jane Crosby, ... 168
Miss Cynthia Bullock, ... 180
Miss Daphne S. Giles, ... 192
Miss Alice Holmes, ... 207
Achievements of the Blind in the Learned Professions:
Section I. Progress in the Sciences, . . . 217
" II. Divines, Lawyers and Physicians, . 234
Achievements of the Blind in the Industrial Pursuits:
Section I. Mechanics, ... 249
" II. Miscellaneous Occupations, . . . 261
Achievements of the Blind in Poetry and Music:
Section I. Some explanation of the method by which the Born Blind gain a knowledge of the extension, magnitude and appearance of distant objects, . . 280
Section II. Blind Musicians, . . 299

PAGE

Autobiographical sketch of Lemuel Rockwell, . . 310
Collected Poems, by L. V. Hall, and other blind Authors:
Reminiscences of Uncle Toby, . . . 328
Teresa, or the Peasant Mother, . . . 337
View of the Mind released from Matter, . . 339
Thoughts on Creation, ... 340
Love's Chain, ... 342
Twilight Shadows, ... 343
A Fable, ... 344
A Fragment, ... 350
Reflections in Youth, ... 350
The Voyage of Life—A Song, . . . 351
Lines written on the first of April, . . 352
A Legend, ... 353
The Harper, ... 355
Autumn, ... 358
The Dying Sister, ... 359
The Forest Tree, ... 360
The Voice of the Sea, ... 362
Thoughts on Niagara, ... 363
The Voice of the Falling Leaves, . . . 365
Blacklock's Picture of himself, . . . 367
Epitaph on a favorite Lap-dog, . . . 369
The Young, ... 369
The God of the World, ... 371
The Eclipse, ... 373
Autumn, ... 374
Farewell to the Flowers, ... 375
The Last of the Jagellons, . . . 377
The Spectre of the Hearth, ... 380
The Lonely Mother, ... 381
The Friend of our Darker Days, . . . 383
We are growing Old, ... 384
Songs of our Land, ... 386

INTRODUCTION.

We will not weary the reader's patience with an elaborate preliminary, nor with apologies for offering the present work to the public. We have been induced to enter the arena of bookmakers, by a desire to disseminate a more correct and extended knowledge of blindness, and its effects upon mental and physical development, than the reading public has hitherto possessed. In this way we hope to remove some of the most formidable obstacles that hedge up the way to usefulness and independence, for all who are placed in this condition; a condition to which, by the vicissitudes of life, every person is exposed, and in whose dark and inauspicious night more than five hundred thousand of our race are at present enshrouded In almost every state of our Union, as well as in those of Europe, Charity, with her angelic hand, has raised up, within the present century, institutions dedicated to the sacred purpose of giving the light of science, and a knowledge of some of the useful arts, to those who behold not the beautiful earth and the serene sky. But sad experience has taught us, that until society in general better understands and appreciates the abilities of the blind, all the knowledge and skill we can acquire at these establishments, are not available as means of self-support, but tend only to awaken a keener sense of our privation and dependence. To illustrate: A young man graduates at one of our institutions for the blind, after receiving a thorough course of instruction in the theoretical and practical sciences. Elated with the hope of henceforth being able to earn for himself a respectable livelihood, as a teacher of music or of some other science, he hears of a vacant situation, and he makes the necessary application, but is informed that, as he cannot see, he cannot, of course, discharge the requisite duties. The next time an opportunity offers he determines to go in person, say a hundred miles, and in winter, too, to show that he is qualified. If a knowledge of music is required, he performs with proficiency; if of literature, philosophy or mathematics, he is ready and clear, and proves himself competent to the discharge of all the duties of the employment which he seeks. But the idea that one who can see is more serviceable than one who cannot, still erects an impenetrable wall between him and success. And thus the prejudice which his condition creates, opposes him on every side.

Without hesitation we say, that all the most painful disadvantages with which we have been obliged to contend under the absence of sight, have arisen entirely from ignorance, on the part of community, of our capabilities and resources. And why all this incredulity and want of confidence? Does not history introduce us to scores of individuals, who have triumphed over all the difficulties of blindness, and have become the most illustrious performers and instructors of their age? Reader peruse our work with candor, then answer.

It is not surprising that under such formidable opposition and depreciating influences, the blind themselves have, generally speaking, lost sight of the examples which their illustrious pre decessors set before them, and have adopted the degrading sen timent of—"can't do anything." Having lost all confidence in themselves, they beg without shame or compunction of con science, and advert only to their sightless eyes as an excuse for choosing this disgraceful method of protracting life, when we need not the sagacity of a philosopher to discover that, in ninety-nine hundredths of these cases, their dependence might be more justly attributed to a want of industry and an enterprising spirit, and perhaps a little kindly encouragement on the part of community. Notwithstanding the magnanimous efforts that have been made to elevate the social, moral and intellectual condition of this class, we find an appeal to sympathy painfully prevalent in almost all their transactions with society.

We need but turn to the Prefaces of most of the literary productions of the blind, to discover how much they have countenanced the ignorance and prejudice so prevalent among the public, for the sake of obtaining sympathy where they despaired of inspiring confidence, though eminently deserving. For example, we quote the following: "Any one familiar with the process of composing, and particularly of writing verses, will understand how great the advantages of being able to commit to paper, for preservation or correction, the passages interrupted from day to day, and how immense the labor of bear ing them, in fragments or in whole, in the memory, through all delays and interruptions. Such thoughts disarm our criticism, where seeming haste has marred the rhythm or measure of a line, or left some link of fancy loose."

Such remarks are as erroneous as they are depreciating. Had not Homer, Ossian, Milton, Blacklock, and scores of others, composed and sung their immortal verses while their vision was muffled, deep and dark as the drapery of night, we might be constrained to use metaphysical arguments to expose the inconsistency and vagueness of such methods to obtain favor, and ward off criticism. But they seem now uncalled for. Those who hew and carve poetry, as a toy-maker whittles out his articles, may find a supply of stationery a *sine qua non.* But a true poetic spirit or genius seems never to have depended upon such agents. We utterly abominate and detest every remark or insinuation that tends to hold up in the light of sympathy the literary efforts of a class, who have in every age won the fairest laurels, and enriched the commonwealth of letters. It has been our object in the present work, to point out to the blind, and the public in general, the achieving abilities of our order.

Reason as well as experience proclaims to us, in tones unmistakable, that until the efforts of the blind are weighed in the balance of merit, it is impossible for us to succeed in any undertaking. Sympathy, like the atmosphere, surrounds us on every side, but like this, it is too light to sustain life. To acknowledge that our present work may have faults and imperfections, is only to admit that it has been produced by human agency. But we certainly cannot ask to have them *excused* or *loved* in consequence of our peculiar condition. No: attribute them to our ignorance, carelessness or stupidity, but we pray thee, reader or critic, attribute them not to blindness, for this we must deem rather an advantage than an inconvenience in the art of composition.

Our subject is one of which so many false notions have been entertained and disseminated by speculative writers, that we have deemed it expedient to give the facts we wish to illustrate in connection with the lives of some of the most distinguished of our class, as we could in such connections best guard against being misunderstood. The characters we have chosen are from almost every age, country, occupation and class of society; so that, though we have dealt somewhat largely in biography, we hope that the facts, trials and triumphs presented may still produce an agreeable variety. The questions so frequently asked with touching pathos, by those who lose their sight in mature life,—"Is there benevolence in this world? Must charity supply my wants? Will there be always some hand to lead me? Have the blind ever a home in any heart? Does anything ever cheer them? Are their lives always useless? Is there anything they can do?"—these interrogatories are, we think, herein fully answered. To accomplish this work, we have spared no time, pains nor expense. All the information relative to the sightless condition, that could be obtained from the records of our Institutions for this class, was, through the kindness of their Principals, placed at our command; and we have imported from Europe for this purpose, numerous valuable works written by the blind, never before possessed by an American public. From these writings, as from many others of our class, we have made a sufficient number of extracts to put beyond question the literary taste and capacity of our order.

It is frequently not uninteresting to the reader, to know something of the author whose thoughts he is perusing. But upon the history of our lives we shall say but little. The principal scenes of life's drama in which we have acted, during our short peregrinations over the rugged face of old mother earth, are so much like those of our class in general, given in other connections, that we shall not here enter into detail. We will therefore only say, for the satisfaction of the curious, that we were born in Western New York, somewhere within the vicinity of twenty-five years ago; that ARTMAN lost his sight at the age of eighteen; that HALL's privation was congenital; that we were both educated at the New York Institution for the Blind, and have for the last four or five years been endeavoring to force a subsistence from nature and society, in various, and of course HONORABLE, occupations.

If this, our first effort in a literary capacity, should find favor with the public, more from us may be heard hereafter.

THE AUTHORS.

Dansville, 1856.

Achievements of the Blind.

MEMOIRS OF EMINENT BLIND AUTHORS,

WITH BEAUTIES FROM THEIR WRITINGS.

THAT man must indeed be depraved, who does not discover in himself some reflection of a divine image, though sin may have blotted and mutilated its form. The whole field of science does not open up to the mind a more pleasing subject for contemplation, or one fraught with more intense interest, than the study of its own mysterious nature. What are the elements that enter into its composition? Can it exist as distinct from matter, or is it merely the result of physical organization, as sound is the result of vibration? Is the brain only a system of organs, conspiring to produce thought, as melody is produced by musical instruments? How did the mind come in possession of its own identity, or that inward consciousness of a separate existence as distinct from the laws of nature which silently govern matter? How does it put forth volition? In what way do outward manifestations awaken painful or pleasant emotions, and why should it possess that fearful power of perverting its own affections, or destroying its own energies? These are themes upon which every contemplative mind loves to dwell. Speculative philosophy is, however, not without its attendant evils; it may ripen into rank infidelity if not carefully guarded. Investigations of mental phenomena should be conducted with a prayerful heart. The relations which the creature sustains to its Creator, should be kept constantly in view, and no apparent discrepancy or incongruity, should be allowed to shake our faith in the wisdom and goodness of a Supreme Being.

Next to an earnest and careful inquiry after God's revealed will to man, the study of man himself is paramount to all others. He who best knows himself, is best able to judge others. Yet, without revealed religion, it is impossible to determine what is laudable in ourselves, without studiously observing what traits of character are lovely or hateful in others. Hence it happens, that biography has been read and admired in all ages, and is found to be of such vital importance to the young. In the history of a great and good man, the youth finds a pattern by which he may mould his character. It is much easier to imitate good examples, than to act well from wise suggestions. It is less hazardous to follow closely in the footsteps of a virtuous and prudent man, whose path has led to honor and distinction, than to mark out for one's self a new course in life.

> Tread you my steps! 'Tis mine to lead the race,
> The first in glory, and the first in place.

AN ACCOUNT OF THE LIFE OF HOMER.

So little is known of this truly great man, that all our most anxious inquiries concerning him, have been but meagerly rewarded. The vague conjectures of his numerous biographers, serve only to thicken the haze that has settled over his long-since faded pathway.

So many fabulous accounts have been given of this prince of poets, by his early biographers, that some rather too skeptical, now deny even his existence. His wonderful poems, however, (the Iliad and Odyssey,) stand as monuments of his true greatness. They are voices from the grave of the past, floating on the tide of time, breathing in poetic numbers the fire of youth and the frenzy of love. The most reliable sources of information concerning Homer are, perhaps—Bibliotheca Græca, by Fabricus, Wood's Essay on the Genius and Writings of Homer, Cumberland's Observer, Lempriere's Classical Dictionary, Herodotus, Plutarch, and the Encyclopedia Britannica.

Various opinions have been entertained respecting the period in which he flourished, the place of his birth, and even his true name. These have been subjects of heated controversies among the learned of all ages.

2

In the most important events of his life's history the most of his biographers agree; namely, that he became blind early in life, after which he completed the Iliad and composed the Odyssey; was a wandering minstrel; that the age in which he lived was unworthy of so great a genius; and that he lived and died in the most abject poverty. It is not the design of the present writers to hazard any conjectures of their own respecting the age in which he lived, or which of the seven illustrious cities — Smyrna, Colophon, Chios, Salamis, Rhodes, Argos, or Athenea, had the honor of giving birth to so great a prodigy; nor will we here offer any comments upon his merits. Some suppose Homer to have flourished three hundred and forty years after the siege of Troy; but according to Herodotus about one hundred and sixty-eight years, and six hundred and twenty-two years before the expedition of Xerxes.

The place of his nativity is not certainly known. But the most prevalent opinion among historians is, that he was born at Smyrna, nine hundred years before the Christian era. His mother's name was Crytheis, an orphan left to the care of one Cleonies, her father's friend, by whom she was seduced. This coming to the knowledge of her guardian, he was anxious to conceal it, and accordingly sent her to Smyrna. Crytheis being near her time, went one day to a festival which the inhabitants were celebrating on the banks of the river Melis, where she was delivered of the immortal Homer, whom she named

Melesigenes. Crytheis was afterwards married to Phemius, a teacher of music and literature in Smyrna, who likewise adopted her son, and soon found in him marks of extraordinary genius. After the death of Phemius, Homer was left to the management of his father's school; but he was soon after induced to embark on a voyage with a person named Mentes. Having then commenced writing his Iliad, he was anxious to visit the places he should have occasion to mention; and he accordingly traveled through all Greece, Asia Minor, and many other places. From Egypt he brought the names of all their gods, the chief ceremonies of their religion, and a more improved knowledge of the arts.

He next sailed to Africa and Spain, and on his return touched at Ithaca, where he was detained for some time with a disease of the eye, which ended ultimately in total blindness. Here he was hospitably entertained by a friend of Mentes, named Mentor, a man of wealth, from whom he learned many things relating to Ulysses, which he afterward made use of in composing his Odyssey.

Mentes, on his return to Ithaca, took Homer with him to Colophon; from thence he returned to Smyrna. Being now reduced to the most extreme want, and still cherishing the fond hope that something might yet be done to restore his sight, our poet removed to Cuma. Here he was received with great joy, and his poems highly applauded. But when he proposed to immortalize their city by writing a poem in its praise, on condition that he should be supported by the public treasury by an annual income, he was told there would be no end of maintaining the Homeroi, or blind men. From this he received the name Homer. Finding his generous offer so ill deserved by the citizens of Cuma, he left that city, uttering this imprecation: "May no poets ever be born in Cuma to celebrate it by their poems." He afterward wandered for several years from place to place, as a minstrel, and finally settled at Chios, where he established a school of poetry, and composed his Odyssey. From this he realized a small profit, married, and had two daughters, one of whom died young; the other became the wife of a very dear friend at Bolyssus. Having now determined to visit Athens, he embarked in a vessel for that city, but was driven on the Island of Samos, where he spent the winter singing at the houses of the great, for a bare subsistence. On the opening of spring he again set sail for Athens; but, landing by the way at Ios, he fell sick, died, and was buried on the sea shore.

"Narrow is thy dwelling now,
Dark the place of thine abode
Deep is the sleep of the dead,
Low their pillow of rest.
When shall it be morn in the grave?
To bid the slumberer awake."

Ossian.

According to some Grecian traditions, both the Iliad and Odyssey were written by Homer after his blindness. Longinus, an eminent Greek critic and philosopher, compares the former to the mid-day, and the latter to the setting sun; and observes, "that though the Iliad claims an uncontested superiority over the Odyssey; yet, in the latter, the same force, the same sublimity and elegance prevail, though divested of their most powerful fire; and that it still preserves its original splendor and majesty, though deprived of its meridian heat."

These two celebrated poems are so frequently met with in this land of books, and so universally admired, that whatever we might here offer in praise of their author's wonderful inventive powers, the purity of his style and his godlike conceptions, would seem superfluous. He has been very justly called the father of Epic Poetry. So charmed was Alexander the Great with his compositions, that he commonly placed them, together with his sword, under his pillow. The Iliad he carefully deposited in one of the most valuable caskets of Darius, in order, said he to his courtiers, "that the most perfect production of the human mind, may be enclosed in the richest casket in the world." It is related of Alcibiades, that he once gave a rhetorician a sound box on the ear, for not having the writings of Homer in his school. The Battle of the Frogs and Mice, and several epigrams, have been ascribed to him; but the most probable opinion is, that there are none of his writings now extant, except the Iliad and Odyssey.

By many of the ancients, Homer was worshiped as a Divinity, and sacrifices were offered to him.

But not until after his death did fame breathe aloud his praise. It has since been echoed through each succeeding age, by applauding millions. "Our author's work," says Mr. Pope, "is a wild paradise, where, if we cannot see all the beauties so distinctly as in an ordered garden, it is only because the number of them is infinitely greater. It is like a copious nursery, which contains the seeds and first productions of every kind, out of which those who followed him have but selected some particular plants, each according to his fancy, to cultivate and beautify. If some things are too luxuriant, it is owing to the richness of the soil; and if others are not arrived to perfection or maturity, it is only because they are overrun and oppressed by those of a stronger nature." In speaking of the growing interest of the Iliad, and the poet's fancy, he says: "It is, however, remarkable that his fancy, which is everywhere vigorous, is not discovered immediately at the beginning of his poem in its fullest splendor: it grows in the progress, both on himself and others, and becomes on fire, like a chariot wheel, by its own rapidity. Exact disposition, just thought, correct elocution, polished numbers, may have been found in a thousand; but this poetic fire, this 'vivida vis animi,' in a very few."

The inimitable writings of Homer, as translated by Pope, we have read with enthusiastic delight. How it is that the blind can derive any degree of satisfaction from descriptive poetry, has long been a subject of speculation and doubt. Nor can we reflect much light upon it. How it is that one who has never seen light and color, is able to form any conception of distance, or extent beyond his reach, or of brilliant objects, as the moon and stars, of the rainbow or the landscape, must remain, to the seeing, enigmatical. We can no more describe to you, fortunate reader, the light which our own fancy sheds around objects, by which our minds take cognizance of them, than you can describe to us the clear light of the sun, or how it pictures upon your mind the objects from which it is reflected.

It may not be uninteresting to those of our readers who have followed us thus far, to give in this connection, a brief description (however vague and imperfect) of our own feelings on reading the wonderful productions of Homer. As our reader gives rapid and distinct utterance to each happily applied word, and as each complete sentence conveys to the mind its full import, every picture drawn by the immortal poet lies before us, glowing with its own poetic fire, and busy with life. Every active, moving and breathing image passes in quick succession before our view, and at their respective distances from each other. Entirely wrapped within ourselves, and excluded from meaner objects without, we are borne unconsciously and irresistibly, on the wings of fancy, to the scenes so vividly described. Our reader is transported with us, and performs a conspicuous part in the drama. He is successively transformed in the several characters; and every word he articulates, grows with significance as the scene heightens.

The writings of Homer must ever stand an indestructible monument of his deathless fame: a sublime structure so well proportioned in all its parts, and so sacred to genius, that it is almost sacrilege to tear from it relics of artistic skill.

FROM THE EIGHTH BOOK OF THE ILIAD.

Jupiter assembles the gods, and commands them not to assist either army. Minerva, however, obtains his consent to aid the Greeks. He afterwards descends to Mount Ida, and balances the fate of the Greeks and Trojans. For force and dignity, this description excels everything we have yet read. The most perfect creations of modern degenerate genius, are mere pigmies when compared with this giant—this twin-brother of perfection.

Aurora now, fair daughter of the dawn,
Sprinkled with rosy light the dewy lawn,
When Jove convened the senate of the skies,
Where high Olympus' cloudy tops arise.
The sire of gods his awful silence broke,
The heavens, attentive, trembled as he spoke:
"Celestial states, immortal gods! give ear!
Hear our decree, and reverence what ye hear!
The fix'd decree, which not all heaven can move,
Thou, Fate! fulfill it; and, ye powers, approve
What god but enters yon forbidden field,
Who yields assistance, or but wills to yield,

Back to the skies with shame he shall be driven,
Gash'd with dishonest wounds, the scorn of heaven:
Or far, oh! far, from steep Olympus thrown,
Low in the dark Tartarean gulf shall groan,
With burning chains fixed to the brazen floors.
And lock'd by hell's inexorable doors;
As deep beneath the infernal center hurl'd,
As from that center to the ethereal world.
Let him who tempts me dread those dire abodes;
And know, the Almighty is the god of gods.
League all your forces then, ye powers above,
Join all, and try the omnipotence of Jove:
Let down our golden, everlasting chain,
Whose strong embrace holds heaven, and earth, and main
Strive all, of mortal, and immortal birth,
To drag, by this, the Thunderer down to earth
Ye strive in vain! If I but stretch this hand,
I heave the gods, the ocean, and the land;
I fix the chain to great Olympus' height,
And the vast world hangs trembling in my sight!
For such I reign, unbounded and above;
And such are men and gods compared to Jove."
Th' Almighty spoke, nor durst the powers reply,
A reverend horror silenced all the sky:
Trembling they stood before their sovereign's look;
At length his best beloved, the power of wisdom spoke:
"Oh, first and greatest! god by gods adored!
We own thy might, our father and our lord!
But, ah! permit to pity human state;
If not to help, at least lament their fate.
From fields forbidden we submiss refrain,
With arms unaiding mourn our Argives slain;
Yet grant my counsels still their breasts may move,
Or all must perish in the wrath of Jove."
The cloud-compelling god her suit approved,
And smiled superior on his best beloved:
Then called his coursers, and his chariot took;
The steadfast firmament beneath them shook:

Rapt by th' ethereal steeds the chariot roll'd;
Brass were their hoofs, their curling manes of gold.
Of heaven's undrossy gold the god's array,
Refulgent, flash'd intolerable day.
High on the throne he snines: his coursers fly
Between th' extended earth and starry sky,
But when to Ida's topmost height he came,
(Fair nurse of fountains and of savage game,)
Where, o'er her pointed summits proudly raised,
His fane breathed odors, and his altars blazed:
There from his radiant car the sacred sire
Of gods and men released the steeds of fire;
Blue ambient mists th' immortal steeds embraced;
High on the cloudy point his seat he placed;
Thence his broad eye the subject world surveys,
The town, and tents, and navigable seas.
  Now had the Grecians snatch'd a short repast,
And buckled on their shining arms with haste.
Troy roused as soon; for on this dreadful day
The fate of fathers, wives, and infants lay.
The gates unfolding pour forth all their train;
Squadrons on squadrons cloud the dusky plain:
Men, steeds, and chariots shake the trembling ground:
The tumult thickens, and the skies resound.
And now with shouts the shocking armies closed,
To lances, lances, shields to shields opposed;
Host against host with shadowy legions drew,
The sounding darts in iron tempests flew;
Victors and vanquish'd join promiscuous cries,
Triumphant shouts and dying groans arise:
With streaming blood the slippery fields are dyed,
And slaughtered heroes swell the dreadful tide.
Long as the morning beams increasing bright,
O'er heaven's clear azure spread the sacred light:
Commutual death the fate of war confounds,
Each adverse battle gored with equal wounas.
But when the sun the height of heaven ascends,
The sire of gods his golden scales suspends

With equal hand: in these explored the fate
Of Greece and Troy, and poised the mighty weight
Press'd with its load, the Grecian balance lies
Low sunk on earth, the Trojan strikes the skies.
Then Jove from Ida's top his horror spreads;
The clouds burst dreadful o'er the Grecian heads:
Thick lightnings flash; the muttering thunder rolls,
Their strength he withers, and unmans their souls.
Before his wrath the trembling hosts retire;
The gods in terror, and the skies on fire.

In the eighth book of the Odyssey, Homer alludes to his condition, if not to himself, in the person of Demodocus. The picture is by no means a sad one, nor is the immortal bard made to feel his blindness a disgrace, or to regret his loss of sight, by the neglect of his friends. The most distinguishing honors are paid him by the king and his courtiers.

Be there Demodocus the bard of fame,
Taught by the gods to please, when high he sings
The vocal lay, responsive to the strings.

In entertaining Ulysses, the royal guest of Alcinoüs, the blind bard is deemed indispensable:

The herald now arrives, and guides along
The sacred master of celestial song:
Dear to the muse! who gave his days to flow
With mighty blessings, mixed with mighty wo;
With clouds of darkness quench'd his visual ray,
But gave him skill to raise the lofty lay.
High on a radiant throne sublime in state,
Encircled by huge multitudes, he sate:
With silver shone the throne: his lyre well strung
To rapturous sounds, at hand Pontinus hung:
Before his seat a polish'd table shines,
And a full goblet foams with generous wines,

His food a herald bore: and now they fed;
And now the rage of craving hunger fled.
Then fired by all the muse, aloud he sings
The mighty deeds of demigods and kings.

Again:

The bard a herald guides: the gazing throng
Pay low obeisance as he moves along:
Beneath a sculptured arch he sits enthroned,
Then peers encircling form an awful round.
Then from the chine, Ulysses carves with art
Delicious food, an honorary part:
"This let the master of the lyre receive,
A pledge of love! 'tis all a wretch can give.
Lives there a man beneath the spacious skies
Who sacred honors to the bard denies?
The muse the bard inspires, exalts his mind:
The muse indulgent loves th' harmonious kind.
The herald to his hand the charge conveys,
Not fond of flattery, nor unpleased with praise.
When now the rage of hunger was allay'd,
Thus to the lyrist wise Ulysses said:
"Oh, more than man! thy soul the muse inspires,
Or Phœbus animates with all his fires:
For who by Phœbus uninform'd, could know
The woe of Greece, and sing so well the woe?
Just to the tale, as present at the fray,
Or taught the labors of the dreadful day:
The song recalls past horrors to my eyes,
And bids proud Ilion from her ashes rise.
Once more harmonious strike the sounding string,
The Epæn fabric framed by Pallas, sing:
How stern Ulysses, furious to destroy,
With latent heroes sack'd imperial Troy.
If faithful thou record the tale of fame,
The god himself inspires thy breast with flame;
And mine shall be the task henceforth to raise
In every land thy monument of praise."

OSSIAN, THE CELTIC BARD.

It is to us a source of no small satisfaction, as it must be to every blind person who has a philanthropic zeal for the honor and elevation of his order, to find so many characters laboring under the same privation, in every period of man's history, who have walked triumphantly the path of fame. Of all the antique literature that has withstood the ravages of time, and at the present day enriches the commonwealth of letters, there is none more justly claiming our admiration, than the poems of this illustrious Celtic bard. As the meteor shoots through blackest night, and pours its glaring light over torrents wild, rocky cliff, and ocean surge, so do the works of this, and the Grecian poet, shine forth with transcendent luster through all succeeding ages.

But as the venerable Ossian flourished in an age when traditional songs supplied the place of written history, we can learn nothing of his long and eventful life, save the few particulars we gather from his poems. So little do we know of him, that even the era of his life has long been a subject of dispute. But from the incidents which the poet mentions, identical in Roman and other authentic histories, we think it may be decided without doubt to have been in the latter part of the third century. In this we agree with McPherson, the translator, and Rev. Dr. Blair, the reviewer, of these sublime poems. Ossian was the last of a line of kings renowned in their time for magnanimity and heroism in war, and clemency and magnificence in peace, who held dominion over Morven, a kingdom comprising that mountainous section of country lying along the north-west coast of Scotland. Fingal, his father, is represented to us as a true hero; though terrible in battle, he displayed many of those ennobling graces found in civilized life. His ancestors, Trathal and Trenmor, are also portrayed in song, possessing such manly virtues as make us forget that they lived in a period when humanity was disgraced at Rome, and heathen darkness, like the dusky curtains of night, spread over the earth.

The following advice of Fingal to his grandson, Oscar, (son of Ossian,) concerning his conduct in peace and war, is an example of true generosity, worthy of the most refined age: "O Oscar, pride of youth. I saw the shining of the sword. I gloried in my race. Pursue the fame of our fathers; be thou what they have been, when Trenmor lived, the first of men, and Trathal, the father of heroes! They fought the battle in their youth. They are the song of bards. O Oscar! bend the strong in arm; but spare the feeble hand. Be thou a stream of many tides against the foes of thy people; but like the gale that moves the grass, to those who ask thine aid. So Trenmor lived; such Trathal was; and such has Fingal been."

While the fire of youth inspired the heroic heart of Fingal, his military aid was solicited by Cormac, king of Ireland, to quell the insurrection and usurpation of Colculla, chief of Atha, where he fell in love with and took to wife Rosecanna, daughter of Cormac, who became the mother of our poet. If the long-established maxim is true, that the first striking event and impressions in one's existence, give the leading impulse to character, it was but natural that Ossian should become a great poet and musician. The wild, animating, and heroic songs of the thousand bards that crowded the halls of Selma, during the life and triumphant career of his father, were perhaps the first sounds that greeted his ear, and formed the lullaby of his early years. It has been the well-founded opinion of our ablest modern literary persons, that an age of uncivilization, when the passions and feelings of men are in unrestrained exercise, is more favorable to poetry than one of nice refinement, when the intellect bows to the deity of arbitrary rules. So prevalent has this opinion become among the literati of our day, that we not unfrequently hear the period known in ancient history as "the dark ages," classically termed the age of poetry.

The method of transmitting history and heroic fame to future times, through poems or traditional songs, which nearly all the nations of antiquity adopted before the art of writing became prevalent, afforded a powerful incentive to the exaltation of poetic genius. A skillful bard, familiar with the history of heroes, and able to poetize with luster what was deemed noble and generous in character, was ever greeted with cordiality at the mansions of the great, and flattered at kingly courts. We are informed that the ancient Spartans were so prejudiced in favor of transmitting their laws and panegyrics in this way, that they never would allow them to be committed to writing. The Germans also preserved monuments of their antique history, and transmitted them orally to quite a modern date, by couching into verse the elegies of their heroes and chief national transactions.

But especially did poetic genius obtain great popularity among the Celtic tribes. Living a roving and indolent life, their highest entertainment in peace, was to gather around the burning oak, or sit in the halls of their fathers, and listen to the praises and exploits of their heroes, from the lips of bards; and in war, these poets rehearsed the deeds of their ancestors to inspire the chiefs with heroic fire. Their greatest incentive to noble deeds was to receive their fame; that is, to become worthy of being celebrated in the songs of bards; and to have their name on the four gray stones. To die unlamented by a bard, was deemed so great a misfortune as even to disturb their ghosts in another state. "They wander in thick mists beside the reedy lake; but never shall they rise, without the song, to the dwelling of winds."

Julius Cæsar informs us, that this class of men comprised many of the first rank, possessing superior talents, highly respected in state, and was supported by public establishment. So thorough a knowledge of ancient historical poetry was requisite, before be ing initiated into this order, that, with many, a course of diligent study for a term of twenty years was required.* In this way the Celtic bards transmitted, as a sacred charge, their poems through successive generations. Consequently, we not unfrequently hear them termed, in ancient verse, the sons of future times. Their persons were held so inviolable, that they were ever secure against personal outrage from foes. "He feared to stretch his sword to the bards, though his soul was dark." When this institution had attained to its meridian excellence, and the capital of Morven was enriched and embellished, to a degree of magnificence before unknown among the nations of north-western Europe, the voice and harp of Ossian woke their echoes in the halls of Selma, the first among a thousand bards. The heroic splendor and peculiar institutions of Ossian's age, formed a conjunction of circumstances highly favorable towards developing a poetic spirit. "Ossian himself," says Dr. Blair, "appears to have been endowed

* Under an institution like this, it is not strange that the best poems produced and preserved of those times, were the compositions of blind bards. Their extraordinary concentrative and retentive powers, and natural fondness for poetic numbers, must have given them great superiority over their cotemporaries.

by nature with an exquisite sensibility of heart; prone to that tender melancholy which is so often an attendant on great genius, and susceptible equally of strong and of soft emotion." His first adventure of which we have any account, was his contest with the chiefs of Erin, for Ever-allin, the beautiful daughter of Branno, king of Ireland, in which he was triumphant, and Ever-allin became his wife, and mother of his only son, Oscar, who was treacherously assassinated by Cairbar, a chief of Erin, and his young spouse Melvina was left in Cona, to mourn the fall of her beloved hero. She became the solace of Ossian in his age and blindness, and it is to her that many of his most beautiful poems are addresed. At what age or period of his life, or from what circumstances, Ossian lost his sight, we cannot definitely determine from his poems; but it must have been at a considerably advanced age, for he sings of expeditions and battles in which he fought, when in the full vigor and strength of manhood, in company with his son Oscar. That these poems were written, however, after he was blind, appears evident from the fact that he, in nearly all of them, adverts to and laments his sightless condition. Notwithstanding the almost universal applause and admiration which these compositions have received from all lovers of true poetry, and their translation into almost every refined language in the civilized world, as Ossianic, every reader in the least acquainted with their history, must be aware that their authorship has been a subject of long and earnest dispute since their first publication. The idea that poems of so pure a style, abounding in such exquisite tenderness and sublimity, should have been produced in an age so rude in every other respect, and transmitted by oral tradition without corruption, through a period of nearly fourteen hundred years, has shocked the credulity of many intelligent and well-disposed persons. This has been looked upon by many literary characters, especially those of England, as so far out of the ordinary course of things, that they have by some been attributed to McPherson, who, it is maintained, wrote and ascribed them to an ancient bard, to avoid the criticism and envy of his cotemporary writers.

Much light had been thrown upon this subject, from time to time, by the numerous methods instituted for this purpose, until Dr. Blair, in his critical dissertation concerning the poems of Ossian, so thoroughly canvassed the subject, and by facts, deductions, and arguments, proved them to be the genuine poems of Ossian, that there is scarcely room left for a doubt. There yet remains, however, unemployed, one argument with which, had it been at the command of this clear-minded and profound writer, he would have dispelled all speculation on this subject, as flee the shadows of night before the morning sun. This argument is predicated upon the perfect delineations of feeling in which these poems abound, intuitive in the bosom of every blind person. No less than twenty times does the author refer to this deprivation, in a manner so striking, that every blind person acquainted with his own thoughts and emotions, cannot fail to recognize them as kindred to those awakened in his own breast. Were these the only proofs in favor of their being the poems of Ossian, his claim would be established firm as the pyramids of Egypt, defying all the armies of literary dabblers and cavilers that have ever questioned their authorship. We do not pretend to deny, that poems whose themes and imagery are drawn from the universal field of nature, to which every author has access, may sometimes be imitated, with considerable exactness; but these are the emotions and vibrations of the soul's intensest struggles, and are as proof against forgery, as the voice of the earthquake. One of the writers of this article, having possessed the advantages of sight, until at a considerable mature age, he can fully appreciate the difficulty under which he labors to make himself understood on this point, by those who have never felt the peculiar emotions awakened by a sense of blindness. There are peculiarities in all the descriptive writings of the blind, so striking, especially when portraying their own condition, or that of others under similar circumstances, that we find no difficulty whatever in tracing their identity.

But that these marks of recognition are not so apparent to the seeing, is clearly manifest from the following remarks of Dr. Kitto, relative to Homer and his writings: "The fact that he was blind," says this celebrated author, "could not, we apprehend, be collected from his works; but we may accept without dispute the ancient and universal tradition of his being in that condition." With all due deference to the doctor's clear perception, we beg leave to affirm, that while the account of Demodocus remains in the Odyssey, and the description of the Cyclopean giant, (whose huge eye Ulysses put out,) in the ninth book of that poem, this master-work will be claimed by the blind, though every tradition of its author should sink into oblivion.

These remarks are alike applicable to Milton, Dr. Blacklock, Rev. Dr. Lucas, and others. So numerous and striking are the pictures which these authors have drawn of their own peculiar privations, that they form true mirrors in which every blind person may behold reflected his own condition. In the third book of "Paradise Lost," and in the dramatic poem, "Samson Agonistes," their inimitable author has left such glaring images of blindness, as must forever betray the privation under which they were conceived, though all incidents of his life were erased from the pages of history.

How forcibly and pathetic do the following senti ments address themselves to our own hearts:

> Thus with the year
> Seasons return; but not to me returns
> Day, or the sweet approach of even or morn,
> Or sight of vernal bloom, or summer's rose,
> Or flocks, or herds, or human face divine ·

But cloud instead, and ever-during dark
Surrounds me! * * * *
So much the rather thou, celestial Light!
Shine inward, and the mind through all her powers
Irradiate; there plant eyes; all mist from thence
Purge and disperse; that I may see and tell
Of things invisible to mortal sight.

Dr. Blacklock, also, in the following expressive lines, not only paints his own experience, but that of his entire class:

Wide o'er my prospect rueful darkness breathes
Her inauspicious vapor; in whose shade,
Fear, grief, and anguish, natives of her reign,
In social sadness gloomy vigils keep;
With them I walk, with them still doomed to share
Eternal blackness, without hope of dawn.

But among all the eminent poets of this order, there is none who has more strikingly portrayed the emotions native to a sense of blindness, than the venerable Ossian. In almost every poem in this entire collection, he laments over his sightlessness, in strains so touching, as are not only indicative of condition, but prove to us that the emotions awakened by this affliction have been the same in every age of the world and state of society. In the fourth book of Fingal, in a strain of sublimity that portrays the deep emotions of his soul, he thus sadly mourns over his deprivations: "Daughter of the land of snow, I was not so mournful and blind, I was not so dark and forlorn, when Ever-allin loved me!"

Again, in the same book of that poem, he thus addresses Malvina: "But I am sad, forlorn, and blind: no more the companion of heroes! Give, lovely maid, to me thy tears."

In Carthon, he beautifully speaks of feeling and hearing, the two senses on which every blind person most depends. "I feel the sun, O Malvina! leave me to my rest. Perhaps they may come to my dreams. I think I hear a feeble voice! The beam of heaven delights to shine on the grave of Carthon. I feel it warm around." And again, in the fifth book of Fingal, lamenting the fall of that hero: "I hear not thy distant voice on Cona. My eyes perceive thee not. Often forlorn and dark, I sit at thy tomb, and feel it with my hands. When I think I hear thy voice, it is but the passing blast. Fingal has long since fallen asleep, the ruler of the war!" In the characters of Crothar, Lamor, and Barbarduthal, who are represented blind, Ossian so perfectly delineates the gestures and feelings consequent upon such a state, as could be done by no author to whom these were not prompted by experience. In Croma, the poet, speaking of his interview with Crothar, and that hero, referring to the shield presented to him by Fingal, thus speaks: "Dost thou not behold it on the wall? for Crothar's eyes have failed. Is thy strength like thy father's, Ossian? let the aged feel thine arm! I gave my arm to the king; he felt it with his aged hands."

These quotations, in connection with what has been said in the foregoing, we deem sufficient to substantiate the position we have taken relative to the authorship of the poems in question. But should any one argue that passages like these could be pilfered from the writings of the blind, and so patched into the compositions of another as not to discover theft, we can only say, he betrays such an ignorance of the true spirit of poetry, that we fear no opposition from this source. While heroic themes, robed in nature's own beauty and majesty, can interest the intelligent reader, the poems of "Blind Ossian" will be read with undiminished interest, and we cannot close this article without offering a few extracts, that may not only serve to throw light upon their author's history, but recommend this collection to all lovers of true poetry.

OSSIAN'S ADDRESS TO THE SUN.

O thou that rollest above, round as the shield of my fathers! Whence are thy beams, O Sun? thy everlasting light? Thou comest forth in thy awful beauty; the stars hide themselves in the sky; the moon, cold and pale, sinks in the western wave; but thou thyself movest alone. Who can be a companion of thy course? The oaks of the mountain fall; the mountains themselves decay with years; the ocean shrinks and grows again; the moon herself is lost in heaven: but thou art forever the same, rejoicing in the brightness of thy course. When the world is dark with tempests, when thunder rolls and lightning flies, thou lookest in thy beauty from the clouds, and laughest at the storm. But to Ossian thou lookest in vain, for he beholds thy beams no more: whether thy yellow hair flows on the eastern clouds, or thou tremblest at the gates of the west. But thou art, perhaps, like me, for a season; thy years will have an end. Thou shalt sleep in thy clouds, careless of the voice of the morning. Exult then, O Sun, in the strength of thy youth! Age is dark and unlovely; it is like the glimmering light of the moon, when it shines through broken clouds, and the mist is on the hills: the blast of the north is on the plain, the traveler shrinks in the midst of his journey.

FROM THE POET'S LAST SONG.

Lead, son of Alpin, lead the aged to his woods. The winds begin to rise. The dark wave of the lake resounds. Bends there not a tree from Mora with its branches bare? It bends, son of Alpin, in the rustling blast. My harp hangs on a blasted branch; the sound of its strings is mournful. Does the wind touch thee, O harp, or is it some passing ghost? It is the hand of Malvina! Bring me the harp, son of Alpin. Another song shall rise. My soul shall depart in the sound. My fathers shall hear it in their airy hall. Their dim faces shall hang, with joy, from their clouds; and their hands receive their son. The aged oak bends over the stream. It sighs with all its moss. The withered fern whistles near, and mixes, as it waves, with Ossian's hair. Strike the harp, and raise the song: be near, with all your wings, ye winds. Bear the mournful sound away to Fingal's airy hall. Bear it to Fingal's hall, that he may hear the voice of his son: the voice of him that praised the mighty! The blast of the north opens thy gates, O king! I behold thee sitting on mist dimly gleaming in all thine arms. Thy form now is not the terror of the valiant. It is like a watery cloud, when we see the stars behind it with their weeping eyes. Thy shield is the aged moon: thy sword a vapor half kindled with fire. Dim and feeble is the chief who traveled in brightness before. But thy steps are on the winds of the desert. The storms are darkening in thy hand. Thou takest the sun in thy wrath, and hidest him in thy clouds. The sons of little men are afraid. A thousand showers descend. But when thou comest forth in thy mildness, the gale of the morning is near thy course. The sun laughs in his blue fields; the gray stream winds in its vale. The bushes shake their green heads in the wind. The roes bound towards the desert.

There is a murmur in the heath! the stormy winds abate! I hear the voice of Fingal. Long has it been absent from mine ear! Come, Ossian, come away, he says. Fingal has received his fame. We passed away like flames that have shone for a season. Our departure was in renown. Though the plains of our battles are dark and silent; our fame is in the four gray stones. The voice of Ossian has been heard. The harp has been strung in Selma; come, Ossian, come away, he says, come, fly with thy fathers on clouds. I come, I come, thou king of men! The life of Ossian fails. I begin to vanish on Cona. My steps are not seen in Selma. Beside the stone of Mora I shall fall asleep. The winds whistling in my gray hair shall not awaken me. Depart on thy wings, O wind, thou canst not disturb the rest of the bard. The night is long, but his eyes are heavy. Depart, thou rustling blast.

BEAUTIES FROM THE WRITINGS OF JOHN MILTON.

"But Milton next, with high and haughty stalks,
Unfettered in majestic numbers walks;
No vulgar hero can his muse engage,
Nor earth's wide scene confine his hallowed rage."

There is much in the long and eventful life of this great and good man, worthy of detail, and eminently calculated to interest the general reader. But so many excellent memoirs of him have been given to the public, in connection with his works, from pens eloquent with praise, and glowing with fervent admiration of his genius, that we purpose, in this article, to confine ourselves mainly to that period of his life subsequent to the loss of his sight. He was born, it appears, at London, in 1608; greatly impaired his sight by hard study in youth; took the degree of A. M. at Christ College, in his twenty-fourth year; zealously embarked in the political and religious controversies of the times, and, while engaged in writing his defense of the English people, again overtasked his eyes, and brought on a *gutta serena*, which ended in the total extinction of his sight, in the forty-fourth year of his age. Of this melancholy result he was, however, forewarned by his physician, but, in the alternative of evils, preferred, it seems, the loss of sight to the dereliction of his duty.

As clouds collect around them dark, floating vapors, and seem to convert into blackness the bright blue sky itself, so great afflictions accumulate sorrow, until every glad beam of hope and joy is shut out from the heart. Very much about this time, Milton was called to mourn the death of his wife, who left to his protection three orphan daughters. He did not, however, long remain in this friendless situation, but shortly after married Catharine, daughter of Captain Woodcock, of Hackney, who seems to have been the object of his fondest affection, but who died within a year after their marriage.

This new accession of sorrow again brought back his helpless and forlorn condition, and no doubt cast a deeper gloom over his spirits than either of his former afflictions had done. It forms the subject of that beautiful and melting sonnet to his deceased wife. This sonnet is found in Milton's collected poems, and possibly lives in the reader's memory, as one of its brightest and purest images of thought. But as it brings out some valuable ideas in relation to the dreams of the blind, and offers us the welcome opportunity of drawing upon our own experience, we gladly give it room:

Methought I saw my late espoused saint
  Brought to me, like Alcestis from the grave,
  Whom Jove's great son to her glad husband gave,
  Rescued from death by force, though pale and faint.
Mine as whom wash'd from spot of child-bed taint

Purification in the old Law did save,
And such, as yet once more I trust to have
Full sight of her in Heaven without restraint;—
Came, vested all in white, pure as her mind:
Her face was veil'd; yet to my fancied sight
Love, sweetness, goodness, in her person shined
So clear, as in no face with more delight.
But, O, as to embrace me she inclined,
I waked; she fled; and day brought back my night.

The sudden transit of the blind from a day of dreams to a night of realities, could not have been more happily or correctly described. Yet some coarse critics as ignorant of the true spirit of poetry as of the sensations of disappointment, experienced by the blind on awakening to a world of darkness, have presumed to pronounce the last line of this sonnet a conceit, and even faulty in construction. It may be interesting to those who would sometimes gladly close their eyes, and even memory, from the busy and active scenes of life, but who welcome with joy the first glad ray of morning, to know that to those who lose their sight late in life, night alone can restore a world of light and color, of bright eyes and happy familiar faces, of woods, streams, flowers, and merry sunshine. But what is more strange, we are able to recognize, in dreams, persons with whom we may have formed an acquaintance subsequent to blindness: sometimes by that peculiar expression of countenance with which fancy may have invested them, but more commonly by the familiar sound of their voices.

To those who have never seen light, (and hence are

ignorant of darkness,) the world of dreams and that of realities are the same, except that in the latter, fancy is controlled by will and reason, and the senses are awake to external impressions. In dreams, the imagination presents to our fancied touch, strange or familiar objects, bearing marks of recognition, with smooth and rough surfaces, differing in form and dimension, and sometimes frightful scenes, such as buildings on fire, assassins in pursuit of their victims, armies in deadly strife, the boisterous ocean, flying clouds, and, in short, every phenomenon of which it is possible to gain a knowledge from description.

Milton, finding himself a second time a widower, employed Dr. Paget to aid him in making choice of a third consort, who was Elizabeth Minshul, of Cheshire. By the assistance of his three daughters, who, under his instruction, had become very serviceable, he was now able to prosecute his studies with nearly as much pleasure and profit, as when he depended upon his own resources for information. His two elder daughters are said to have been able to pronounce the Latin, Greek, and Hebrew languages, and to read in their respective originals whatever authors he wished to consult, though they understood none but their mother tongue. But notwithstanding all these advantages, no one, perhaps, ever felt his loss of sight more deeply, or described it more pathetically, than Milton. In view of the ills that followed in its train, this affliction was no doubt to him a source of bitter regret; but to the world, it will ever be regarded as a blessing. For had not this night closed upon his political career, shut out from his view objects of sense, and left his great soul to concentrate its powers in sublime contemplation, and to find utterance only in glowing images of thought, "Paradise Lost," would never have been written. Not that darkness is likely to produce new mental phenomena, or favor a more extended research into physical sciences; but that the absence of sight does aid reflection, concentration, and the imagination, few will deny.

Milton, it is true, like Homer, had collected much of his material of thought, before the loss of his sight. He had visited the classic grounds of Italy, and had seen nature robed in her brightest and richest attire. While a student of Christ's College, he composed many Latin poems, and is said to have been the first Englishman who wrote Latin verse with classical elegance. His "Mask of Comus," "L 'Allegro," and "Penseroso," bear the unmistakable impress of true genius; and would have been sufficient to render his name immortal, had he left no other monuments of his greatness. But as stars fade at the approach of morning light, so these recede before the noonday splendor of "Paradise Lost;" an epic poem only inferior to the "Iliad," in force and heroic fire, and not in profound contemplation. The description of Satan's escape from his dungeon, and ascent through the realm of chaos, up to light, in the second book of this poem, is perhaps one of the loftiest conceptions that ever sprang from the human intellect. And we are fully persuaded, that, had not the author been surrounded by the hollow darkness which he here describes; and wholly shut in with self and thought, while ever-during night kept sentinel without, this scene could never have been rendered so complete. The view presented to Satan, sin and death, on the opening of the infernal gates, set forth in the following, in point of sublimity is certainly without a parallel:

Before their eyes in sudden view appear
The secrets of the hoary deep; a dark
Illimitable ocean, without bound,
Without dimension, where length, breadth, and height,
And time, and place, are lost; where eldest Night
And Chaos, ancestors of Nature, hold
Eternal anarchy, amidst the noise
Of endless wars, and by confusion stand:
For hot, cold, moist, and dry, four champions fierce,
Strive here for mast'ry, and to battle bring
Their embryon atoms; they around the flag
Of each his faction, in their several clans,
Light-arm'd or heavy, sharp, smooth, swift, or slow,
Swarm populous, unnumber'd as the sands
Of Barca or Cyrene's torrid soil,
Levied to side with warring winds, and poise
Their lighter wings. To whom these most adhere,
He rules a moment; Chaos umpire sits,
And by decision more embroils the fray,
By which he reigns: next him, high arbiter,
Chance governs all. Into this wild abyss,
(The womb of nature, and perhaps her grave,)
Of neither sea, nor shore, nor air, nor fire,
But all these in their pregnant causes mix'd
Confusedly, and which thus must ever fight,
(Unless the Almighty Maker them ordain

His dark materials to create more worlds ;)
Into this wild abyss the wary fiend
Stood on the brink of hell, and look'd a while
Pondering his voyage.

After much difficulty this divine poem was licensed for the press, and published first at London, in 1667. To show how little the age in which Milton lived was worthy of so great a genius, we need only mention that on the completion of this great work, the poet could sell the copy for no more than fifteen pounds, the payment of which depended upon the sale of three large editions; and his widow afterwards sold her claims for eight pounds. Three years after the publication of "Paradise Lost," he published "Samson Agonistes," a tragedy in the purest style of the Greek Drama; and "Paradise Regained," the subject of which is said to have been suggested by the following circumstance: Elwood, a Quaker, who had read "Paradise Lost," in manuscript, on returning it, put this quaint interrogation: "What hast thou to say to Paradise Found?"

We have only farther to mention that, worn out by the gout, our poet paid the debt of nature in 1674, in his sixty-sixth year.

The following sublime and affecting production was but lately discovered among the remains of our great epic poet, and is published in the recent Oxford edition of Milton's Works:

I am old and blind!
Men point at me as smitten by God's frown;
Afflicted and deserted of my kind;
Yet I am not cast down.

I am weak, yet strong;
I murmur not that I no longer see;
Poor, old, and helpless, I the more belong,
Father supreme! to thee.

O, merciful one!
When men are farthest then thou art most near;
When friends pass by me, and my weakness shun,
Thy chariot I hear.

Thy glorious face
Is leaning towards me; and its holy light
Shines in upon my lonely dwelling place—
And there is no more night.

On my bended knee
I recognize thy purpose clearly shown:
My vision thou hast dimm'd, that I may see
Thyself—Thyself alone.

I have nought to fear;
This darkness is the shadow of thy wing;
Beneath it I am almost sacred; here
Can come no evil thing.

O! I seem to stand
Trembling, where foot of mortal ne'er hath been,
Wrapp'd in the radiance of thy sinless land,
Which eye hath never seen.

Visions come and go:
Shapes of resplendent beauty round me throng;
From angel lips I seem to hear the flow
Of soft and holy song.

Is it nothing now,
When heaven is opening on my sightless eyes?—
When airs from paradise refresh my brow
The earth in darkness lies.

In a purer clime
My being fills with rapture—waves of thought
Roll in upon my spirit—strains sublime
Break over me unsought.

Give me now my lyre!
I feel the stirrings of a gift divine:
Within my bosom glows unearthly fire
Lit by no skill of mine.

REV RICHARD LUCAS, D. D.

There is no other period in the history of England that produced as many able polemic writers, as the seventeenth century. The enthusiasm and cruel persecutions that attended the first outbreak of the reformation in that country, had then much subsided, and both the great leading powers (Protestant and Papal) were made willing to consecrate their faith and creeds at the shrine of reason and revelation. This concession, so long sought for by the reformers, inspired and brought into the field many of the most learned and distinguished men of those spirit-stirring times. Their fervent discussions of holy writ, tempered with that moderation and zeal which an earnest inquiry after the truth always inspires, resulted in the discovery and establishment of those vital doctrines, in the propagation of which the Christian church has since been so eminently successful. In this arena of giant intellects, was spent the life of our author, a bright luminary, lighting up the path of the inquirer after truth, and by his profound learning vanquishing the advocates of error on every side.

This eminent divine was of Welsh origin, the son of Mr. Richard Lucas, of Resteign, in Radnorshire, England, and was born in that county in the year

1648. He early evinced a strong desire for knowledge, and after a thorough training in the common branches of science, he was sent to Oxford, and entered a student of Jesus College, in 1664.

Having taken both his degrees in arts, he entered into holy orders about the year 1672, and was afterwards master of the free school at Abergavenny; but being much esteemed for his talents in the pulpit, he was chosen vicar of St. Stephen's, Coleman-street, London, and lecturer of St. Olave, Southwark, in 1683. His sight began to fail in his youth, but he lost it totally about this time.

The privation of this important sense, in the full vigor of life and highest sphere of usefulness, might have been considered by some, (less noble,) a justifiable excuse for a retirement from the duties and re sponsibilities of public life. But he, true to that excellency of soul that characterized his former career, made up in energy and perseverance what he lost in sight, and continued to devote himself to the public good with such well-directed zeal as must merit the highest respect of all succeeding generations.

Early in life, at an age when most young men spend their time in trifling amusements, this champion of the cross consecrated all his powers to the service of his divine Master, and was, therefore, meekly resigned to whatever privation or affliction a benign Providence might assign him.

As a testimonial of his resignation we quote the following from the preface of the author's work, entitled "Enquiry after Happiness:" "It has pleased God, that in a few years I should finish the more pleasant and delightful part of life, if sense were to be the judge and standard of pleasure, being confined (I will not say condemned) to retirement and solitude.

"In this state conversation has lost much of its former air and briskness; study, which is the only employment left me, is clogged with this weight and incumbrance, that all the assistance I can receive from without, must be conveyed by another's sense, not my own; which, it may easily be believed, are instruments or organs as ill fitted and awkwardly managed by me, as wooden legs and hands by the maimed. Should I ambitiously affect to have my name march in the train of those, although not all equally great ones, Homer, Appius, Aufidius, Didymus, Walkup, Père Jean l'Aveugle, &c., all of them eminent for their service and usefulness, notwithstanding their affliction of the same kind with mine, even this might seem almost a commendable infirmity; for the last thing a mind truly great and philosophical puts off, is the desire of glory. But this treatise owes neither its conception nor birth to this principle; for, besides that I know my own insufficiency, I must confess I never had a soul great enough to be acted by the heroic heat which the love of fame and honor has kindled in some."

Notwithstanding the inconvenience of this privation, Dr. Lucas continued to discharge the duties of his holy calling, with such zeal and ability as brought him to the notice and favor of some of the leading men of his day. He took the degree of doctor of divinity, and was installed prebendary of Westminster, in 1696. He died, June, 1715, and was interred in Westminster Abbey.

> "So, peaceful rests, without a stone, a name,
> That once had titles, piety, and fame."
>
> "How loved, how honored once, avails thee not,
> To whom related, or by whom begot;
> A heap of dust alone remains of thee;
> 'Tis all thou art, and all the proud shall be!"

Dr. Lucas wrote many valuable works, namely: "A Treatise on Practical Christianity;" "The Morality of the Gospel;" "A Guide to Heaven;" "An Enquiry after Happiness;" "Christian Thoughts for every Day of the Week;" "The Duty of Servants;" and "Sermons," in five volumes. He also made a Latin translation of the "Whole Duty of Man," which was published in 1680.

Of Dr. Lucas, Mr. Orton has given the following from Dr. Doddridge's Mss.: "His style is very peculiar: sometimes exceedingly fine, nearly approaching to conversation; sometimes grand and sublime; generally very expressive. His method not clear, but his thoughts excellent; many are taken from attentive observation of life; he wrote as entirely devoted to God, and superior to the world." His "Practical Christianity" is most valuable, and also his "Enquiry after Happiness," especially the second volume. Orton speaks of reading the latter work a sixth time. The pious Mr. Hervey, in speaking of his work, says: "May I be permitted to recommend as a treasure of inestimable value, Dr. Lucas' 'Enquiry after Happiness;' that part, especially, which displays the method, and enumerates the advantages of improving life, or living much in a little time; chapter iii, page 158 of the 6th edition. An author in whom the gentleman, the scholar, and the christian, are most happily united; a performance which, in point of solid argument, unaffected piety, and a vein of thought amazingly fertile, has, perhaps, no superior. Nor can I wish my reader a more refined pleasure, or a more substantial happiness, than that of having the sentiments of this entertaining and pathetic writer woven into the very texture of his heart." The treatise on "Practical Christianity" is earnestly recommended, also, by Sir Richard Steele, in the Guardian, No. 43. To these great names we must add that of Rev. John Wesley, who warmly recommends the "Treatise on Happiness" to his people, as one of the most valuable books a Christian can read.

What has been said in the foregoing sketch, respecting the life and commendable characteristics of this great man, may have raised a wish in our readers to have a specimen of his writings. We therefore copy at length from his inimitable work. We do it the more cheerfully, from the conviction that none of the literary productions of this author, so eminent in his own country, have ever been before the American public.

[From "Enquiry after Happiness," published in London, in 1806.]

ADDRESS TO THE YOUNG.

You are now in your bloom. What glorious fruit may you bring forth! what honor may you do God! what service may you render your relations and your country! and what joys and blessings may you not heap on yourselves! Time and tide seem to wait on you; even the providence and grace of God, with reverence be it said, seem to attend and court you.

But, ah! remember, they will not do so forever; these smiles and invitations of heaven and nature will not last continually; your infidelity or ingratitude, your folly and sensuality, will soon blast and wither all these fair hopes, turn all your pleasures into gall and wormwood, and all your blessed advantages into the instruments of your ruin, and aggravations of it, too. Grace will soon retire, nature degenerate, time grow old, the world despise you, the God of it frown upon you, and conscience, guilty conscience, will be either stupefied and benumbed, or fester and rage within you, and death will come, and then judgment; and how soon it will come, ah! who knows? Sudden and early deaths ought to convince you on what uncertain ground you stand. The scythe of death stays not always till the harvest be ripe, but promiscuously mows down the young and old. Ah! begin, begin, then, to live! seize upon pleasure and happiness while they stand courting and inviting you; pursue virtue and glory immediately, while the difficulties are fewer, your strengths and aids greater, your judgments being not yet corrupted by the maxims or rather the fancies of the world, nor your wills yet disabled and enslaved by a custom of sin.

Ah! venture not to devote your youth to vanity and folly, on presumption of devoting your age to repentance and religion; for if this were a rational and just design in itself, yet it is to you a very unsafe and doubtful one. For which way can you insure life, or on what ground can you confide on the morrow? "Boast not thyself of to-morrow, for thou knowest not what a day may bring forth." Prov. xxvii, 1.

I know what opposition will be raised against this kind of exhortation, and with what rude reflection they will be treated. Come, say they, this is our spring, let us enjoy ourselves whilst we have time and vigor; religion looks too grave and formal for these years: we shall have time enough to be dull and melancholy. Come on, then; let us enjoy ourselves as becomes our youth; this is our portion, and our lot is this; and whatever they who have now outlived themselves, whose blood is sour and spirits low, may gravely talk against these things, they, too, when time was, admired what they now would have us despise as vanity, and committed themselves what they now condemn in us.

In answer to this, let us pass over the briskness and the flourish, and examine the sense and reason of this sort of talk. The substance of it may be reduced to three heads :

First. Youth is the season of pleasure, i. e. sin and folly. Inclination and opportunity conspire to invite you to it ; therefore you indulge it. What a strange argument is this! Is there any period of our life, from our cradle almost to our coffin, I mean from the moment we arrive at the use of reason to our grave, wherein some sin or other is not in season? May not manhood defend ambition, and old age covetousness, by the same argument by which you do your sinful pleasures? If inclination to a folly would justify our commission of it, in what part of life should we begin to be wise and virtuous? It will be hard to find the time wherein we shall have no inclination to any sin or folly ; or rather, if this be so, who can be guilty? The adulterer will impute his uncleanliness to the impetus of his lust ; the murderer his bloodshed to the violence of his rage ; i. e. each of them their sins to the strength of their inclinations ; and if your argument be good they will be innocent. But do not deceive yourselves ; then is your obedience, as most acceptable to God, so most indispensable in itself, when you lie under temptations to sin, and heaven is proposed as a reward, not of following, but conquering your inclinations.

The second part of the objection is, that religion doth not look very graceful in young men. This I could never well understand. If you be so foolish as to think religion consists in sour faces, or an affected moroseness and sullenness, or in stupidity and melancholy, I must confess you have little reason to be fond of it; for this becomes no age, and much less the more verdant one.

But if by religion you understand devotion toward God, reverence towards your parents and superiors, temperance and chastity in yourselves, and such like virtues, I must needs say, nothing can appear to me more great and lovely than religion in youth. What can better become those who possess the gifts of nature in their own perfection, than gratitude to the God of nature? What can be a greater glory to the young, than obedience to parents, and reverence to their elders and superiors? What does more preserve or better become strength, than sobriety and temperance? What is a more charming or more lasting ornament to beauty, than modesty and chastity? After all this, it is a vain thing to comfort yourselves with saying, that the grave and wise, when they had the same inclinations you now have, did as you do—indulge and gratify them; for, *first*, this is not generally true; and, *secondly*, the less they did it, the more were they honored and beloved; but *thirdly*, if they did, it is certain that they have bitterly condemned it and repented it. And is it not strangely absurd, that you should propose to yourselves nothing in the lives of the wise and virtuous but their frailties and errors, for your example; that you should pitch upon that only for your imitation, which all the wise and good detest and bemoan, as their sin and shame, and think it their highest wisdom to do so.

To conclude this address to the younger sort, unless there be any who are possessed with a spirit of infidelity, against which I will not now enter the lists, all the pretences you can possibly form for your deferring to devote yourselves instantly to wisdom and religion, are founded in two suppositions, of which the one is false, and the other absurd. The false one is, that sin is a state of pleasure; virtue of trouble and uneasiness; the contrary of which is, I think, sufficiently demonstrated through this whole treatise; and would you but be prevailed with to taste the pleasures of a sincere virtue, your experience would soon confute this fancy. What madness, then, is it to be afraid of becoming happy too soon! Ah! how differently are we affected under the maladies of the mind and of the body! Did the lame or blind, the lepers, the lunatics, or demoniacs, ever entreat our Lord to defer their cure, and give them leave to enjoy their miseries, diseases, and devils, a little longer?

The other supposition is absurd; which is, that you will repent hereafter. Must you then repent hereafter? Must this be the fruit of all your sinful pleasures, guilt and remorse, grief and fear, distress and agony of soul? Do revelation and reason, death and judgment, do all your sober and retired thoughts preach you this one lesson, *repentance?* And yet can you resolve to plunge yourselves in that filthiness which must be washed off with tears? Can you resolve to indulge those cheating and deceitful lusts which will one day fill your soul with shame and sorrow, with distraction, horror, and amazement?

Ah, infatuation! ah, bewitchery! that ever a rational creature should live in such an open defiance and hostility against his reason! And yet, if repentance, after many years, and innumerable sins, would be more easy; if your sins would be more easily conquered, or more easily atoned; this frenzy would not want some little color. But how contrary is this to truth.

THE LIFE OF T. CAROLAN,

THE CELEBRATED IRISH MUSICIAN AND LYRICAL WRITER

"Erin from her green throne surveys
The progress of her tuneful son,
Exulting as the minstrel plays,
At the applause his harp has won.
Then grieve not for the loss that shades
Fair nature's landscape from your view;
The genius that no gloom invades,
She gave in recompense to you."

Carolan was born in 1670, in the village of Nobber, in the county of Westmeath. He is among the last of the Irish bards of any distinction. His father was a poor farmer, the humble proprietor of a few acres, which yielded him a scanty subsistence. Car-:lan lost his sight at a very early age, by the small-pox. He soon evinced a fondness for music and poetry, and received every encouragement from his friends that their limited means would allow. At twelve years of age he commenced a thorough course of musical study, under a proficient master, who instructed him upon the harp; but unfortunately for him, his remarkable genius was not coupled with that rigid application so requisite to success. Genius seldom makes diligence her companion: her perfect creations appear at her bidding, and if nature does not give them breath, she disowns her offspring.

Carolan spent the most of his life as an itinerant musician, singing at the houses of the great, where he never failed to meet with a cordial welcome. He thought the tribute of a song due to every house in which he was entertained, and never failed to pay it, choosing for his subject either the head of the family, or some one of its loveliest members. He is said to have composed upward of four hundred pieces; and contributed much towards correcting and enriching the style of national Irish music, by his productions. He alternately tried almost every style of music, the elegiac, the festive, the amorous, and the sacred; and has so much excelled in each, that we scarcely know to which of them his genius was best adapted. Among the numerous instances in which he displayed a knowledge of harmony and purity of taste, not common to the Irish at that period, the following is perhaps the most striking:

His fame as a musician having reached the ears of an eminent Italian music-master in Dublin, he devised a plan for putting his abilities to a very severe test. He singled out an elegant piece of music in the Italian style; but here and there he altered or mutilated it, in such a manner that none but a real judge could detect the alterations. Carolan, quite unaware that it was intended as a trial of his skill, gave the deepest attention to the performer who played the piece, thus altered, in his presence. He then declared it to be an excellent piece of music; but, to the astonishment and satisfaction of the company, added humorously, 'but here and there it limps and stumbles.' He was then requested to rectify the errors, which he accordingly did. In this state the piece was sent back to Dublin; and the Italian master no sooner saw the amendments, than he cordially pronounced Carolan to be a true musical genius.

Aside from his superior musical abilities, he was a very fair poet, and has left coupled to his music many fine lyric poems. As music always tends to soften and refine the feelings, and to kindle in the soul deep and ardent passions, Carolan was by no means exempt from this rule. Being frequently dependent upon others for kind offices, and perhaps sometimes accused by them of ingratitude, he no doubt felt most keenly, at times, his forlorn and friendless condition. When he grew to manhood, there was a time when his harp could only reëcho the impulses of love. About this time he became warmly attached to a young lady by the name of Bridget Cruise. But Bridget, it appears, did not unite her lot with his; and he afterward loved and married Mary Maguire, of a good family, in the county of Fermanagh. After this event, he built him a neat little house, on a small farm near Mars-hill, where he lived, it is said, more merrily than wisely.

An interesting anecdote is related of our blind poet and musician, in which it appears he was able to recognise a very dear friend, who had long been ab sent, by the shape of her hand. Many years after his marriage, he went on a pilgrimage to St. Patrick's Purgatory, a cave in the island of Soughderg, Donegal ; and on returning to the shore, met several pilgrims waiting the arrival of the boat that conveyed him. On assisting some of these into the boat, his hand unexpectedly met one which caused him to start, and he instantly exclaimed, "This is the hand of Bridget Cruise!" His sense of feeling had not deceived him. It was the hand of her he had once loved so passionately. It is by no means uncommon for the blind to recognise their friends by touching their hands; yet the narrator of this anecdote, (as though fearful the account might be thought fabulous and legendary in a few generations,) adds: "I had this anecdote from his own mouth, and in terms which gave me a strong impression of the emotion which he felt on meeting the object of his early affection."

By many it is thought wonderful, that blind persons should be able to recognise their friends by the sound of their voices, or the peculiar form of their hands. To us, it appears no more strange, than that the seeing should recognise a friend by the countenance he is in the habit of wearing every day; to say nothing of the one he has in reserve for extra occasions. The reserve is only a counterfeit of the one nature gave him, though perhaps a little more highly carved and polished. If there are some faces more striking than others, there are some voices more attractive than others. When men habitually wear a face expressive of severity, constantly clouded with frowns, the voice is sure to indicate it. It is no more surprising that the blind should discover marks of recognition in the hand, or voice, than that the seeing should observe differences in figure and dress. Almost any one can distinguish a friend from a stranger, even in the dark, by the sound of his voice; yet, because the loss of sight compels one to resort to this method, it is made a matter of wonderment and surprise, even among those who can do it themselves.

At a period in Carolan's life when he most needed the attention of a kind friend, he was called to mourn the loss of an affectionate wife. After this sad event Carolan lived but five years. While on a visit at the house of Mrs. McDermott, of Alderford, in the county of Roscommon, he died, in March, 1738, in the sixty eighth year of his age.

A monody, composed by him, on the death of his wife, we subjoin:

ON THE DEATH OF MARY MAGUIRE.

Were mine the choice of intellectual fame,
  Of skillful song and eloquence divine,
Painting's sweet power, philosophy's pure flame,
  And Homer's lyre and Ossian's harp were mine,—
The splendid arts of Erin, Greece, and Rome,
  In Mary lost, would love? their wonted grace;
All would I give to snatch her from the tomb,
  Again to fold her in my fond embrace!

Desponding, sick, exhausted with my grief,
  Awhile the founts of sorrow cease to flow,
In vain I rest, and sleep brings no relief;
  Cheerless, companionless, I wake to woe.
Nor birth, nor beauty, shall again allure,
  Nor fortune win me to another bride;
Alone I'll wander, and alone endure,
  Till death restore me to my dear one's side.

Once every thought and every scene was gay,
  Friends, mirth, and music, all my soul enjoyed;
Now doom'd to mourn my last sad years away;
  My life a solitude, my heart a void.
Alas! the change, to change again no more,
  For every comfort is with Mary fled;
And ceaseless anguish shall her loss deplore,
  Till age and sorrow join me with the dead.

Adieu! each gift of nature and of art,
  That erst adorn'd me in life's earliest prime;
The cloudless temper and the social heart,
  The soul ethereal, and the flight sublime.
Thy loss, my Mary, chas'd them from my breast!
  Thy sweetness cheers, thy judgment aids no more
The muse deserts a heart with grief oppress'd,
  And lost is every joy that charm'd before!

A SONG.

[The following lines were addressed to a young lady, written perhaps, while yet our poet's harp was rapturously tuned to the sweet plaints of love:]

To thee harmonious powers belong,
That add to verse the charms of song,
Soft melodies with numbers join,
And make the poet half divine.

As when the softly blushing rose,
Close by some neighboring lily grows,
Such is the glow thy cheeks diffuse,
And such their bright and blended hues!

The timid luster of thine eye
With nature's purest tints can vie;
With the sweet blue-bell's azure gem,
That droops upon the modest stem!

The poets of Ierni's plains
To thee devote their choicest strains;
And oft their harps for thee are strung,
And oft thy matchless charms are sung.

Since the fam'd fair of ancient days,
Whom bards and worlds conspir'd to praise,
Not one like thee has since appear'd,
Like thee to every heart endear'd.

How blest the bard, O lovely maid!
To find thee in thy charms arrayed;
Thy pearly teeth, thy flowing hair,
Thy neck beyond the cygnet fair.

Even he, whose hapless eyes no ray
Admit from beauty's cheering day;
Yet though he cannot see the light,
He feels it warm, and knows it bright.

In beauty, talents, taste refined,
And all the graces of the mind,
In all, unmatch'd thy charms remain,
Nor meet a rival on the plain.

THOMAS BLACKLOCK, D. D.

So much has been said in praise of this excellent man by his numerous admirers, that a volume of the present size could not contain even their encomiums, much less a detailed account of his eventful life, together with the selections we wish to make from his writings. We purpose, therefore, to give, in this connection, only a few of the most interesting particulars of his life's history.

Rev. Dr. Blacklock was born at Annan, Dumfrieshire, Scotland, in 1721. His parents were of a highly respectable class, though in humble circumstances. His father was by trade a bricklayer. When but six months old, he was attacked by that most loathsome of all diseases, the small-pox, which entirely destroyed his sight. This misfortune, it was supposed, unfitted him for any of the mechanical pursuits, nor was it thought possible for him to attain any of the higher professions. His early education, however, was not entirely neglected. His father, to whom he so affectionately alludes in some of his poems, took great pleasure in reading for his sightless boy; at first such publications as were best calculated to amuse and instruct him, and afterward such works as Allan Ramsay, Prior's Poems, and the Tattler, Spectator and Guardian. In this way, young Blacklock soon acquired a fondness for reading, and a love for poetry.

Quite early in life, Milton, Spenser, Pope and Addison were his favorite authors. At twelve years of age, he commenced writing verses in imitation of them. Some of these early productions, it is said, were not inferior to many of the premature compositions by schoolboys possessing the best advantages. At the early age of nineteen, his father was accidentally killed by the falling of a malt-kiln. The loss of parents, at any period of one's life, is a trying affliction; and it may well be supposed that the young poet felt his loss most deeply. The few hopes he had built upon his father's probable success in life, were suddenly destroyed. Thus deprived of the support on which his youth had leaned, and left in destitute circumstances, every bright prospect of future fame faded before him, leaving only clouds of despondency which, later in life, sometimes threw their dark shadows across his pathway. After this sad event, he lived about a year with his mother, and was considered, among his personal friends, a young man of uncommon ability.

His remarkable talents and poetical genius soon attracted the notice of Dr. Stephenson, an eminent physician in Edinburgh, who came to Dumfries on a professional visit. In him, Blacklock found a warm friend and benefactor. This kind-hearted gentleman placed him at a grammar school in the Scotch metropolis, and generously volunteered to defray the expenses of his education. Here he remained under the patronage of Dr. Stephenson, until 1745. He then returned to Dumfries, where he resided for some time with his brother-in-law, in whose house he was treated with kindness and affection.

In 1746, he published a small collection of his poems, at Glasgow. Shortly after, he returned to Edinburgh, and entered the University, where he pursued his studies for six years longer. He soon became master of Latin and Greek, and, it is said, could converse quite fluently in the French.

In 1754, he published at Edinburgh a second edition of his poems, greatly improved and enlarged, to which was prefixed an account of his life. This publication attracted the notice of Mr. Spence, Professor of Poetry at Oxford, who was first to call the attention of the public to the true native genius and high intellectual attainments of this blind student, and to his originality, as a poet. Through the influence of the celebrated David Hume, a warm friend and admirer of Blacklock, a third edition of his poems was published in London, in 1756, under the superintendence of Mr. Spence, together with an account of the author's life, and a very elaborate dissertation upon his character and superior merits.

About this time, he published at Edinburgh a pamphlet on Universal Etymology, or the Analysis of a Sentence.

During his course of study at the University, he acquired a knowledge of the various branches of philosophy and theology, nor was polite literature neglected by him. In 1757, he formed the design of establishing a school for the instruction of young men in oratory. But meeting with some discouragement from his friends, he abandoned the project, and commenced a thorough course of theological study, with the intention of going into the church ; and was accordingly licensed, in 1759, by the presbytery of Dumfries, to preach the gospel. In 1760, he published an able sermon, on the Right Improvement of Time. " The sentiments it contains," says Mr. Wilson, " are just and solid, and the advice is calculated to be useful at all times, particularly in the the prospect of national danger or distress." In 1761, he published a lengthy discourse, on Faith, Hope, and Charity, in 8vo.

In 1762, he married Miss Sarah Johnston, of Dumfries, a lady of highly respectable parentage. Her fine talents and generous nature, (personal charms most attractive to the blind,) combined with a sweetness of temper, and true devotion to the interests of her husband, made her a companion worthy of his love and confidence, and a star in the evening of his life, whose mild face was never hid among clouds of disappointment. Shortly after this event, he was ordained minister of the church at Kirkcudbright, on the presentation of the Earl of Selkirk. But the people, on account of their prejudices toward one deprived of sight, refused to receive him as their spiritual guide. "Though undoubtedly blind enough themselves," says Mr. Bowen, "they did not like the idea of having a blind clergyman." After a legal dispute of nearly two years, he was at last induced to compromise the matter, by resigning his situation and receiving a small annuity instead.

A very interesting anecdote is related of him, which shows his mental anxiety at this time, and deserves a place in Dr. Abercrombie's chapter on Somnambulism. It occurred at an inn in Kirkcudbright. "Dr. Blacklock, one day, harassed by the censures of the populace, whereby not only his reputation, but his very existence was endangered, and fatigued with mental exertion, fell asleep after dinner. Some hours after, he was called upon by a friend, answered his salutation, and rose and went with him into the dining-room, where some of his companions were met. He joined with two of them in a concert, singing, as usual, with taste and elegance, without missing a note, or forgetting a word; he then went to supper, and drank a glass or two of wine. His friends, however, observed him to be a little absent and inattentive; by and by he began to speak to himself, but in so low and confused a manner as to be unintelligible. At last, being pretty forcibly roused, he awoke with a sudden start, unconscious of all that had happened, as, till then, he had continued fast asleep."

In 1764, he removed to Edinburgh, and opened a boarding-house for young men, whom he proposed to instruct in philosophy and the languages. Shortly after, the University of Aberdeen conferred upon him the degree of Doctor of Divinity. In 1767, he published a work entitled Consolation, deduced from Natural and Revealed Religion. In 1773, he published a satirical poem at Edinburgh, in 8vo. He was also the author of a heroic ballad, in four cantos. It may not be generally known that the article "Blind," in the Encyclopedia Britannica, published in 1783, was written by him. He died in 1791, in the seventieth year of his age, and was interred in the burying-ground of Ease Chapel.

> "Peace to thy gentle shade, and endless rest!
> Bless'd in thy genius, in thy love, too, bless'd!"

We cannot place before our readers a richer literary feast, than our poet's beautiful soliloquy, copied from his Edinburgh edition:

A SOLILOQUY,

Occasioned by the author's escape from falling into a deep well where he must have been irrecoverably lost, if a favorite lap-dog had not, by the sound of its feet upon the board with which the well was covered, warned him of danger.

> "Quid quisque viret, nunquam homini satis
> Cautum est in horus." *Horat.*

Where am I!—O Eternal Power of Heaven!
Relieve me; or, amid the silent gloom,
Can Danger's cry approach no generous ear,
Prompt to redress the unhappy? O my heart!
What shall I do, or whither shall I turn?
Will no kind hand, benevolent as Heaven,
Save me, involv'd in peril and in night?
Erect with horror stands my bristling hair;

My tongue forgets its motion; strength forsakes
My trembling limbs; my voice, impell'd in vain,
No passage finds; cold, cold as death, my blood,
Keen as the breath of winter, chills each vein.
For on the verge, the awful verge of fate
Scarce fix'd I stand; and one progressive step
Had plunged me down, unfathomably deep
To gulfs impervious to the cheerful sun
And fragrant breeze; to that abhorr'd abode,
Where Silence and Oblivion, sisters drear!
With cruel Death confed'rate empire hold,
In desolation and primeval gloom.
Ha! What unmans me thus? What, more than horror,
Relaxes every nerve, untunes my frame,
And chills my inmost soul?—Be still, my heart!
Nor fluttering thus in vain attempt to burst
The barrier firm, by which thou art confin'd,
Resume your functions, limbs! restrain those knees
From smiting thus each other. Rouse, my soul!
Assert thy native dignity, and dare
To brave this king of terrors; to confront
His cloudy brow, and unrelenting frown,
With steady scorn, in conscious triumph bold.
Reason that beam of uncreated day,
That ray of Deity by God's own breath
Infus'd and kindled, reason will dispel
Those fancied terrors: reason will instruct thee,
That death is Heaven's kind interposing hand,
To snatch thee timely from impending woe;
From aggregated misery, whose pangs
Can find no other period but the grave.
For, oh! while others gaze on Nature's face,
The verdant vale, the mountains, woods and streams;
Or, with delight ineffable, survey
The sun, bright image of his parent God;
The seasons, in majestic order, round
This varied globe revolving; young-eyed Spring,
Profuse of life and joy; Summer, adorn'd
With keen effulgence, brightening heaven and earth,

Autumn, replete with Nature's various boon,
To bless the toiling hind; and Winter, grand
With rapid storms, convulsing Nature's frame:
Whilst others view heaven's all-involving arch,
Bright with unnumber'd worlds; and lost in joy,
Fair Order and Utility behold;
Or, unfatigued, the amazing chain pursue,
Which in one vast, all-comprehending whole,
Unites th' immense, stupendous works of God,
Conjoining part with part, and through the frame
Diffusing sacred harmony and joy;
To me those fair vicissitudes are lost,
And grace and beauty blotted from my view.
The verdant vale, the mountains, woods, and streams,
One horrid blank appear; the young-eyed Spring,
Effulgent Summer, Autumn decked in wealth
To bless the toiling hind, and Winter grand
With rapid storms, revolve in vain for me:
Nor the bright sun, nor all-embracing arch
Of heaven, shall e'er these wretched orbs behold.
O Beauty, Harmony! ye sister train
Of graces; you, who, in th' admiring eye
Of God your charms displayed, ere yet transcrib'd
On Nature's form, your heavenly features shone,
Why are you snatched forever from my sight,
Whilst in your stead, a boundless waste expanse
Of undistinguish'd horror covers all!
Wide o'er my prospect rueful darkness breathes
Her inauspicious vapor; in whose shade,
Fear, Grief, and Anguish, natives of her reign,
In social sadness, gloomy vigils keep:
With them I walk, with them still doom'd to share
Eternal blackness, without hope of dawn.
Hence, oft the hand of Ignorance and Scorn,
To barbarous Mirth abandon'd, points me out
With idiot grin: the supercilious eye
Oft, from the noise and glare of prosperous life
On my obscurity diverts its gaze,
Exulting, and, with wanton pride elate,

Felicitates its own superior lot:
Inhuman triumph! Hence the piercing taunt
Of titled insolence inflicted deep.
Hence the warm blush that paints ingenuous shame
By conscious want inspir'd; th' unpitied pang
Of love and friendship slighted. Hence the tear
Of impotent compassion, when the voice
Of pain, by others felt, quick smites my heart,
And rouses all its tenderness in vain.
All these, and more, on this devoted head,
Have with collected bitterness been pour'd.
Nor end my sorrows here. The sacred fane
Of knowledge, scarce accessible to me,
With heart-consuming anguish I behold;
Knowledge, for which my soul insatiate burns
With ardent thirst. Nor can these useless hands,
Untutored in each life-sustaining art,
Nourish this wretched being, and supply
Frail nature's wants, that short cessation know.
Where now, ah! where is that supporting arm
Which to my weak, unequal infant steps,
Its kind assistance lent?* Ah! where that love,
That strong assiduous tenderness, which watch'd
My wishes yet scarce form'd; and to my view,
Unimportun'd, like all-indulging Heav'n,
Their objects brought? Ah! where that gentle voice
Which, with instruction, soft as summer dews
Or fleecy snows, descending on my soul,
Distinguish'd every hour with new delight?
Ah! where that virtue, which amid the storms
The mingled horrors of tumultuous life,
Untainted, unsubdued, the shock sustain'd!
So firm the oak which, in eternal night,
As deep its root extends, as high to Heaven
Its top majestic rises; such the smile
Of some benignant angel, from the throne
Of God dispatch'd, ambassador of peace;

* The character here drawn is that of the author's father, whose unforeseen fate had just before happened: he was killed by the fall of a malt kiln.

Who on his look impress'd his message bears,
And pleas'd, from earth averts impending ill.
Alas! no wife thy parting kisses shar'd;
From thy expiring lips no child receiv'd
Thy last, dear blessing, and thy last advice.
Friend, father, benefactor, all at once,
In thee forsook me, an unguarded prey
For every storm, whose lawless fury roars
Beneath the azure concave of the sky,
To toss, and on my head exhaust its rage.
Dejecting prospect! soon the hapless hour
May come; perhaps this moment it impends,
Which drives me forth to penury and cold,
Naked, and beat by all the storms of heaven,
Friendless and guideless to explore my way;
Till on cold earth this poor unshelter'd head
Reclining, vainly from the ruthless blast
Respite I beg, and in the shock expire.
Me miserable! wherefore, O my soul!
Was, on such hard conditions, life desir'd?
One step, one friendly step, without thy guilt;
Had plac'd me safe in this profound recess,
Where, undisturb'd, eternal quiet reigns
And sweet forgetfulness of grief and care.
Why, then, my coward soul! didst thou recoil?
Why shun the final exit of thy woe?
Why shiver at approaching dissolution?
Say, why, by nature's unresisted force,
Is every being, where volition reigns
And active choice, impell'd to shun their fate,
And dread destruction as the worst of ills;
Say, why they shrink, why fly, why fight, why risk
Precarious life, to lengthen out its state,
Which, lengthen'd, is at best protracted pain?
Say, by what mystic charms, can life allure
Unnumber'd beings, who, beneath me far
Plac'd in th' extensive scale of nature, want
Those blessings Heaven accumulates on me!
Blessings superior; though the blaze of day

Pours on their sight its soul-refreshing stream,
To me extinct in everlasting shades:
Yet heaven-taught music, at whose powerful voice
Corrosive care and anguish, charm'd to peace,
Forsake the heart, and yield it all to joy,
Ne'er soothes their pangs. To their insensate view
Knowledge in vain her fairest treasure spreads.
To them the noblest gift of bounteous Heaven,
Sweet conversation, whose enlivening force
Elates, distends, and, with unfading strength,
Inspires the soul, remains forever lost.
The sacred sympathy of social hearts;
Benevolence, supreme delight of heaven;
Th' extensive wish, which in one wide embrace
All beings circles, when the swelling soul
Partakes the joys of God, ne'er warms their breasts.
  As yet, my soul ne'er felt th' oppressive weight
Of indigence unaided; swift redress,
Beyond the daring flight of hope, approached,
And every wish of nature amply bless'd,
Though, o'er the future series of my fate,
Ill omens seem to brood, and stars malign
To blend their baneful fire: while the sun
Darts boundless glory through th' expanse of heaven,
A gloom of congregated vapors rise,
Than night more dreadful in her blackest shroud,
And o'er the face of things incumbent hang,
Protruding tempest; till the source of day
Again asserts the empire of the sky,
And o'er the blotted scene of nature, throws
A keener splendor. So, perhaps, that care,
Through all creation felt, but most by man,
Which hears with kind regard the tender sigh
Of modest want, may dissipate my fears,
And bid my hours a happier flight assume.
Perhaps, enlivening hope! perhaps my soul
May drink at Wisdom's fountains, and allay
Her unextinguish'd ardor in the stream:
Wisdom, the constant magnet, where each wish,

Set by the hand of Nature, ever points,
Restless and faithful, as the attractive force
By which all bodies to the center tend.
What then! because th' indulgent sire of all
Has, in the plan of things, prescrib'd my sphere;
Because consummate Wisdom thought not fit,
In affluence and pomp, to bid me shine;
Shall I regret my destiny, and curse
That state, by Heaven's paternal care design'd
To train me up for scenes, with which compar'd,
These ages, measured by the orbs of heaven,
In blank annihilation fade away?
For scenes, where, finish'd by th' Almighty art,
Beauty and order open to the sight
In vivid glory; where the faintest rays
Out-flash the splendor of our midday sun?
Say, shall the Source of all, who first assign'd
To each constituent of this wondrous frame
Its proper powers, its place and action due,
With due degrees of weakness, where results
Concord ineffable; shall he reverse
Or disconcert the universal scheme,
The general good, to flatter selfish pride
And blind desire?—Before th' Almighty voice
From non-existence call'd me into life,
What claim had I to being? What to shine
In this high rank of creatures, form'd to climb
The steep ascent of virtue unrelax'd,
Till infinite perfection crown their toil?
Who, conscious of their origin divine,
Eternal order, beauty, truth, and good,
Perceive, like their great Parent, and admire.
Hush! then, my heart, with pious cares suppress
This timid pride, and impotence of soul:
Learn, now, why all those multitudes which crowd
This spacious theater, and gaze on heaven,
Invincibly averse to meet their fate,
Avoid each danger; know this sacred truth,
All-perfect Wisdom, on each living soul,

Engrav'd this mandate, to preserve their frame
And hold entire the general orb of being.
Then, with becoming reverence, let each pow'r,
In deep attention, hear the voice of God;
That awful voice, which, speaking to the soul,
Commands its resignation to his law!
For this, has Heaven to virtue's glorious stage
Call'd me, and placed the garland in my view,
The wreath of conquest; basely to desert
The part assigned me, and with dastard fear,
From present pain, the cause of future bliss,
To shrink into the bosom of the grave?
How, then, is gratitude's vast debt repaid?
Where all the tender offices of love
Due to fraternal man, in which the heart
Each blessing it communicates, enjoys?
How then shall I obey the first great law
Of nature's legislator, deep impress'd
With double sanction, restless fear of death,
And fondness still to breathe this vital air?
Nor is th' injunction hard; who would not sink
Awhile in tears and sorrow, then emerge
With ten-fold luster, triumph o'er his pain,
And with unfading glory, shine in heaven?
Come, then, my little guardian genius! Cloth'd
In that familiar form, my Phylax, come!
Let me caress thee, hug thee to my heart,
Which beats with joy of life preserved by thee.
Had not thy interposing fondness stay'd
My blind precipitation, now, e'en now,
My soul, by nature's sharpest pangs expell'd
Had left this frame; had pass'd the dreadful bounds,
Which life from death divides, divides this scene
From vast eternity, whose deep'ning shades,
Impervious to the sharpest mortal sight,
Elude our honest search.—But still I err.
Howe'er thy grateful, undesigning heart,
In ills foreseen, with promptitude might aid;
Yet this, beyond thy utmost reach of thought,

Not e'en remotely distant couldst thou view.
Secure thy steps the fragile board could press,
Nor feel the least alarm, where I had sunk;
Nor couldst thou judge the awful depth below
Which, from its watery bottom, to receive
My fall, tremendous yawn'd. Thy utmost skill.
Thy deepest penetration here had stopt
Short of its aim; and in the strong embrace
Of ruin struggling, left me to expire.
No—Heaven's high sovereign, provident of all,
Thy passive organs moving, taught thee first
To check my heedless course, and hence I live.
Eternal Providence! whose equal sway
Weighs each event, whose ever wakeful care,
Connecting high with low, minute with great,
Attunes the wondrous whole, and bids each part
In one unbroken harmony conspire;
Hail! sacred Source of happiness and life!
Substantial Good, bright, intellectual Sun!
To whom my soul, by sympathy innate,
Unwearied tends; and finds in thee, alone,
Security, enjoyment, and repose.
By thee, O God! by thy paternal arm,
Through every period of my infant state
Sustain'd, I live to yield thee praises due.
O! could my lays with heavenly raptures warm,
High as thy throne, reëcho to the songs
Of angels; thence, O! could my prayer obtain
One beam of inspiration, to inflame
And animate my numbers; Heaven's full choir,
In loftier strains, th' inspiring God might sing;
Yet not more ardent, more sincere than mine.
But, though my voice, beneath the seraph's note,
Must check its feeble accents, low depress'd
By dull mortality: to thee, great Soul
Of heaven and earth! to thee my hallow'd strain
Of gratitude and praise shall still ascend.

LIFE OF HUBER.

It has been observed by writers, that there is no misfortune to which mankind is exposed, that so effectually shuts from us the book of nature and knowledge, as that of physical blindness. Yet, when we take into consideration the scores of blind persons, (many of them so from birth or early in life,) in almost every age and country, whose names are registered high on the scroll of fame, for their attainments in literature and the arts, and their important service in the development of science, since its early dawn upon mankind, we are at an utter loss to determine from what strange oracle these writers have received such disparaging impressions, or what mode of reasoning they have adopted, to arrive at such conclusions.

It is a well known matter of fact, as well as history, that there is scarcely a single branch of natural science yet developed, requiring the minutest calculation or profoundest thought, in which blind persons have not been celebrated proficients. The most intricate problems of mathematics they have demonstrated with ease; to the beautiful science of chemistry they have added many valuable experiments; hydrostatics, hydraulics, acoustics, and optics, have been to them themes of entertainment and delight; and even the motion of the heavenly bodies they have determined with accuracy, and the two noblest poems that yet gem the literary heavens, at this Augustin age, are the productions of the blind.

With such truths before us, refulgent as the noonday sun, we cannot help thinking that, whoever seeks to maintain that the immortal mind of man must remain ignorant and unemployed, for the only reason that one of its avenues to the external world of knowledge has become obstructed, is guilty of the grossest inconsistency, and shows himself destitute of the most important of all senses — common sense.

To receive that knowledge through other mediums of the mind, usually conveyed through that of the eye, is, we confess, in many instances inconvenient; but whoever has not sufficient force of character to grapple with such difficulties in the pursuit of knowledge, would, under the most favorable circumstances, arrive at no great celebrity. How the difficulties which the loss of sight occasions, may be overcome by ingenuity and perseverance, even in the investigation of those sciences requiring the minutest observation, the achievments of this naturalist have cheeringly illustrated.

Francis Huber was born at Geneva, on the 2d of July, 1750, of an honorable family, in which originality and vivacity of mind formed a distinguishing characteristic. His father, John Huber, had the reputation of being one of the most witty men of his age, a trait which was frequently noticed by Voltaire, who valued him for the originality of his conversation. He was an agreeable musician, and no inferior poet. To these accomplishments he joined the taste and art of observing the peculiarities of the animal creation.

His love of natural history as well as his brilliancy of mind were completely inherited by his son. The latter attended from his childhood the public lectures at the college, and, under the guidance of good masters, he acquired a predilection for literature, which the conversation of his father served to develop. He derived his fondness for science from the lessons of De Saussure, and from manipulations in the laboratory of one of his relatives, who ruined himself in searching for the philosopher's stone.

At the age of fifteen, his general health and his sight began to be impaired. The zeal with which he pursued his studies, constituting his highest pleasure, and his unremitting application to reading by the feeble light of a lamp, or that of the moon, were, it is said, the causes which threatened at once the loss of health and of sight. His father took him to Paris, to consult Tronchin on account of his health, and Venzel, on the condition of his eyes.

With a view to his general health, Tronchin sent him to an agricultural district near Paris, to divert his attention from all laborious study. He there practiced the life of a simple peasant, engaging in those rural concerns that never fail to give quietude of mind, and healthful activity to the body. This recreation proved happily effectual, and Huber ever after not only retained confirmed health, but a tender recollection and decided taste for rural life.

But Venzel, his oculist, was not so successful. The cataracts which had been forming on Huber's eyes were then considered irremovable; it was, therefore, announced to him that he must be doomed to utter blindness. But before his departure, he found a congenial spirit in the person of Maria Aimée Lullin, a daughter of one of the syndics of the Swiss republic; and such a mutual love was cherished by them as the age of seventeen is apt to produce. But fearing that the loss of sight might unfavorably affect the dearest object of his affections, he resorted to dissimulation. While he could discern a ray of light, he acted and spoke as if he could see perfectly, and often beguiled his own misfortune by such pretences. But M. Lullin, possessing the true heart of woman, and being inspired by that love not based upon mere policy or expediency, remained constant to the favorite companion of her youth, notwithstanding the determined opposition of her father. As soon as she had attained her majority, she presented herself at the altar with him who had been her choice, and to the amelioration of whose sad misfortune she now determined to devote her life.

Madame Huber proved, by her attachment to his interest, herself worthy of so true and ardent a lover. During the forty years of their union, she never ceased to bestow upon her husband the kindest attention. She was his reader, his secretary, his observer and she removed, as far as possible, all those embarrassments which would naturally arise from his deprivation. Her husband, in alluding to her small stature, would say of her, "mens magna in corpore parvo." As long as she lived, said he, I was not sensible of my misfortune.

We have known the blind to surmount obstacles in the pursuit of knowledge, that made them the wonder of their age; but it was reserved for Huber to give a luster to his class, in the sciences of observation, and upon objects so minute that the most clear-sighted investigator can scarcely observe them. The reading of the works of Reaumer and Bonnet, and the conversation of the latter, directed his curiosity to the history of bees. His habitual residence in the country inspired him with the desire, first, of verifying some facts, then of filling some blanks in their history; but this kind of observation required not only the finest optical instruments, but an intelligent assistant. For this latter purpose he instructed his servant, named Francis Burnens, (remarkable for his sagacity and devotion to his master,) whom he directed in his researches, and by questions adroitly combined, aided by his wife and friends, he rectified the assertions of his assistant, and became enabled to form, in his own mind, a perfect image of the minutest facts. "I am much more certain of what I declare to the world than you are," said he to his friend one day smiling; "for you publish what your own eyes only have seen, while I take the mean among many witnesses."

The publication of his first observations appeared in 1792, in the form of letters to Ch. Bonnet, under the title of " Nouvelles Observation sue les Abeilles." This work made a strong impression upon many naturalists, not only from the novelty of its facts, but from their rigorous exactness, and the amazing difficulty which the author overcame with so much ability. But his investigations were neither relaxed by the flattering reception of his first publication, (which might have been sufficient to gratify his self-love,) nor even by his separation from his faithful Burnens.

The origin of the wax was, at that time, a point in the history of bees much disputed by naturalists. By some it was asserted, though without sufficient proof, that it was fabricated by the bee from the honey. Huber, who had already happily cleared up the origin of the propolis, confirmed this opinion with respect to the wax, by numerous observations; and showed very particularly (what baffled the skill of all naturalists before him) how it escaped in a laminated form from between the rings of the abdomen.

During the course of his observations with Burnens, his wife and son for assistants, he instituted laborious researches to discover how the bees prepare it for their edifices. He followed step by step the whole construction of those wonderful hives, which seem, by their perfection, to resolve the most delicate problems of geometry; he assigned to each class of bees the part it takes in this construction, and traced their labors from the rudiments of the first cell to the completed perfection of the comb. He made known the ravages which the sphinx atropos produces in the hives; he made ingenious inquiries respecting the locality and history of the bee's senses; he discovered that they consume oxygen gas like other animals, and how by a particular motion of their wings, they renovate the atmosphere in the hive.

Since the days and brilliant achievements of Huber, naturalists have not been able to add any considerable discovery to the history of bees. The second volume of his observations was published in 1814, and was edited in part by his son. Huber was considered by his cotemporaries worthy of a place in the class of special observers. Most of the academies of Europe (and especially those of Paris) admitted Huber, from time to time, among their associates.

But his valuable contributions to science were not the only tributaries to his fame. As a writer, he possessed more than ordinary merit. The elegance of his style, the height of imagination, and correctness of his imagery, lead us to infer that he might have been a poet as well as naturalist. In the various relations of life, he displayed such sweetness of temper as made him beloved by all his large circle of friends. He spent the evening of his life at Lausanne, under the care of his daughter, Madame de Molin.

Huber retained his faculties to the last. At the age of eighty-one, in a letter to one of his friends, he writes thus: "There is a time when it is impossible to remain neglectful; it is when separating gradually from each other, we may reveal to those we love all that esteem, tenderness, and gratitude have inspired us with towards them." He farther adds: "Resignation and serenity are blessings which have not been refused." He wrote these lines on the 20th of December, 1831, and on the 22d he was no more. His life became extinct, without pain or agony, while in the arms of his daughter.

None of his writings previous to this have been published in the United States. We favor our readers with several extracts, from a copy of his work on bees, imported by ourselves for this purpose. A few ingenious experiments, elucidating portions in their history, dark to naturalists prior to his researches, must, however, suffice.

EXPERIMENTS RELATIVE TO THE FORMATION OF SWARMS

I now proceed to experiments proving that an old queen always conducts the first swarm:

One of my glass hives consisted of three parallel combs, placed in frames opening like the leaves of a book. It was well peopled, and abundantly provided with honey and wax, and with brood of every differ ent age. On the 5th of May, 1787, I removed its queen, and, on the 6th, transferred all the bees from another hive into it, with a fertile queen at least a year old. They entered easily and without fighting, and were in general well received. The old inhabitants of the hive, which, since privation of their queen, had begun twelve royal cells, also gave the fertile queen a good reception; they presented her with honey, and surrounded her in regular circles. However, there was a little agitation in the evening, though confined to the surface of the comb where we had put the queen, and which she had not quitted, for all was perfectly quiet on the other side.

On the morning of the 7th, the bees had destroyed the twelve royal cells; but, independent of that, order continued prevalent in the hive; the queen laid the eggs of males in the large cells, and those of workers in the small ones respectively.

Towards the 12th, we found the bees occupied in constructing twenty-two royal cells, of the same species described by M. de Reaumur; that is, the bases not in the plane of the comb, but appended perpendicularly by pedicles or stalks of different length, like stalactites, on the edge of the passage made by the bees through their combs. They bore considerable resemblance to the cup of an acorn, the longest being only about two lines and a half in depth from the bottom to the orifice.

On the 13th, the queen seemed already more slender than when introduced into the hive; however, she still laid some eggs, both in common cells and those of males.

We also surprised her this day laying in a royal

cell; she first dislodged the worker there employed, by pushing it away with her head, and then supported herself by the adjoining cells while depositing the egg.

On the 15th, the size of the queen was yet farther reduced; the bees continued their attention to the royal cells, which were all unequally advanced, some to the height of three or four lines, while others were already an inch long; thus proving that the queen had not laid in the whole at the same time. At the moment when least expected, the hive swarmed on the 19th; we were warned of it by the noise in the air, and hastened to collect and put the bees into a hive purposely prepared. Though we had overlooked the facts attending the departure of this swarm, the object of the experiment was fulfilled; for, on examination of all the bees, we were convinced they had been conducted by the old queen, by her that we introduced on the 6th of the month, and which had been deprived of one of the antenæ. Observe, there was no other queen in this colony. In the hive she had left we found seven royal cells close at the top, but open at the side, and quite empty. Eleven more were sealed, and some others newly begun; no queen remained in the hive. The new swarm next became the object of our attention; we observed it during the rest of the year, in winter and the subsequent spring; and, in April, we had the satisfaction of seeing another depart with the same queen at its head that had conducted the former one in May of the preceding year.

You will remark, sir, that this experiment is positive. We put an old queen in a glass hive while laying the eggs of males; the bees received her well, and at that time began to construct royal cells; next she laid in one of them before us; and in the last place she led forth the swarm.

We have repeated the same experiment several times with equal success. Thus it appears incontestible, that the old queen always conducts the first swarm, but never quits the hive before depositing eggs in the royal cells, from which other queens will proceed after her departure. These cells are prepared by the bees only while the queen lays male eggs, which is attended by a remarkable fact, namely, that after this laying terminates, her belly being considerably diminished, she can easily fly, whereas it is previously so heavy that she can hardly drag it along. Therefore, it is necessary she should lay, in order to be in a state for undertaking her journey, which sometimes may be very long.

But this single condition is not enough. It is also requisite that the bees be very numerous—they should be even superabundant, and it may be said that they are aware of it, for, if the hive is thin, no royal cells are constructed when the male eggs are laid, which is done solely at the period that the queen is able to conduct a colony. This fact was proved by the following experiment on a large scale:

On the 3d of May, 1788, we divided each of eighteen hives, whose queens were about a year old, into two portions. Thus each portion of the hives had but half the bees that were originally there. Eighteen halves wanted queens, but the other eighteen had very fertile ones. They soon began to lay the eggs of males; but the bees being few, they did not construct royal cells, and none of the hives threw a swarm.

Therefore, if the hive containing the old queen is not very populous, she remains in it until the subsequent spring, and, if the population is then sufficient, royal cells will then be constructed; she will begin to lay male eggs, and, after depositing them, will issue forth at the head of a colony, before the young queens are produced.

ON THE RESPIRATION OF BEES.

The respiration of insects accumulated together in a confined space, where the air can be renewed with difficulty, offers a new problem to the naturalist. Such is the case with regard to bees. Their hive, whose dimensions does not exceed one or two cubic feet, contains a multitude of individuals, all animated, active, and laborious. Its entrance, which is constantly very restricted, and often obstructed, by crowds of bees departing and arriving during the heats of summer, is the only opening admitting the air, yet it suffices for their exigencies. The hive, besides being internally plastered over with wax and propolis by its inhabitants themselves, and closed up with lime from without by the cultivator, has none of the conditions necessary for preserving a current of natural air.

If a lighted taper be placed in a vessel of equal capacity as a hive, with an aperture larger in proportion than its entrance, the flame grows pale in a few minutes, then burns bluish, and is extinguished. Animals in the same situation would soon expire, yet how do the bees survive in their dwelling?

ARTICLE I. PROOFS OF RESPIRATION.

Experiment 1. Bees in the receiver of an air pump were not affected by the first strokes of the piston; but when the mercury sunk to a quarter of an inch above the level of the cistern, they fell down motionless. Exposure to the open air revived them.

2. I took three empty flagons, each capable of holding sixteen ounces of water, and introduced two hundred and fifty workers into the first, the same number into the second, and one hundred and fifty males into the third. The first and last were shut close, the second only restrained the escape of the bees, that they might serve for comparison. In a a quarter of an hour the workers in the close vessel began to testify signs of uneasiness; their rings contracted and dilated with greater rapidity; they per-

spired copiously and seemed strongly affected, because they licked the humid sides of their vessel. In another quarter of an hour a cluster, which had formed around a bit of straw, suddenly separated, and each of the bees fell to the bottom of the vessel, incapable of rising. All became asphyxiated in three quarters of an hour; nevertheless, when removed and exposed to the air, they recovered. The males were affected more fatally, for none survived; but the bees in the vessel admitting the air did not suffer. We found the air of the others greatly altered; the oxygen gas was almost totally consumed, and bees now introduced into it perished.

3–4. Experiment demonstrated, that a new supply of oxygen gas restored the asphyxiated bees. When this gas was pure, some of them put among it lived eight times as long as in common air, but all were suffocated by its conversion into carbonic acid gas.

ARTICLE III. RESEARCHES ON THE MODE OF RENEWING THE AIR IN HIVES.

While investigating all the faculties of bees themselves, which might affect renewal of the internal air, we were struck with the vibration of the wings. We suspected that, having sufficient action to produce the continual buzzing heard within, it might be for the purpose of displacing the air vitiated by respiration.

During fine weather, a certain number of bees always appear before the entrance of the hive occupied in this manner, but still more are found to be engaged in the interior. The ordinary place of ventilation is on the board—those outside of the entrance have their heads turned in towards it; those within have them turned in an opposite direction. We may affirm, that they arrange themselves regularly, to ventilate more at ease. Thus they form files, terminating at the entrance of the hive, and sometimes disposed like so many diverging rays. But this order is not uniform. probably it is owing to the necessity for the ventilating bees giving way to those going and coming, whose rapid course compels them to range themselves in a file, to avoid being hurt or thrown over every instant. Sometimes about twenty bees ventilate at the bottom of a hive; at other times their number is more circumscribed, and their employment of various duration. We have seen them engaged in it during twenty-five minutes, only taking breath, as it were, by the shortest interruption of the vibration. On ceasing, they are succeeded by others, so that there never is any intermission of the buzzing in a populous hive.

EXPERIMENTS DEMONSTRATING THE ORIGIN OF WAX.

The existence of the organs above described, and the scales seen under different gradations, induce us to believe them appropriated for the secretion of wax. But, in common with other animal and vegetable secretions, the means by which this is accomplished appears to be carefully vailed by nature.

Our researches by simple observation thus being obstructed, we felt it essential to adopt other methods for ascertaining whether wax actually is a secretion or the collection of a particular substance.

Providing it were the former, we had first to verify the opinion of Reaumur, who conjectured that it came from an elaboration of pollen in the stomach, though we did not coincide with him that bees then disgorged it by the mouth. Neither were we disposed to adopt his sentiments regarding its origin; for, like Hunter, it had struck us that swarms newly settled in empty hives do not bring home pollen, notwithstanding they construct combs, while the bees of old hives, having no cells to build, gather it abundantly. We had, therefore, to learn whether bees, deprived of pollen for a series of time, would make wax, and all that this required was confinement.

On the 24th May, we lodged a swarm which had just left the parent stock, in a straw hive, with as much honey and water as necessary for the consumption of the bees, and closed the entrances so as to prevent all possibility of escape, leaving access for the renewal of the air.

At first the bees were greatly agitated; but we succeeded in calming them by carrying the hive to a cool, dark place, where their captivity lasted five days. They were then allowed to take flight in an apartment, the windows of which were carefully shut,

and where the hive could be examined conveniently. The bees had consumed their whole provision of honey; but their dwelling, which did not contain an atom of wax when we established them in it, had now acquired five combs of the most beautiful wax, suspended from its arch, of a pure white, and very brittle. We did not expect so speedy a solution of the problem; but before concluding that the bees had derived the faculty of producing wax from the honey on which they fed, a second experiment, susceptible of no other explanation, was necessary.

The workers, though in captivity, had been able to collect farina; while they were at liberty they might have obtained provisions on the eve or on the day itself of their imprisonment, and enough might have been in the stomach, or on the limbs, to enable them to extract the wax from it that we had found in the hive.

But if it actually came from the farina previously collected, this source was not inexhaustible; and the bees being unable to obtain more, would cease to construct combs, and would fall into absolute inaction. Before proceeding to the second experiment, which was to consist in prolonging their captivity, we took care to remove all the combs they had formed in that preceding. Burnens made them return to the hive, and confined them again with a new portion of honey. The experiment was not tedious. From the evening of the subsequent day, we observed them working in wax anew; and on examining the hive on the third day, we actually found five combs as regular as those they had made during their first imprisonment.

The combs were removed five times successively, but always under precaution of the escape of the bees from the apartment being prevented, and during this long interval, the same insects were preserved and fed with honey exclusively. Undoubtedly the experiment, had we deemed it necessary, might have been prolonged with equal success.

On each occasion that we supplied them with honey, they produced new combs, which puts it beyond dispute that this substance affected the secretion of wax in their bodies, without the aid of pollen. As the reverse of the preceding experiment would prove whether the pollen itself had the same property, instead of supplying our bees with honey, we fed them on nothing except fruit and farina. They were kept eight days in captivity, under a glass bell with a comb, having only farina in the cells; yet they neither made wax, nor were scales seen under the rings.

Could any doubt exist as to the real origin of wax? We entertained none.

BIOGRAPHICAL SKETCH OF JAMES HOLMAN,

A CELEBRATED BLIND TRAVELER.

The history and writings of this wonderful man cannot fail, we think, to especially interest those of our readers who are wholly unacquainted with the progress which the blind of all ages have made in the intellectual pursuits, and with the various methods adopted by them for the acquisition of knowledge. By those who know but little of the ardent wishes cherished by this class of persons, to make themselves active and useful members of society, the first inquiry will very naturally be—What pleasure will one derive from traveling who cannot look out upon this beautiful world, with all its gay and varied scenery; its green earth; its starry skies; its gay flowers, with their endless variety of sweet faces waving in the clear sunlight; the sloping lawns and rich meadows; the mountains, the woods, and, in short, all that is truly grand and beautiful in nature? This inquiry deserves a kind consideration; and we cannot better meet it than by copying Mr. Holman's own answer to like interrogations:

"I am constantly asked, and I may as well answer

the question here once for all, what is the use of traveling to one who cannot see? I answer, Does every traveler see all he describes? and is not every traveler obliged to depend upon others for a great portion of the information he collects? Even Humboldt himself was not exempt from this necessity. The picturesque in nature, it is true, is shut out from me, and works of art are to me mere outlines of beauty, accessible only to one sense; but perhaps this very circumstance affords a stronger zest to curiosity, which is thus impelled to a more close and searching examination of detail, than would be considered necessary to a traveler who might satisfy himself by the superficial view, and rest content with the first impressions conveyed through the eye. Deprived of that organ of information, I am compelled to adopt a more rigid and less suspicious course of inquiry, and to investigate analytically, by a train of patient examination, suggestions and deductions, which other travelers dismiss at first sight; so that, freed from the hazard of being misled by appearances, I am the less likely to adopt hasty and erroneous conclusions.* I believe that, notwithstanding my want of vision, I do not fail to visit as many interesting points, in the course of my travels as the majority of my contemporaries; and by having things described to me on the spot, I think it is possible for me to form as correct a judgment as my own sight would enable me to do; and to confirm my accuracy, I could bring many living witnesses to bear testimony to my end less inquiries and insatiable thirst for collecting information.

"Indeed, this is the secret of the delight I derive from traveling, affording me, as it does, a constant source of mental occupation, and stimulating me so powerfully to physical exertion, that I can bear a greater degree of bodily fatigue than any one could suppose my frame to be capable of supporting. I am frequently asked how I take my notes. It is simply thus: I keep a sort of rough diary, which I fill up from time to time as opportunities offer, but not from day to day, for I am frequently many days in arrear, sometimes, indeed, a fortnight together; but I always vividly remember the daily occurrences which I wish to retain, so that it is not possible that any circumstances can escape my attention. I also collect distinct notes on various subjects, as well as particular descriptions of interesting objects, and when I cannot meet with a friend to act as my amanuensis, I have still a resource in my own writing-apparatus, of which, however, I but seldom avail myself, as the process is much more tedious to me than that of dictation. But these are merely rough notes of the heads of subjects, which I reserve to expatiate upon at leisure, on my return to old England."

It is thought by many that the lack of sight always presupposes both mental and physical debility, dull perceptions, feeble imagination, and, as a natural sequence, sluggish energies, a tasteless and melancholy existence. But these false conclusions have been drawn from instances of restlessness and inactivity among the blind, which were not the result of their peculiar situation, and should not be attributed to their blindness.

It was evidently not a roving disposition, which some have thought a characteristic of the blind, that prompted our worthy author to go abroad, but rather a wish to place himself among eminent travelers, and to increase his sphere of usefulness, by presenting to the world facts that always escape the more superficial observer. "I have been conscious," says he, "from my earliest youth, of the existence of this desire to explore distant regions, to trace the varieties exhibited by mankind under the different influences of different climates, customs, and laws, and to investigate, with unwearied solicitude, the moral and physical distinctions that separate and diversify the various nations of the earth. I am bound to believe that this direction of my faculties and energies has been ordained by a wise and benevolent Providence, as a source of consolation under an affliction which closes upon me all the delights and charms of the visible world."

Mr. James Holman, R. N., (a sketch of whose life we have the honor of publishing for the first time in this country, together with some extracts from his writings,) was born at Exeter, in the year 1786. He lost his sight at the age of twenty-five years, while on service on the coast of Africa, as a lieutenant in the royal navy. In 1820, strange as it may appear, he traveled through France and Italy, and, in 1822, favored the public with an account of his interesting travels, which work was favorably received. In the same year, he undertook an arduous journey through Russia, Siberia, Poland, Austria, Saxony, Prussia, and Hanover. These travels he published in 1825, in two vols. 8vo. The object which Mr. Holman had in making this tour is developed by himself in the following words: "On the 19th of July, 1822, I embarked in the Saunders Hill schooner, commanded by Captain Courtney, then lying in the London docks, and bound for St. Petersburgh, with the ostensible motive of visiting the Russian empire; but my real intention, should circumstances prove propitious, was to make a circuit of the whole world." He was, however, unfortunately prevented from carrying his plans into execution, for after having traveled thousands of miles, and spending some months in the midst of Siberia, he was apprehended as a spy, and was conducted from thence, a state-prisoner, to the frontiers of Austria. In Russia, Mr. Holman was called the "blind spy," an appellation wholly unworthy of our hero, and still more ludicrous in view of his peculiar situation. He gives a most interesting account of the manners and customs of the Russians, their buildings, shipping, commerce, &c.

Being obliged to leave Moscow, his mind was seriously occupied with various reflections. "My situation," says he, "was now one of extreme novelty, and my feelings corresponded with its peculiarity. I was engaged, under circumstances of unusual occurrence, in a solitary journey of a thousand miles, through a country, perhaps the wildest on the face of the earth, and whose inhabitants were scarcely yet accounted within the pale of civilization, with no other attendant, than a rude Tartar postillion, to whose language my ear was wholly unaccustomed; and yet, I was supported by a feeling of happy confidence, with a calm resignation to all the inconveniences and risks of my arduous undertaking; nay, I even derived a real inward gratification in the prospect of retirement from the eternal round of pleasure and social enjoyments, in which I had been participating, to a degree of satiety that began to be oppressive. Again and again I interested myself, by contrasting voluntary exile with the constrained banishment of the numerous unfortunate wretches who have been known to languish away in the inhospitable wilds I was about to traverse, the remnant of a protracted existence, aggravated by an eternal separation from all the blessings that they have deemed most dear to them in life."

After an absence of two years and one day from his native country, our author ultimately landed at Hull, on the 24th of June, 1824.

"Sweet is the hour that brings us home,
  Where all will spring to meet us;
Where hands are striving, as we come,
  To be the first to greet us.
When the world has spent its frowns and wrath,
  And care been sorely pressing,

'Tis sweet to turn from our roving path,
And find a fireside blessing.
Ah, joyfully dear is the homeward track,
If we are but sure of a welcome back!"

No one, we think, can fail to discover in Mr. Holman the elements of a noble and active mind, a force of character, and strength of purpose that would have done honor to a Cæsar. Yet some may urge, (while at the same time they laud his perseverance,) that, had our author lost his sight in infancy, his passion for traveling would never have developed itself. Such an inference would scarcely be just, for now that Locke's philosophy is exploded, no one dare deny the existence of ruling desires, in germ, even at birth. It will be seen that the loss of our highest external sense, (viz, sight,) does not necessitate any faculty of the mind to remain dormant, when we take into consideration the superior culture which the remaining senses receive, and more especially if the physical organism be strong and vigorous. True, happy circumstances aid greatly in nourishing genius, and exercise alone gives health and vigor to the mental, as well as to the physical constitution. The eye may embrace, at one glance, (though superficially,) what would occupy weeks to examine by the sense of touch ; yet we do not know that this is so great an advantage, nor do we believe that the loss of sight precludes the possibility of scientific investigation, deep and profound thought, and even a high appreciation of the beautiful. Nor does external blindness shut out from inner vision the glad face of Nature. Objects which inspire the seeing with emotions of grandeur and sublimity, excite in us the same feelings, and frequently more intense.

We may, at some future time, favor the reading public in this country, with Mr. Holman's entire work; but at present, we shall be obliged to make a few brief extracts suffice.

Mr. Holman, in commenting upon the characters and customs of the French inhabitants of Fernando Po, says, "I shall indulge my own particular feelings and partialities in entering upon that part of my observations which relates more exclusively to the fairer and softer portion of this aboriginal people. The infinite modifications of person, mind, and manners, exhibited by the sex in the different grades of society throughout the world, whether formed by the influences of climate, government or education, presents a most interesting subject to the speculative observer of human nature; and to one who, from early life, both by profession and inclination a traveler, has wandered under every temperature of our eastern hemisphere, who has studied and admired the sex under every variety of character, no wonder that the contemplation of woman, as nature left her, inartificial, unsophisticated, simple, barbarous, and unadorned, should seem fraught with peculiar interest. Are there any who imagine that my loss of eye-sight must necessarily deny me the enjoyments of such contemplations? How much more do I pity the mental darkness which could give rise to such an error, than they can pity my personal calamity! The feelings and sympathies which pervade my heart, when in the presence of an amiable and interesting female, are such as never could be suggested by *viewing* a mere surface of colored clay, however shaped into beauty, or however animated by feeling and expression. The intelligence still allowed me by a beneficent Providence, is amply sufficient to apprise me of the existence of the more real—the diviner beauties of the soul; and herein are enjoyments in which I am proud to indulge. A soft and sweet voice, for instance, affords me a two-fold gratification;—it is a vehicle of delight, as operating on the appropriate nerves, and, at the same time, it suggests ideas of *visible* beauty, which, I admit, may, by force of imagination, be carried beyond *reality*.* But, supposing I am deceived, are my feelings the less intense?—and, in what consists my existence, but in those feelings?

* What Mr. Holman avers to be true of himself, in relation to ideas of visible beauty, suggested by pleasant voices, the present writers of this volume most cheerfully endorse. It is corroborated by the experience of almost every blind person with whom we are acquainted, and those are not a few. As nature speaks of tranquillity in the low whisper of the winds, or of might and contention in the roar of the ocean, so the soul has a voice, blended with the natural utterance of speech, or the sound of the human voice. To us, the voice as clearly indicates moral worth, intelligence, and personal beauty, as does the expression of countenance to the seeing. The voice is as truly an index of the mind, as the face; nor can the mind be highly cultivated, without perceptibly changing the tone of voice.

Is it otherwise with those who *see?* If it be, I envy them not. But are those who think themselves happier, in this respect, than I am, sure that the possession of a more exquisite sense than any they enjoy, does not, sometimes at least, compensate the curtailments to which the ordinary senses, and particularly the one of eye-sight, is liable? and if they should think so, let them not, at least, deny me the resources I possess. I shall not, however, persist further in a description of that situation, those circumstances and those consolations, which the all-feeling comprehension of the poet hath so justly caught in one of its diviner moods of inspiration :

'And yet he neither drooped nor pined,
Nor had a melancholy mind;
For God took pity on the boy.
And was his friend, and gave him joy,
Of which we nothing know.'

"The personal appearance of the females of Fernando Po, is by no means attractive, unless (degustibus non est dis pretandum) a very ordinary face, with much of the contour of the baboon be deemed so.

"Add to this the ornaments of scarification and tattooing, adopted by the sex to a greater extent than by the men, and the imagination will at once be sen sible how much divinity attaches to Fernandian beauty. Like the men, the women plaster the body all over with clay and palm-oil, and also, in a similar manner, wear the hair long, and in curls or ringlets, well stiffened with the above composition. The children of both sexes, or those who have not attained the age of puberty, have the hair cut short, and are not permitted to use any artificial covering to the body. One trait is, perhaps, peculiar to the women of this country, and may be regarded by some as an indication of their good sense—that they have no taste for baubles, or, at all events, do not appear to desire them more than the men. With respect to articles of clothing, they are equally exempt from such incumbrances as the other sex.

> Happy the climate where the beau
> Wears the same suit for use and show,
> And at a small expense, your wife,
> If once well pink'd, is clothed for life.

" Their lords and masters contrive to keep them in great subjection, and accustom them to carry their burdens; they evince also a considerable degree of jealousy, and show evident marks of displeasure, whenever strangers pay attentions to them. As, however, this is equally the case whether the lady be young or old, it is not improbable that it may, in some measure, arise from their considering it too great a condescension on their parts, to notice persons whom they deem so inferior."

Mr. Holman's view from Adam's Peak, in Ceylon, will give the reader a faint idea of the pleasure he derived from traveling, and the exquisite delight, with which his inner vision drank in scenes of beauty. "We reached the summit," says he, "just before the sun began to break, and a splendid scene opened upon us. The insulated mountain, rising up into a peak of 7,420 feet above the level of the sea, flanked on one side by lofty ranges, and on the other by a champagne country, stretching to the shore, that formed the margin of one immense expanse of ocean. I could not see this glorious sight with the visual orbs, but I turned toward it with indescribable enthusiasm. I stood upon the summit of the Peak, and *felt* all its beauties rushing into my heart of hearts."

It is to be regretted that Mr. Holman did not give to the world, more of his own observations and reflections. As a writer, he might have been useful to the world in a two-fold sense. Having possessed perfect sight during the early part of his life, his vivid recollections of light and shade, nature's smiles and frowns, and the various combinations of color, enabled him to draw, with an imaginative pencil, every scene that could be described to him. The knowledge which he gained of new and interesting objects, by adroitly managing the eyes of others, was as correct, no doubt, as though they had been painted upon his own mind. He, therefore, found no difficulty in describing all that other travelers describe, or in gathering as much useful information as other travelers collect. To him, phases of the human character were presented, which are commonly hidden from the seeing. We allude to those higher feelings of wild and savage nature, that only the misfortunes of others can sometimes bring out. Wild, sweet flowers are sometimes found among brambles, and the crudest nature has in it something refined. Most blind persons find the study of character a source of unbounded satisfaction. Our author's peculiar situation, and comparative helplessness, might have opened up to him, among the numerous tribes he visited, an endless field of useful labor. We are, however, not disposed to find much fault with the course Mr. Holman pursued. His writings have amused and interested the public, and have gained for their author a high character in the literary world.

LIFE OF JAMES WILSON, THE BLIND BIOGRAPHER.

"I go, I go! And must mine image fade
From the green spots wherein my childhood played
By my own streams?
Must my life part from each familiar place,
As a bird's song that leaves the woods no trace
Of its lone themes?"

JAMES WILSON was born May 24th, 1779, in Richmond, Virginia. His father, John Wilson, was a native of Scotland, who emigrated to this country when eighteen years of age, to manage the estate of his uncle, which he afterward inherited. After the death of his uncle, he married Elizabeth Johnson, of Baltimore. But, unfortunately for him, at the commencement of the revolutionary war, he found his predilections for monarchy too strong to relish the doctrines of liberty or death, and joined the royal cause. In consequence of this, a band of enraged incendiaries attacked and burned his dwelling, and laid waste his plantation. He served during five campaigns, in a detachment under the command of Lord Cornwallis, and was taken prisoner at Yorktown, where General Washington gave the finishing stroke to the war.

On being released, he found his health much impaired, and being perhaps much grieved to see the star spangled banner, which he strove so hard to humble in the dust, now wave in proud triumph over the Colonies, he decided to take his family and return to England. Bound for Liverpool, the vessel set sail under the guidance of Captain Smith. But they had scarcely lost sight of land, when Mr. Wilson was attacked with severe illness, and twenty days after the ship had left New York harbor, he died.

Mrs. Wilson, being at this time in delicate health, was so shocked by this sad event, that she expired in twenty minutes after. They were both wrapped in one hammock, and committed to a watery grave! And James Wilson, their only surviving offspring, at the tender age of four years, was left a poor, friendless, fortuneless orphan. Nor was this the end of his misfortune; seized by the small pox, and for want of a mother's care and proper medical aid, this most loathsome disease deprived him of his sight. After a long and tedious voyage, the captain was compelled to put into Belfast harbor for repairs. Young Wilson, having not yet recovered from his illness, was immediately sent to the city and placed in charge of the church warden; and to prevent him from becoming a charge to the parish, the benevolent Captain Smith put in the warden's hands a sum of money sufficient to defray his expenses for five years.

When about seven years of age, his right eye was couched by Surgeon Wilson, and restored to partial sight. But shortly after, on crossing the street one day, he was attacked and badly bruised by an ill-natured cow, which nearly cost him his life, and deprived him of the sight he had recovered. He early manifested great mental as well as physical activity, and was held in high esteem by his youthful associates, for daring exploits and inventive genius. So perfect a knowledge did he acquire of every street, nook, and principal building in Belfast, that he was not unfrequently a guide to strangers, with perfect sight, who groped about in midnight darkness, unable again to find their lodgings.

His first effort for self-maintenance, when about twelve years of age, was in carrying letters to and from the different offices of merchants and professional gentlemen, and was afterward employed by Mr. Gordon, editor of the Belfast News Letter, to deliver the papers to subscribers on the days of publication. While in this employment, he was often compelled to call at the residences of gentlemen four or five miles out of the city. But having a perfect knowledge of the surrounding country, he was enabled to execute his business with correctness and dispatch. His indigent circumstances and friendless condition, rendered his opportunities for acquiring knowledge exceedingly limited. But his native genius soon suggested plans to overcome these embarrassments, which his indomitable perseverance at length carried into full effect.

It seems to be indispensably necessary, that a mind destined to be truly great should be first disciplined in the school of rigid self-denial, and its progress hedged up with the most formidable obstacles. For proof of this, we have but to turn over the annals of ancient and modern record, where we find mention of but few personages whose deeds brighten the pages of man's history, or who have been considered illustrious benefactors of their race, that have not risen from humble and embarrassing situations in life. The path leading to true intellectual greatness is fraught with such incessant toil, that there are few surrounded with wealth and affluence, who do not prefer their ease to walking therein. Hence the development of science and the fine arts, in every age, has been left to men of low estate, and often those seeming to labor under the greatest disadvantages.

A vigorous and aspiring intellect cannot be suppressed by mere physical circumstances; but like old Ocean's tide, it gathers strength from impediments, pressing forward with irresistible force, and scales in triumph the loftiest summits of opposition. To the truth of this remark, the trials and triumphs of Mr. Wilson during his long and eventful life bear testimony. When we behold him a poor, sightless, and friendless boy, groping his way through the populous city of Belfast, delivering letters and papers from door to door, while the winter storms howled dismally through the narrow alleys, and the sleety rains fell upon his thin-clad form, a feeling of surprise unconsciously steals over us, that his young and tender heart did not give way under the mountain of affliction that seemed to rest upon it. But He, without whose notice not a sparrow falls to the ground, "who feedeth the young ravens when they cry," has also made the never-failing promise to be a Father to the fatherless.

When Wilson was about fifteen years of age, being destitute of the means requisite for his attending school, he appropriated a part of his scanty earnings each week for educational purposes. With this he purchased such publications as are usually attractive to boys of that age, and employed his young associates to read to him during their leisure hours. A few years subsequent to this time, desiring a more lucrative employment, he chose that of an itinerant dealer; but he found this occupation ill adapted to his circumstances.

"The want of sight," says he in his memoir, "made it difficult for me to steer my course aright, and I was often exposed both to hardships and danger. Many a time have I heard the thunder roll over my head, and felt the teeming rain drench me from head to foot, while I have unknowingly passed by a place of shelter, or stood like a statue, not knowing which way to turn, though within a few paces of a house. Still, however, while reflecting on all these circumstances, and on the sympathy which I was sure to meet with after my sufferings, I have been often led to conclude that the balance was in my favor, when compared with many who enjoyed the use of every sense. There is no rose without its thorn, neither is there any state without its comforts."

During his peregrinations through the country, he was frequently exposed to the most imminent dangers, from which he sometimes narrowly escaped with his life; for example, we give the following as related by himself. "From Ballymena I was one day going out to the Rev. Robert Stewart's. At the end of the town the road divides; one branch leads to Ballymena, and the other to Broughshane. In the forks an old well was opened for the purpose of sinking a pump. It being two o'clock in the day, the workmen were all at dinner, and I was groping about with my staff to ascertain the turn in the road, when a man called out to me to stand still and not move a single step. I did so, when he came forward and told me, that two steps more would have hurried me into a well eighty feet deep, and half full of water. He held me by the arm, and made me put forth my staff to feel and be convinced of my danger, when I found that I was actually not more than one yard from the edge! The blood ran cold in my veins; I was scarcely able to stand erect,

'And every limb, unstrung with terror, shook.'"

In the year 1800, a temporary Institution was established at Belfast, for the instruction of those destitute of sight, in such mechanical pursuits as were best adapted to their peculiar situation. Of this, James Wilson became an inmate, and soon acquired a knowledge of the upholstery business; a trade, by the pursuit of which, under the patronage of his friends, he rendered his circumstances more easy. In 1803, a number of young men formed a reading society in Belfast, and, although they were all mechanics, some of them were also men of taste, and possessed considerable talent. Into this association Wilson was admitted a member, which was the dawning of a brighter day in his literary pursuits. One of its members, to whom he was warmly attached, kindly offered to read to him such books as he could procure. Their stated time for this employment was from nine o'clock in the evening until one in the morning, in the winter season, and from seven until eleven in the summer. In this way he committed to memory a vast collection of pieces, both in prose and verse. "So ardent," says he, "was my desire for knowledge at that time, that I could never bear to be absent a single night from my friend; and often, when walking in the country, where I could have been comfortably accommodated, I have traveled three or four miles, in a severe winter night, to be at my post in time. Pinched with cold and drenched with rain, I have many a time sat down and listened for several hours together, to the writings of Plutarch, Rollin, or Clarendon." This course of reading he continued for seven or eight years, during which time he was made acquainted with almost every work in the English language.

Aided by a retentive power cultivated to a surprising degree, it may well be supposed that Mr. Wilson had by this time accumulated a large store of useful knowledge. So tenacious was his memory, that, during the French revolution, being somewhat interested in politics, he served as an army and navy list to the illiterate who had relations in either of these departments. To illustrate how fully, we give the following anecdote as related by himself: "Being invited by a friend to spend an evening at his house, I had scarcely sat down when three gentlemen entered, and the conversation turning on the news of the day, I was requested by my friend to repeat the names of as many of the ships of the British navy as I could recollect, telling me, at the same time, that he had a particular reason for making the request. I commenced, and my friend marked them down as I went along, until I had repeated six hundred and twenty, when he stopped me, saying I had gone far enough. The cause of the request was then explained. One of the gentlemen had wagered a supper that I could not mention five hundred; he expressed himself much pleased, however, at the loss, having been, as he acknowledged, highly entertained by the experiment." In another place, in adverting to his memory, he says: "In relation to geography, I became acquainted with every place of note on the habitable globe, so that on being examined by some who were either curious or doubtful of my knowledge, my descriptions have been found to coincide with the best constructed maps. Respecting history, the reader will best judge of the power of my memory, by the following relation: To a few select friends who wished to prove my knowledge of English history, I repeated, to their entire satisfaction, an epitome of the history of England, from the Norman conquest till the peace in 1783, invasions, conspiracies, insurrections, and revolutions; the names of all the kings and queens; the years of their accessions; the length of their reigns, and the affinity each had to his predecessors; together with the names and characters of all the great statesmen, heroes, philosophers, and poets, who flourished in the different reigns. In consequence of this and similar rehearsals, I was termed 'the Living Book,' and a 'Walking Encyclopedia.'"

We hear it sometimes remarked, that those deprived of sight, are *naturally* endowed with extraordinary retentive powers. But *we* claim, that memory, like all other faculties of the mind, is only strengthened by continued exercise. The surprising and almost unparalleled degree of perfection which Mr. Wilson attained in this respect, he ascribes mainly to this cause. The power of retaining facts and impressions, of recorded events, and linking together by association a chain of occurrences, is strikingly analogous to the magnet, which, if allowed to lie inactive and to corrode, soon loses its mysterious affinity for the objects that have clustered about it, and they drop one by one like lost remembrances. But if strengthened by daily accession, its power may be cultivated to an almost illimitable degree.

Wilson was married in the 23d year of his age, to

a respectable young lady with whom he had been acquainted for some time. Her unassuming manners, amiable disposition, industrious habits, and assiduous devotion to his interests, made her not only an agreeable companion of his youth, but a solace in declining age. They had eleven children, only four of whom were living when he published his memoirs, in 1838. His merits as an author, and fine literary attainments, recommended him to the notice of many distinguished cotemporary writers, among whom were Dr. Percy, bishop of Dromore, last of that illustrious school of which Johnson, Goldsmith, and Burke were members; and the Rev. H. Boyd, well known in the literary world as translator of Dante.

Quite early in life, at the solicitation of his friends, our author published a small work in verse. Though this production would not, perhaps, commend itself to the mercy of literary cudgelers, *we* think it quite creditable, and shall favor our readers with a few selections.

He afterward formed the design of publishing a history of the blind, which he accomplished, though attended with immense labor, in 1820. To this work we are greatly indebted for many valuable statistics.

TO MEMORY.

Come, Memory, and paint those scenes
  I knew when I was young,
When meadows bloomed, and vernal greens,
  By nature's band were sung.

I mean those hours which I have known,
  Ere light from me withdrew—
When blossoms seemed just newly blown,
  And wet with sparkling dew.

Yet, ah! forbear, kind Memory, cease
  The picture thus to scan!
Let all my feelings rest in peace,
  'Tis prudence' better plan;

For why should I on other days
  With such reflections turn,
Since I'm deprived of vision's rays,
  Which sadly makes me mourn!

And when I backward turn my mind,
  I feel of sorrow's pain,
And weep for joys I left behind,
  On childhood's flowery plain;

Yet now, through intellectual eyes,
  Upon a happier shore,
And circled with eternal skies,
  Youth sweetly smiles once more

Futurity displays the scene,
  Religion lends her aid;
And decks with flowers forever green,
  And blooms that ne'er can fade,

Oh, happy time! when will it come,
  That I shall quit this sphere,
And find an everlasting home,
  With peace and friendship there?

Throughout this chequer'd life 'tis mine
 To feel affliction's rod;
But soon I'll overstep the line
 That keeps me from my God.

A DREAM.

Night o'e rthe sky her sable mantle spread,
And all around was hushed in sweet repose,
Nor silence suffered from intrusive noise;
Save now and then the owl's unpleasant scream
From yon old pile of ancient grandeur sent,
Broke in, obtrusive on the tranquil hours.
Reflection took my mind, and o'er my thoughts
Unnumbered visions flit with rapid speed.
I thought on man, and all his childless joys,
From rosy infancy to palsied age—
And yet the sigh of recollection stole,
Then heaved my breast with sorrow's poignant throb;
For ah! I feel what some have never felt,
That is, to be in one continued night,
From January's sun till dark December's eve;
And strange it is, when sleep commands to rest,
While gloomy darkness spreads her lurid vail,
That then by being blind I suffer most!
O sight! what art thou? were my final words
When sleep with leaden fingers seal'd my eyes.
Now free from care and tumult's torturing din,
Young fancy led me from my humble cot;
And far through space, where suns unnumbered burn,
I with her took a grand excursive flight,
Then back again to Erin's hill of green,
I with her wandered; nor did night, nor gloom,
One step intrude to shade the prospects round.
I saw sweet Scarvagh, in her loveliest garb,
And all her trees in summer's dress were clad·

Her honored mansion, seat of peace and love,
Gave rapture to my breast, for there I've found
True hospitality, which once did grace
The hall's of Erin's chiefs of old;
But soon, alas! the hum of nightly bands
And vagrants, strolling on in quest of sin,
Bore fancy from me with her golden train,
And once more left me in the folds of night.

BEAUTIES FROM "A BLIND MAN'S OFFERING,"

TOGETHER WITH A SKETCH OF THE AUTHOR'S LIFE.

"Offerings there are, of moral worth and talents,
Sacrificed to lust and love of gain,
To envy, hatred, loves inordinate,
And all the baser passions of the soul.
But thine are offerings sacred to the shrine
Of reason, truth and sentiment, replete
With beauties rare, and treasures of the mind."

MAN'S nature, like veneering, may be warped to almost every condition in life. It may be bent to angular circumstances, or shaped to infirmities; it may be marred and chafed by care and want; and still present a surface susceptible of the highest polish. Misfortunes which may seem at first almost insupportable, may grow in favor, like Crusoe's pet spider, and at length come to be regarded as old and tried friends, if not positive blessings. Afflictions are but the seasonings of life's dish, and without them it would be tasteless and insipid. Without the ills of life, we should be illy prepared to enjoy its blessings. By opposites, alone, we judge of the nature of things. Contrast is the betrayer of every object in nature. Were it not for darkness, or the absence of light, we should remain forever ignorant of the existence of light itself. Wrong is the only rule by which we can measure right action; and were there no pain there would be no pleasure. Sorrows are but ill-timed joys—wrong, right inverted—error, reason's blunders — disappointment, only the broken links in life's chain of pleasant associations, and often, from the common ills of life spring our choicest blessings. It is folly to pine at misfortune, while the world is full of time, and effort is fruitful of success. The mind that is truly great, will rise above the petty annoyances of this world, and though the visible universe be shrouded in midnight darkness, knowledge will enter, if only at the finger's ends. True, thoughts, like plants, reach up for the light, but it is the light of truth; and he who is blind to this light, is blind indeed.

Mr. Bowen, author of the work above alluded to, in his reflections on cheerfulness, says: "The smile that wreathes the lip with gladness comes not from the sunshine without, but from within. The physical world is not beautiful until the soul has breathed upon it. The highest happiness of which we are capable can proceed only from the heart that has been sanctified by sorrow." In the same connection he adds: "We can never be too grateful to God for so arranging the allotments of his providence that there is always something in the situation of every one, which exerts an alleviating influence."

The truth of the Roman adage, that all things are not possible to all men, has been verified, we doubt not, in the experience of most persons. And tha the same amount of knowledge, or degree of happiness is not within the reach of every man, is equally true. Yet there is something we are convinced in the condition of every one, in a measure, compensatory for all his privations and afflictions. But how far the loss of sight, or the loss of either of the other senses, is made up to us by the superior development of the remaining faculties, from the degree of culture which they must necessarily receive, or by creating new incentives to efforts, by awakening new desires, directing the thoughts and affections in new channels, and opening up new fields of enterprise, is difficult to determine. Every station in life, however humble or exalted, has its advantages, and with them its own sources of joy and grief. The highest privilege may be abused, and the purest and noblest affections of the soul may be perverted. The rich man may be happy in the possession of great wealth, or he may be indeed more wretched than the poor man, who labors to earn a scanty subsistence; or even the miserable beggar by the wayside. The blind man may see more in the world that is truly worthy of his admiration, than the man who is blessed with perfect sight. Much, we are persuaded, depends upon the medium through which we view our allotments. A false glass gives not only a false coloring to objects, but may greatly magnify or distort them. Habitual cheerfulness tends rather to diminish than increase the burden of afflictions, while despondency is sure to cast a gloom over all that is bright and beautiful in nature. A cheerful submission to whatever is manifestly irremediable, can never fail to be productive of the most happy results.

It is not wonderful that ancient philosophers were forced to acknowledge the necessity of a more perfect revelation from God, in order to understand his arrangements. In the light of divine revelation, he has not only exhibited the beauty and perfection of his own character, but the intrinsic excellence of all created objects, the end for which they were designed, and the true relation of the creature to its Creator. Through this medium alone, do we behold nature in her true aspect. And it is by this light alone that we are enabled to discover the justice of each divine dispensation. Before it every shadow of doubt and despondency, gloom and fear, must vanish like the shades of night before the king of day.

It is to us a source of no small satisfaction, to find in the writings of all blind persons whose works have fallen into our hands, this spirit of christian resignation and implicit trust in Him who doeth all things well; but in none is it more beautifully exemplified than in the life and writings of Mr. Bowen, our gifted American author.

Mr. B. B. Bowen, author of the "Blind Man's Offering," was born in the town of Marblehead, Massachusetts, in the year 1819. At the early age of six weeks he was deprived of sight, and when but six years old he lost his mother. He early manifested great physical activity, and owing to his father's indigent circumstances, he was forced to rely upon his own efforts for maintenance. When but ten years of age, he was employed in carrying fresh fish, as they were daily caught, to the different houses in the place, receiving for his services twenty per cent.

His destitute circumstances, and the great inconvenience under which he labored, secured to him, as might naturally be supposed, the patronage of the wealthy. Although the few pennies earned in this way were barely sufficient to supply his immediate wants, his reliance upon this humble occupation for means of support not only fostered a spirit of independence, but early developed those firm principles which always form the basis of a great and noble character. With Burns, we like the glorious privilege of being independent. Self-dependence we regard as the main prop of manliness. As freedom of will forms the basis of present and eternal happiness, so self-dependence is the pillar of every ennobling virtue.

At the age of fourteen, he was selected by Dr. Howe as one of the six blind children, with whom the first experiments in the instruction of this class were made in the United States. His first two years at this institution were spent mainly at manual labor, but subsequent to this more of his attention was given to study; and at the expiration of his term he maintained a respectable standing in all the principal studies of the first class, except higher mathematics.

In music he had also made considerable proficiency, and after an honorable discharge from the institution, in 1838, he returned to his native town, where he employed his time in teaching music, and those handicrafts which he had learned at the institute. Being desirous that all laboring under similar privations should share the benefit which these institutions afford, he at length embarked as an itinerant lecturer, endeavoring to awaken public interest in behalf of the blind.

Feeling deeply impressed with the idea expressed in the Garden of Eden, namely, "that it is not good for man to be alone," he sought and obtained the hand of one who has thus far strewn the rugged pathway of his life with flowers. In alluding to this event, he thus beautifully remarks: "I could tell you of one who, free from the intense selfishness in which so many hearts seem shrouded, with graces of person made more attractive by a brilliant intellect, and a heart of untainted purity, left her father's halls, and the society of her early associates, to share the humble lot of one who could never see her face, or return her glance of deep affection. It was not that she was actuated by a morbid sensibility, nor with the thought that she was making any greater sacrifice than if she had shared the destiny of one less unfortunate. *No!* It was because she honored him whom she loved; because her education had made her superior to vulgar prejudices, that she was willing to adorn the humble home of a blind man."

In 1847, he published a work in 12mo, comprising over four hundred pages of prose and verse, entitled "A Blind Man's Offering," of which he has person ally sold about eighteen thousand copies. This pro duction has been favorably reviewed, and everywhere received and read with interest. We cannot better recommend it to our readers, than by giving the fol lowing, which is, we think, a just example of the el· egant style in which it is written :

MUSIC.

"The man that hath not music in his soul,
And is not moved by the concord of sweet sounds,
Is fit for treasons, stratagems and spoils."

There is but one universal language, one idiom, by which we can express those feelings, sentiments and ideas common to all. This language, this idiom, is *music*. It pervades all nature. And it is this which seems to connect us, by a thousand mystic ties, to every created thing, and makes us feel, in our silent, contemplative moments, a sympathetic relationship with every object by which we are surrounded, or with which we have been associated. The tree, beneath whose shade we played in our childhood, why is it that we yet remember it? And why do we yet feel that between it and us there once existed a strange but undefinable companionship? Never, amid the din and noise of the world, the selfishness and activity of life, can we entirely forget the music of its rustling leaves, or the thoughts it awakened, as it echoed, at quiet evening, the vesper hymn of the flowers, or answered, at noonday, to the song of the rills. Why is it that we yet retain recollection of those we love, when their image no longer dwells in our mind? It is the music of the voice divine, that can never die. For the tones of love survive the glance of affection.

O Music! divinest of all the arts! deepest of all mysteries! In thee is embalmed the memory of the past, and from thee comes the hope of the future. Thou only revealest the coming blessedness of the race; thou only prophesiest of universal harmony. The phenomena of light, like that of sound, is the result of innumerable vibrations. Everything in nature seems to be in perpetual agitation, and each, in its own way, is ever chanting a gladsome strain, that blendeth in a common chorus, to the Maker of all. From the low song of the flowers, so sweet and plaintive, to the chorus of the spheres, so grand and majestic, there is perpetually ascending to the Fountain of all, a hymn of gratitude and praise. In this universal harmony, there is but one exception, one discord. Of all created things, man alone mars this pæan of nature. Yes, "the harp of a thousand strings," made capable of such high music, formed for such divine strains, withholds its tribute to the universal harmony, or mars with its broken cadence.

The heart of humanity, from which once issued

such holy melodies, where is now its primeval minstrelsy? Over its broken strings sweeps no more the spirit of love. The fiend of selfishness has broken the instrument, made by the hand of God for the holiest purposes; and where erst an angel caroled, there shrieks a demon. Sad and mournful comes the dirge from him who should have foremost sung the gladsome song in nature's universal orchestra. O man! must it ever be thus? Must thou forever sing, in broken strains, the requiem of thy departed joys—of thy lost glory? Shall there gush no more from out thy heart that deep delight that made thy early Eden vocal with thy praises? Shall thy wondrous voice, formed for such lofty eloquence, be tuned no more in unison with nature? Must thy bitter wailing never cease? and all thy life seem but a mockery?

> No! it shall not always be thus with thee,
> Thou greatest of all earth's mystery;
> Thy noblest song is not yet sung,
> Thy highest work is not yet done.

What the world most needs is a benefactor; one who shall expound to our race the laws of harmony, the observance of which shall place men in true relationship to each other and to nature. A poet or a prophet, whose burning words shall awaken, in the mighty heart of humanity, a deeper consciousness of its unity and its harmonies, that shall kindle once more in the bosom of man the flame of seraphic minstrelsy, and revive again those beautiful affinities that once united him to all intelligences. Then will music, the divinest of all the arts, become what it once was —the medium of all true thought and expression.

There are times, when oppressed by the conceptions and aspirations of the soul, we strive in vain for utterance. There are no words that can convey our ideas. Then it is that we have recourse to music, for it is then only that we can truly understand its significance and power. We strive to make ourselves heard and understood, but our yearnings and our struggles meet with no response. The dark world is too much engrossed in its selfishness and sensuality. We commune only with the voices of the past, with the spirits of the departed. Are we sad and sorrowful, we crave the deep sympathy of Beethoven. If we would raise ourselves above this poor life, and catch a glimpse of a higher destiny, we listen with gratitude and admiration to Mozart and Hayden. There are a host of others, who come at our bidding, and with their deep, impassioned strains assuage our griefs and elevate our joys. It is at such times that we cease to be conscious of that dark pall that, from our infancy, hath vailed from us the beautiful in earth and sky.

From my earliest days I have felt within me a striving to be free, that music can only adequately express: a longing for a deeper sympathy, a closer communion with the good, the true, the beautiful. In childhood, those blessed and balmy days, when the fragrance of the flowers and the music of the birds thrilled my heart with deep delight, I felt within —I knew not what—a spirit, whose plaintive, earnest voice wept and smiled, and ever yearned for a fuller, brighter manifestation. 'Twas all in vain I strove to express its meaning. To each dear, cherished thing, around which affection twined, the voice within replied, "It will not do." The spirit cried aloud for something more. But once, but only once, it gave me rest. O, that happiest hour of all my life, that deepest joy I ever knew! The sun's last rays had kissed the verdant hill-top and trailed in beauty along the evening sky. The soft zephyr, laden with the perfume of a thousand flowers, distilled its grateful incense upon all around. The birds had caroled their last sweet lay and gone to rest. A deep, delicious languor overspread all nature. At that holy hour, when solemn thoughts, that, like the stars, come forth at night to shine within the soul's serener sky, when nature everywhere seems wrapped in meditation deep, profound,—I wandered forth alone, for unto me both day and night are one. Yet, dearest of all time is summer eve, for it was at such an hour, that I first felt the mystery of that voice divine, that awoke within me such unutterable delight, that called forth from my heart such deep response, as music only hath power to awaken. O! if I had but fitting words to tell how all-absorbing, how uncontrollable, was the love awakened by those dulcet tones, that softly trembled on the evening air. At that blessed hour, most blessed of all my life, when she, my Isadora, accompanied by her guitar, breathed forth this impassioned lay :

"Give me the night, the calm, beautiful night,
When the green earth reposes in heaven's own light;
When the moon and the stars keep their vigils above,
And nought is awake save the spirit of love.

'When visions of memory visit the heart,
Like the dreams of the past, which too soon must depart.
And the soul fondly dwells on the scenes of delight,
Give me the night, the calm, beautiful night.

"Spirit of love, in you isles of the blest,
Where the bright and the beautiful ever have rest,
Spread thy wings o'er the earth, now so smiling and fair
And breathe all thy tenderness, loveliness there.

"Though the tear will escape as the heart heaves a sigh,
And thoughts, all too deep for emotion, reply,
Yet the soul lingers still o'er the scene of delight,—
Give me the night, the calm, beautiful night."

She ceased; but in my soul, that, until then, had not known aught of companionship, there was created a sense of fullness and deep joy, an all-pervading consciousness that I was blessed, supremely blessed. Years have passed away, but memory of that hour shall live forever.

My Isadora, but for thee,
E'en doubly dark this world would be.

He who may never hope to gaze upon earth or sky, who can never behold the light of the sun, nor look upon the face of a friend, can only adequately appreciate the music of the human voice. To him only can music impart its highest delight, and change his midnight darkness to a noonday splendor. Who can estimate fully the influence of music upon the heart and the life? What can do more to soften and refine the feelings? to purify and elevate the whole nature? And why should it not exert as great a power now, as in the earlier ages of society? Why not have as much influence upon the civilized, as the savage man? Those who have been the most constantly affected by it, who are best capable of appreciating its effects, tell us that there is nothing that can so exalt and ennoble the moral and religious element. Who can calculate the influence it exerts in our churches? What is so well designed to lift the mind from earth to the contemplation of heaven? And then, too, consider the influence of music upon our social feelings. There is nothing like the concord of sweet sounds that can so move the heart to noble deeds and lofty daring, and that, at the same time, can prompt to that spirit of kindness and disinterestedness that softens and beautifies our social intercourse. However, the power to appreciate music is the gift of God. Shall I not say it is one of the noblest vouchsafed to man? Blessed is he who possesses it, and can appreciate it. For amidst all the vicissitudes of this strange life, he has within him that which can sustain and cheer him. It is a pleasant thing to see the smiling faces of those around you, tc look upon the speaking countenances of your friends, to read the burning thoughts that come forth in each glance of the eye. But the beautiful face soon becomes pale and emaciated; the eye soon loses its brilliancy and luster, the form its grace, and the step its elasticity; but the music of the voice can never die. Like the soul, it is divine and immortal. Great is his privilege for whom nature, with its myriad objects of beauty, has power to delight—who can look upon the green, beautiful earth—who can gaze upon the heavens, adorned with its innumerable lights. But there is yet a greater boon, there is a depth in music which transcends all else.

> "O, say, is there a star above,
> Like the low, sweet voice of one you love?"

There is no faculty I possess with which I would not part, rather than relinquish the high satisfaction which music affords. Gladly would I open these sealed orbs, and look out upon the vast, magnificent universe; but I would not accept so great a boon, if it must be obtained at the sacrifice of the deep delight, of the inexpressible joy, of the unutterable happiness, which music alone can impart.

MRS. S. H DE KROYFT.

"The darksome pines that o'er your rocks reclined,
Wave high, and murmur to the hollow wind,
The wandering streams, that shine between the hills,
The grots that echo to the tinkling rills,
The dying gales that pant upon the trees,
The lakes that quiver to the curling breeze;
No more these scenes my meditation aid,
Or lull to rest the visionary maid:
But o'er the twilight groves and dusky caves,
Long-sounding aisles, and intermingled graves,
Black melancholy sits, and round her throws,
A death-like silence, and a dread repose;
Her gloomy presence saddens all the scene,
Shades every flower, darkens every green,
Deepens the murmur of the falling floods,
And breathes a browner horror on the woods."

In the preceding biographical sketches, it has been our uniform purpose to collect all the authentic statistics, relative to the lives of our authors, we could find in either European or American literature, and form a chain of events, interspersed with such original remarks as the occasion and our own experience under similar circumstances, seemed to suggest.

But in noticing our present authoress, having been unable to procure any accounts of her strangely eventful and interesting history, save those she has given to the public in her beautiful and universally admired volume, entitled, "A Place in Thy Memory," we deem it proper to digress from our former rule, and give them principally in her own language and connection.

The beautiful metaphoric drapery thrown around these references to her life and misfortunes, and the simple, natural, and deeply feeling manner in which she tells her tale of woe, form paragraphs so sacred that it seems like ruthless sacrilege to divest them of their original attire.

The following tender and pathetic lines, that must move every reader to tears, susceptible in the slightest degree to feel for others' woes, serve us as a partial introduction to her history:

ROCHESTER, *October*, 1846.

"DEAR CLARA:—'Tis autumn, and to-day the winds howl mournfully among the trees. Four long weeks I have been pillowed on a sick couch, and though with much of its drapery around me, I can to-day sit in an easy chair. Fever still burns on my cheeks, and my brow is pressed with throbbing pain. Last night they fed me opium, and I slept a pleasant sleep, I dreamed of other days. I thought that we again, arm in arm, paced the halls of the old seminary, and talked confidingly of bright realities in the future. The chime of the welcome school-bell again rang in my ears, and I heard the halls echo with the familiar tread of many feet, and mingling voices, all buoyant with hope and love. This morning, I engaged a friend to write for me, while I fancy myself whispering in your ear the story of all that grieves me, and wrings every joy from my heart. 'Truth is often stranger than fiction,' and the tale I shall tell you, needs no coloring. Clara, I *am blind!* forever shrouded in the thick darkness of an endless night. And now, when I look down the current of coming years, a heavy gloom settles on me, almost to suffocation.

"Is there any sympathy in your heart? Oh, then weep with me, for now, like an obstinate prisoner, I feel my spirit struggling to be free. But oh, 'tis all in vain, 'tis all over, misery's self seems stopping my breath, hope is dead, and my heart sinks within me. Clara, I am in a land of strangers, too. Stranger voices sound in my ears, and stranger hands smooth my brow, and administer to my wants. I see them not, but I know they have learned the laws of kindness. I love them, and pray Heaven to hold them in remembrance. But let me change the subject. The first year after we parted at school, my love of knowledge increased every day. I continued Italian with a success that pleased me. I read various French authors, besides translating most of the Old Testament Scriptures, reviewed Rollin, &c.

"In June last, Dr. DeKroyft was seized with hemorrhage of the lungs. He sent for me and I came to him. Every day his lips grew whiter, and the deep paleness on his brow alarmed me. Now, in a half-coughing tone, I hear him say, 'Helen, I fear the hand of consumption is settling on me, and my days will soon be numbered!

"On the afternoon of the Fourth he visited me, went out, and returned no more. Our wedding-day came. It was his wish, and by his bedside our marriage was confirmed. Soon after, I saw him die. They laid him in the ground, and I heard the fresh dirt rattle on his narrow home, and felt as if my hold on life had left me. I lingered in R. a few weeks longer. How I got through the days I do not know. William's room, his books, and the garden where I wept, are all I remember, until I awoke one morning and my eyes were swollen tight together. I could no more move them, or lift up the lids, than roll the mountains from their places. They were swollen with an inflammation that, three days after, made me forever blind—oh, the word! Like the thunders of Niagara, it was more than I could bear.

"Thus, dear Clara, in simplicity, I have told you all. No, not the half. Words can never reach the feelings that swell my heart, imagination can never paint them. They are known only to me. Sorrow, melancholy, blighted hopes, wounded love, grief and despair, clad in hues of darkness, all brood upon my silent heart, and bitter fear is in all my thoughts. Oh, what will become of me? Is there benevolence in this world? Must charity supply my wants? Will there be always some hand to lead me? Have the blind ever a home in any heart? Does anything ever cheer them? Are their lives always useless?

Is there any thing they can do? So I question, and wonder, until with morphine they quiet my distracted thoughts. When my eyes were swelling as if they would quit their sockets, and my entire being was racked with pain, forgive me, Clara, I did question if there be a God in heaven who is always merciful. But to-day, in the calmness of better feelings, my confidence is unmoved, and, 'though he slay me, yet will I trust in him.' Though I do not feel all the self-abnegation of Fenelon, yet I am certain my heavenly Father loves me, and will grant me ever his protecting care and sustaining grace. Adieu, but think of me, and pray for me sometimes."

Tears, and such deep anguish of soul as we find portrayed in the above, stoics have attributed to weakness and imbecility of mind; but, instead of coinciding with such philosophy, we are persuaded that precisely the opposite is true. The sluggish stream that moves torpidly in its encumbered course, can be suddenly stopped without agitating its smooth and languid surface; but the crystal torrent, cheered by misty clouds and rainbow tints, that rushes down the mountain side in power and majesty, if impeded, foams in fury, and impetuous waves in desperation wild, dash to and fro, till freed again to move forward in its resistless course. The dull and selfish being who plods along without comprehending either his design or destiny, or cheered with no higher hope than mere physical gratification, is ever secure against overwhelming spiritual depression. The loftiest minds that have ever gemmed the canopy of fame, wept most over suffering humanity and blighted hopes. A distinguished editor, adverting to her misfortune, says: "Humanity must view the change with weeping surprise and wonder at the ways of Providence. Surely angels of pity must hover around her, and the blessed in heaven drop a tear of sympathy at the necessity of a sacrifice so deplorable for the admonition of the world."

But her ever active mind, richly stored with the choicest treasures of science, could not long thus recoil upon itself, and pine over irretrievable misfortunes. Soon after her melancholy privation, through the influence of kind and official friends, she obtained permission to spend a term of one year at the New York Institution for the Blind, hoping there to dissipate, in the pursuit of knowledge, the bitter sorrows that oppressed her heart. But her former opportunities having advanced her far beyond the literary pale of this Institute, it could but serve as an altar or tower of retreat from the cold world, until she could collect her scattered powers and concentrate them upon some object, in the pursuit of which she could provide for herself the necessaries of life. The chaste, elegant, and magic eloquence of her literary composition, was not long in recommending her to public favor, and she soon hit upon the happy expedient of publishing a book, and engaging personally in its sale.

Her modest and highly intelligent appearance, and the laudable object for which she toiled, secured friends and public patronage beyond her most sanguine hopes. We cannot better do her justice, in this connection, than by copying the following summary editorial:

"How few who may read this paragraph, would think it possible for them, entirely without means, to get up a book, transact all the business contracts and operations necessary, and then, without a single ray of light to guide their steps, go out personally to sell it, day after day, patiently ferreting out dark, lonely streets, and climbing winding stairs; thereby to secure food and raiment. Such enterprise is worthy of praise, and deserves the encouragement of every patron of honest industry. This looks to us like the ambition of Napoleon crossing the Alps, or gathering his scattered army after his discomfiture at Moscow.

The purpose of this blind lady is, to secure for herself "a little cottage and a little plat," which she may call her home. Her cottage must be built. Every book sold, piles one stone on its walls, and all who enjoy a good home, and who can look upon its dear and loved inmates, cannot better add to the zest of its enjoyments than by mingling with them the consciousness of having contributed to provide the same for one who is eminently qualified to enjoy and ornament domestic life, and upon whom has fallen this unparalleled succession of bereavements, thus described in her own words: "I was in one short month a bride, a widow, and blind."

Such men as our late President Taylor, Mr. Clay, General Waddy Thompson, Senator Dawson, Mr. Burt, General Greene, Rev. Dr. Nott, and Dr Turner of New York, and his excellency, Governor Floyd of Virginia, and many other distinguished individuals, both of the clergy and laity, together with the prin cipal editors of New York, Washington, Charleston, S. C., Boston, Salem, Portland, and other places, have lent their influence to this work; and, moreover, Mrs. DeKroyft brings with her letters from many of the most gifted ladies of our land, one of whom, from Washington, says: "That Mrs. DeKroyft is a lady of more than ordinary interest, we need say only to those who have not had the pleasure of listening to her graceful conversation, or reading one of her charming letters in 'A Place in Thy Memory,' which we are happy to say, ornaments almost every drawing-room in Washington City. It is a book which may be read with profit by the most talented, as well as the most common reader. It occurs to us that this book is really one of the most interesting and useful Gift Books for the season. It is no fiction from 'this flood' of literature that is now upon us, but a true, an interesting, and a peculiar phase of real life, that will do good wherever it is read and pondered. The book is embellished with an engraving of the author, and the New York Institution for the Blind."

We will not anticipate with further detail, the memoirs of her life, with which we hope she will at some time favor the public. A true history of her trials and triumphs, in her own magic style, would stimulate forcibly those under similar privations, to shake off the fetters of dependence, and grapple successfully with the difficulties of their situation.

The following is an example of her composition, which, in point of majesty and sublimity of thought, we think, is seldom excelled in the English language :

PRAYER TO LIGHT.

Oh, holy light! thou art old as the look of God, and eternal as his breath. The angels were rocked in thy lap, and their infant smiles were brightened by thee. Creation is in thy memory ; by thy torch the throne of Jehovah was set, and thy hand burnished the myriad stars that glitter in his crown. Worlds, new from His omnipotent hand, were sprinkled with beams from thy baptismal font. At thy golden urn, pale Luna comes to fill her silver horn, and Saturn bathes his sky-girt rings ; Jupiter lights his waning moons, and Venus dips her queenly robes anew. Thy fountains are shoreless as the ocean of heavenly love ; thy center is everywhere, and thy boundary no power has marked. Thy beams gild the illimitable fields of space, and gladden the farthest verge of the universe. The glories of the seventh heaven are open to thy gaze, and thy glare is felt in the woes of lowest Erebus. The sealed books of heaven by thee are read, and thine eye, like the Infinite, can pierce the dark vail of the future, and glance backward through the mystic cycles of the past. Thy touch gives the lily its whiteness, the rose its tint, and thy kindling ray makes the diamond's light; thy beams are mighty as the power that binds the spheres; thou canst change the sleety winds to soothing zephyrs, and thou canst melt the icy mountains of the poles to gentle rains and dewy vapors. The granite rocks of the hills are upturned by thee, volcanoes burst, islands sink and rise, rivers roll, and oceans swell at thy look of command. And oh, thou monarch of the skies, bend now thy bow of millioned arrows, and pierce, if thou canst, this darkness that thrice twelve moons has bound me. Burst now thine emerald gates, O morn, and let thy dawning come. My eyes roll in vain to find thee, and my soul is weary of this interminable gloom. My heart is but the tomb of blighted hopes, and all the misery of feelings unemployed, has settled on me. I am misfortune's child, and sorrow long since marked me for her own.

MISS FRANCES BROWN.

Though this fair world so radiant with light,
To thee, lay shrouded in perpetual night;
Creative Genius, conscious of her power,
Framed thee a world with mountain, tree and flower,
And glassy lake, reflecting from its breast
The mirrored forms that there in beauty rest;
And e'en the muse, obedient to thy call,
Kindled thy fancy, and inspired thy soul
To rapturous song, of love and story old,
Of memories faded, and of hearts grown cold

FOR the particulars of the life of Miss Brown, we are chiefly indebted to the celebrated Dr. Kitto, author of "The Lost Senses." She was born, it appears, in 1816, at Stranolar, in the county of Donegal. There is little known of her parents, except that her father was postmaster of the village. When but eighteen months old, she lost her sight by the small-pox. And in consequence of this misfortune, her early education, like that of most blind children, was neglected. It is commonly supposed, that blind persons can derive no benefit from the ordinary methods of instruction used at common schools. This we think is a mistaken notion. It is true, a blind child cannot perform an example in arithmetic on a common slate, or demonstrate a geometrical figure drawn upon the black-board, but he may recite in the classes or mental arithmetic, and receive oral lessons from the teacher in geography, grammar, and, in short, all the branches usually taught at common schools.

Our young author not only gained a knowledge of the rudiments of grammar, but added a considerable stock of words to her vocabulary, by hearing her brothers and sisters con aloud their lessons. From her earliest years, Frances Brown evinced a love for poetry. At seven years of age she made her first attempt at writing verse, by throwing into rhyme the Lord's Prayer. Up to this time a few psalms, of the Scotch version, Watts' Divine Songs, and some old country songs, formed the extent of her poetical knowledge. As she grew older, her memory was strengthened by committing pieces of poetry from the provincial newspapers. These furnished rich food for the mind, and were no doubt well digested, as she was in the habit of frequently repeating them for her own amusement. As books were at this time scarce in her remote neighborhood, Susan Gray, The Gentle Shepherd, Mungo Park's Travels, Robinson Crusoe, were among the first of her book acquaintances. "I have often heard them read by my relatives," says she, "and remember to have taken a strange delight in them, when, I am sure, they were not half understood." These soon created in her a passion for fiction and romance; a taste by no means commendable, but much preferable, we think, to that distaste for all reading which dry history is likely to cultivate, if placed too soon in the hands of young persons. By this we would not be understood to encourage novel reading, yet rather such than none at all. Furnish the mind with food of some kind, or it will devour its own puny offspring, and at last feed upon its own vitality. One who has been blind from infancy, will be likely to suffer most from such neglect.

When the mind cannot look out upon God's perfect work, or be permitted to catch one glance at the book of nature thrown open to the view of kindred minds, yet feels an inward consciousness of powers it cannot put forth, of inspirations and desires it can never gratify, when it has tried in vain to break its prison house and roam at large over the broad field of nature, its gaze is turned inward upon itself; but only sees, by the faint light of its expiring energies, its own moral deformity. Our authoress, however, did not thus pine under her afflictions. Through the sunshine of her young heart floated many a bright vision. Relating in part her early history, she says: "It was a great day for me when the first of Sir Walter Scott's works fell into my hands. It was the 'Heart of Mid Lothian,' and was lent me by a friend, whose family were rather better provided with books than most in our neighborhood. My delight in the work was very great, even then; and I contrived by means of borrowing, to get acquainted in a very short time with the greater part of the works of its illustrious author, for works of fiction, about this time, occupied all my thoughts. I had a curious mode of impressing on my memory what had been read, namely, lying awake, in the silence of the night, and repeating it all over to myself. To that habit I probably owe the extreme tenacity of memory which I now possess; but, like all other good things, it had its attendant evil, for I have often thought it curious that, whilst I never forgot any scrap of knowledge collected, however small, yet the common events of daily life slip from my memory so quickly, that I can scarcely find anything again which I have once laid aside."

Miss Brown had now reached a period in life, when dreams of love and romance lose much of their interest, and fancies gradually give place to facts. Historical novels were laid aside, and the more wonderful romance of history itself now attracted her attention. Baine's History of the French War, and Hume's History of England, were read by her with avidity. About this time, a friend presented her with that voluminous work, the "Universal History," in twenty-two volumes, which made her acquainted with the histories of Greece and Rome, and other ancient nations. The fund of information thus acquired was afterwards increased from many other sources. These historical studies making a knowledge of geography necessary, she began to acquire this in the mode already indicated, viz. by learning the lessons of her brothers and sisters. In order to obtain a more perfect knowledge of the relative situation of distant places, she sometimes requested a friend who could trace maps, to place her finger upon some well known spot, the situation of which was already known to her, and then conduct the fingers of the other hand to any place in the map, the situation of which she desired to ascertain. By this plan, having previously known how the cardinal points were placed, she was enabled to form a tolerably correct idea, not only of the boundaries and magnitude of various countries, but also of the courses of rivers and mountain chains. In her eagerness to gain a knowledge of geography, it seems rather surprising that the present plan of constructing maps for the blind, did not suggest itself to her mind. Had some friend glued upon her map tangible lines, marking the boundaries of the different divisions, and by other elevations indicating the course of rivers, mountain chains, and the localities of principal towns, it would have enabled her to pursue the study of geography with little or no in convenience.

It may be well to remark here, in this connection (and perhaps be better understood,) that blind per sons find no difficulty in retaining images, or ideas of the form of bodies, if their true shape has been once positively ascertained by the sense of touch. Hence, it will be seen that ideal maps and diagrams may be drawn by them, and impressed upon the memory with all their lines and angles distinctly marked. Though these images present no differences in color, there are marked differences in the smoothness, or asperity, of their surfaces. Those who can only retain the impression of objects they have once seen, by their peculiar color, or, in other words, by the contrast of light and shade, will hardly understand how it is that one who has never seen color, and consequently can have no conceptions of the outlines of objects as they appear to the eye, can picture to himself the relative distance of bodies, their magnitude and different proportions, and more particularly, bodies in motion. At a casual glance at the subject, it no doubt appears wonderful that a person entirely depending upon the sense of touch, should be able to form any idea of extent beyond the space he occupies. But it should be remembered that all knowledge was first gained by repeated experiment. Some writers on optics claim that the infant first sees every object inverted; but that the delusion vanishes when he has once ascertained by the sense of touch their true position. Whether this be true or not, it is certain that the most experienced observer cannot always determine the true distances of objects from the eye by their apparent magnitude. Hence, in order to gain a knowledge of extent, figure, and the real magnitude of bodies, a series of experiments seem requisite for the seeing, as well as for the blind.

By a few of Miss Brown's poems, which we propose to subjoin presently, the reader will be able to judge whether their learned authoress was ignorant of the scenes she so vividly describes. Although she could have retained no recollection of visible objects, her imagery is perfect, and her descriptions by no means deficient in warmth and color. Her first poetical efforts were but feeble imitations of everything she knew—from the Psalms to Gray's Elegy. Depending upon the eyes of others for much of her information, Miss Brown had, up to this time, been able only to manage the lighter kinds of reading, by the aid of her young relatives, who took great pleasure in reading to her such publications as most amused and interested themselves. As this kind of reading did not greatly elevate her standard of taste, her powers of invention, for a time, kept pace with her imperfect ideas of poetry.

In a few years her compositions had accumulated into a considerable manuscript. But having read the poems of Burns, and Pope's translation of Homer's Iliad, she became so disgusted with her own feeble attempts at versification, that in a fit of sovereign contempt she committed her whole manuscript to the flames, and resolved never again to insult the muses. In this resolution she persevered for several years. Byron's Childe Harold next made a deep impression on her mind, and served greatly to strengthen her resolution. Her strong inclinations, however, for writing verse, together with the influence of her friends, at length induced her to break the rash promise she had made, and become a contributor to the "Irish Penny Journal." In 1841 she sent a few small poems to the editor of the London Atheneum, with the offer of further contributions, and solicited that a copy of the journal might be sent to her in return. After waiting in anxious suspense some acknowledgment of her voluntary contributions, she had nearly given up as lost her long cherished object, when to her great delight, several numbers of the journal arrived. This encouragement gave a new impulse to her efforts; and with it dawned a brighter day in her life than had hitherto cheered her solitary way, lighting up a fairer prospect in the future than she had yet anticipated.

From that time Miss Brown's writings have been more before the public, and never failed to attract favorable notice. She is at present well known in the literary world as an authoress of some very creditable verse. Her long poem, "The Star of Attigher," is thought by some less meritorious than many of her smaller productions. Her style is brilliant, and her poems abound in metaphor. If they have a fault, it is the sudden transition from one simile to another, illustrating the same idea, somewhat analagous to a rapid modulation in musical composition: a new key is introduced, before the ear is prepared for a new succession of sounds. Her themes, however, are happily chosen, and the construction of her verse is fluent and musical.

To those who see, like herself, by the light which fancy kindles in the imagination, creating for the blind an artificial day, her poems cannot fail to be peculiarly attractive. It is most remarkable that, in her whole collection of poems, there is not a word about blindness. The most probable reason that we can assign for this is, Miss Brown did not wish the sympathy which her supposed unhappy condition might awaken, either to enhance or diminish the intrinsic value of her productions. Sympathy is like an image reflected from a mirror, it only remains while the object is present. It is but an echo of suffering, and seldom more than a faint response from light hearts but imperfectly tuned, to the deep, sad tones of a lonely and desolate heart. Another inducing motive was, we doubt not, her sad experience of the fact, that any allusion to her misfortune would carry with it, to the minds of some, an idea of moral, physical, and intellectual deterioration. Although many think in the dark with their eyes open, their thoughts are not supposed to gather darkness; or if they wish to shut out intruding objects by closing their eyes in the day time, the torch of reason and the fire of genius are supposed to give luster to their imaginings. But when one is compelled to gather his thoughts in the dark, there is great danger, it is thought, that the shades of night will even gather around his mid-day scenes. "Blindness from infancy," says Dr. Kitto, "however deeply to be lamented by those who enjoy sight and know the sources of pleasure and usefulness which it opens, can afford few materials of sorrow to one who knows not this, and can scarcely be practically aware that there is any happier physical condition than her own."

There are few perhaps better able to estimate the loss of sight and the many inconveniences to which such a loss exposes one, than the learned author we have quoted, having himself been deaf from a very early period of life. But our own experience leads us to a conclusion very different from his. It is not strictly true that persons born blind are so blissfully ignorant of their own misfortune. It is quite as reasonable to suppose, that one who has never enjoyed the use of his legs, yet observes how others value them, should be ignorant of the inconvenience to which he is exposed, in pushing himself from place to place by the mere strength of his arms. Though on the principle of the lever, what he loses in velocity he gains in power, (since in the absence of legs his arms are made to subserve a double purpose, thereby acquiring great strength and dexterity,) yet to him this fact is not so consoling after all. The illustration we have used, however, is too strong for the reality; for of the two physical defects, were it left to our own choice, we would gladly choose the former. The dull soul that looks coldly out on the bright aspect of things, upon all the beauties of the visible universe, and feels no chord vibrate with the harmony of nature, no generous response to her theme of universal praise, no deep and fervent emotions of love, nor even rises above the mean and sordid things of earth, can have no sympathy with a spirit fettered and immured in its dark prison-house, ever wishing to pierce the impenetrable vail of darkness, if only to admit one ray of heaven's pure light. There are some who never look up; whose admiration never soars above the pile of glittering dust before them; who imagine they read by its false light God's whole revelation to man, and by its duration they compute their own immortality. True, the gold does not rust, but their reasons will; it will still shine, though the light of intelligence has faded from their eyes. To such, the fair face of nature soon grows wan and familiar; and to such only does her book present a universal blank.

From Frances Brown's volume of collected poems, we have made the following selections as specimens of her style:

THE PAINTER'S LOVE.

The summer day had reach'd its calm decline,
When the young painter's chosen task was done—
At a low lattice, wreathed with rose and vine,
And open to the bright descending sun,
And ancient Alps, whose everlasting snows
And forests round that lonely valley rose;
Yet lovely was the brow, and bright the hair
His pencil pictured—for an Alpine maid,
In blooming beauty, sat before him there,
And well had the young artist's hand portray'd
The daughter of the south, whose youthful prime
Was bright as noontide in her native clime.
Perchance the maiden dreamt not that amid
The changeful fortune of his after days,
That early-treasured image should abide—
The only landmark left for memory's gaze.
Perchance the wanderer deemed his path too dim
And cold for such bright eyes to shine on him;

For silently he went his lonely way—
And like the currents of far parted streams,
Their years flow'd on; but many a night and day
The same green valley rose upon their dreams—
To him with her young smile and presence bright—
To her with the old home-fire's love and light;
For she, too, wander'd from its pleasant bowers,
To share a prouder home and nobler name
In a far land. And on his after hours
The golden glow of Art's bright honors came;
And time roll'd on, but found him still alone,
And true to the first love his heart had known
At length, within a proud and pictured hall
He stood, amid a noble throng, and gazed
Upon one lovely form—which seem'd of all
Most loved of sages, and by poets praised
In many a song—but to the painter's view
It had a spell of power they never knew;
For many an eye of light and form of grace
Had claim'd his magic pencil since its skill
To canvas gave the beauty of that face:
But in his memory it was brighter still;
And he had given life's wealth to meet again
The sunny smile that shone upon him then.
There came a noble matron to his side,
With mourning robes and darkly-flowing vail,
Yet much of the world's splendor and its pride,
Around long-silver'd hair and visage pale;
But at one glance—though changed and dim, that eye
Lit up the deserts of his memory.
It brought before his sight the vale of vines,
The rose-wreath'd lattice, and the sunset sky,
Far gleaming through the old majestic pines
That clothed the Alpine steeps so gloriously
And, oh! was this the face his art portray'd,
Long, long ago beneath their peaceful shade!
The star his soul had worship'd through the past,
With all the fervor of untutor'd truth—
His early loved and longed for—who at last

Gazed on that glorious shadow of her youth!
And youth had perish'd from her—but there stay'd
With it a changeless bloom that could not fade;
The winters had not breath'd upon its prime—
For life's first roses hung around it now,
Unblanch'd by all the waves and storms of time
That swept such beauty from the living brow—
And withering age, and deeply-cankering care,
Had left no traces of their footsteps there.
The loved one and the lover both were changed,
Far changed in fortune, and perchance in soul;
And they whose footsteps fate so far estranged,
At length were guided to the same bright goal
Of early hopes: but, oh, to be once more
As they had been in that sweet vale of yore!
They cast upon each other one long look;
And hers was sad—it might be with regret
For all the true love lost; but his partook
Of woe, whose worldless depth was darker yet,
For life had lost its beacon, and that brow
Could be no more his star of promise now.
And once again the artist silently
Pass'd from her presence. But, from that sad hour,
As though he feared its fading heart and eye,
Forsook all mortal beauty for the power
Of deathless art. By far and fabled streams
He sought the sculptured forms of classic dreams,
And pictured glories of Italian lore,
But looked on living beauty never more.

"Miss Brown," says the learned Dr. Kitto, "uses shade and shadow as synonymous. Of shade she could have an idea, from having herself, when under a tree, realized the consciousness of being screened from the warmth of the sun; but of shadow, as distinct from shade, she does not appear to have had an idea, for whenever she does use it, shade is meant."

One of the present writers, who has been blind from birth, adds, "I have always had a notion of some difference between shade and shadow. Shade appears to me much darker, and more confused than shadow. Shade has no particular form, while shadow takes the shape of the object by which it is cast." We see no reason why Miss Brown should have had a less distinct idea of the difference between shade and shadow than of the difference in the two primary colors, yellow and orange. We are not willing to believe that she was totally ignorant of the import of the words shade and shadow. We give, however, a brief extract from her "Lessons of the Louvre," and leave the reader to judge for himself:

"So spake the sun of Gallic fame,
  When, on his conquering noon,
No dimly distant shadow came
  Of clouds to burst too soon—
But o'er the crown'd and laurel'd brow
  There passed a shade the while,
That dimm'd the dark eye's haughty glow,
  And quench'd the scornful smile."

THE LAND OF LIBERTY

Where may that glorious land be found
  Which countless bards have sung—
The chosen of the nations, crown'd
  With fame, forever young?

A fame that fill'd the Grecian sea,
And rang through Roman skies;
O! ever bright that land must be—
But tell us where it lies!

The rose-crown'd summer ceaseless shines
On orient realms of gold,
The holy place of early shrines,
The fair, the famed of old;
But ages on their flood have borne
Away the loftiest fane,
Yet left upon the lands of Morn
A still unbroken chain.

The West—O! wide its forests wave,
But long the setting sun
Hath blush'd to see the toiling slave
On fields for freedom won;
Still mighty in their seaward path
Roll on the ancient floods,
That miss the brethren of their youth,
The dwellers of the woods.

The North with misty mantle lowers
On nations wise and brave,
Who gather from a thousand shores
The wealth of land and wave;
But stains are on their boasted store—
Though Freedom's shrine be fair,
'Tis empty—or they bow before
A gilded idol there!

The South—the cloudless South—expands
Her deserts to the day,
Where rove those yet unconquer'd bands,
Who own no scepter's sway;
But wherefore is the iron with
Our golden image blent?
For, see, the harem-bars reach forth
Into the Arab's tent.

O! Earth hath many a region bright,
  And Ocean many an isle—
But where on mortals shines the light
  Of Freedom's cloudless smile?
The search is vain! From human skies
  The angel early fled—
Our only land of freedom is
  The country of the dead!

MISS FRANCES JANE CROSBY,

AN AMERICAN AUTHORESS.

"T is bright where'er the heart is;
Nor chain nor dungeon dim,
May check the mind's aspirings,
The spirit's pealing hymn.
The heart gives life its beauty,
Its glory and its power,—
'T is sunlight to its rippling stream,
And soft dew to its flower."

THE poems of this blind lady have been so much and so justly admired by all who have read them, and have so frequently drawn from the pen of reviewers acknowledgments of their superior excellence, almost amounting to adulation, that a few glimpses of her early history will be received no doubt by our readers with interest. To her assiduous efforts as a teacher, the Institution for the Blind at New York, with which she has long been connected, owes much of its present prosperity; and to her aid in many other respects it is, no doubt, indebted for its world-wide reputation.

No one can read her poems and not be struck with the simple beauty and elegance of her style, the correctness of her imagery, and her giddy flights of fancy, as may be seen in the poem entitled, "Visit to a Fixed Star." And more particularly is she happy in the choice of euphonic words, and in the construction of musical and well rounded sentences, which is said to be a characteristic of the blind. In the preface of her first work, the writer of it observes: "That one who, from the earliest period of infancy, has been deprived of sight, and whose entire knowledge of external objects, from which to paint with the imaginative pencil, has been derived from oral description, should be able thus faithfully to present scenes from nature, and in colors so vivid and true as to render the reader incredulous as to the originality of the production, is a subject of surprise, as well as admiration.

As an evidence that Miss Crosby is in some degree a reasoner, as well as poetess, we copy the following lines from her last work, entitled, "Monterey and other Poems:"

TIME CHRONICLED IN A SKULL.

Why should I fear it? Once the pulse of life
Throbbed in these temples, pale and bloodless now?
Here reason sat enthroned, its empire held
O'er infant thought and thought to action grown:
A flashing eye in varying glances told
The secret workings of immortal mind.
The vital spark hath fled, and hope, and love.

* Thoughts suggested to our authoress on placing her watch in a human skull, which was one day put into her hands.

And hatred—all are buried in the dust:
Forgotten, like the cold and senseless clay
That lies before me: such is human life.
Mortals, behold and read your destiny!
Faithful chronometer, which now I place
Within this cavity, with faltering hand,
Tell me how swift the passing moments fly!
I hear thy voice, and tremble as I hear;
For time and death are blended—awful thought!
Death claims his victim. Time that once was his,
Bearing him onward with resistless power,
Must in a vast eternity be lost.
Eternity! duration infinite!
Ages and ages roll unnumbered there;
From star to star the soul enraptured flies,
Drinking new beauties, transports ever new,
Casting its crown of glory at His feet,
Whose word from chaos to existence called
A universe; whose hand omnipotent
Controls the storms that wake the boundless deep,
"And guides the planet in its wild career."

The novel circumstance which formed the subject of this poem, though trivial in itself, was well calculated to inspire our authoress with deep and sublime emotions, and at once suggest to her a train of melancholy reflections.

"Why should I fear it? Once the pulse of life
Throbbed in these temples, pale and bloodless now."

What terror must she have felt, on placing her hands on the dry, hard bones, which once formed the prison-house of an immortal mind! How reluctantly must she have placed her watch in the dark cavity where once sat enthroned a reason, an ever-active intelligence, that thinks, that wills, that knows, and yet knows not itself, or its own destiny!

> "I hear thy voice, and tremble as I hear;
> For time and death are blended—awful thought!"

Among her many creditable performances, this poem unquestionably excels in point of what we conceive to be true merit. It certainly stands unrivaled by any modern production of the blind we have yet seen. It not only possesses many intrinsic beauties, but discovers in the writer a depth of thought, and an appreciation of the sublime truly surprising.

Miss Frances Jane Crosby, an élève of the New York Institution for the Blind, was born in 1820. At the early age of six weeks she lost her sight, by a fit of severe illness. Nor was this her only misfortune. Losing her father about this time, and her mother being left in indigent circumstances, scarcely able to provide for her own maintenance, the early education of her sightless daughter was entirely neglected.

Her unhappy condition at this period we cannot better describe than she herself has done in the following:

> "She sat beside her cottage door,
> Her brow a pensive sadness wore;
> And while she listened to the song
> That issued from that youthful throng,
> The tears, warm gushing on her cheek,
> Told what no language e'er could speak;

While their young hearts were light and gay,
The hours passed heavily away.
A mental night was o'er her thrown,
She sat dejected and alone.
Yet, no; a mother's accents dear,
Came softly on that blind girl's ear.
While all were lock'd in dreamy sleep,
That mother o'er her couch would weep,
And as she knelt in silence there,
Would breath to God her fervent prayer:
'That he all merciful and mild,
Would bless her sightless, only child.'"

This is a sad but no doubt true picture of her childhood. Possessing from her infancy a poetical temperament, quick perceptions, and a sensitive nature, she perhaps felt more deeply her privation. This is not the case, however, with all blind children; their inventive genius soon suggests methods for joining other children in their sports. Parents should be careful to encourage their little sightless charges, who seem to them so helpless, in healthful and playful exercises; allow them to run at will about the yards where they are not exposed to danger, and devote at least a small portion of their time each day to their mental training. In this way they would soon become as active and vigorous, both physically and mentally, as seeing children, and be guilty of quite as many mischievous pranks.

Strange notions have been entertained, by writers of all ages, in relation to blindness. Some suppose it to be not only the greatest calamity that can befal one, but to preclude the possibility of a strong and vigorous constitution. As an instance, we offer the following from the Encyclopedia Britanica: "The sedentary life to which they are doomed, relaxes the frame, and subjects them to all the disagreeable sensations which arise from dejection of spirits; hence the most feeble exertions create lassitude and uneasiness, and the natural tone of the nervous system, destroyed by inactivity, exasperates and embitters every disagreeable impression." This, so far from being true, is strikingly at variance with our own experience and numerous observations. The educated blind are commonly as cheerful as the seeing, and apparently much happier than the deaf mute, who has all his powers of locomotion, aided by perfect sight. He is annoyed by a thousand loathsome and disgusting objects, which, from us, are excluded. Possessing the sense of hearing, cultivated to an astonishing degree, and a delicacy of touch known only by those who look out from the ends of their fingers, we hear beauties in pleasant voices, sweet sounds, and even what may seem to others harsh discord, entirely hidden to the more obtuse senses of those who see. We derive great satisfaction from feeling over glossy surfaces, equivalent, perhaps, to the pleasurable emotions experienced by the seeing from the perception of brilliant colors. Indeed, this charge cannot be true, (though a hypothesis commonly assumed at the present day,) from the fact that the blind, in order to examine objects by their sense of touch, are necessarily compelled to travel over a space of ground which the eye might embrace at a single glance. In short, all blind persons with whom we have ever been acquainted, are more or less addicted to habits of incessant motion, either in walking or oscillating, a motion which Blacklock so good-naturedly describes in his picture of himself.

An opinion is prevalent, even at the present day, that when the grand avenue to the mind is closed from birth, nature most miraculously provides for the deficiency, by digging deep the other channels; or, in other words, rectifying her mistake by endowing her imperfect piece of mechanism with supernatural abilities. Hence, Rochester's idea: "If one sense should be suppressed, it but retires into the rest." Some suppose that when the mind cannot peep out through its natural windows, at the fair face of nature, it listens more intently at what is going on without, and even reaches out through the fingers' ends, to gain a knowledge, not only of the texture of objects, but, *mirabile dictu*, even their very colors, though tinseled with a thousand lights and shades. It is rather surprising that those who entertain such vague notions, are not fearful that some elfish blind person, in groping about among nature's fixings, might tarnish the brilliant colors of the rainbow. These remarks are not meant to be unkind, nor would we be understood as holding in contempt the inferences drawn by the friends of the blind, from the many astonishing exhibitions of their delicacy of touch. Nor do we think these mistaken impressions unworthy of a candid consideration. But, having adverted to them in another place, let us turn from this digression, patient reader, to go in quest of the little desponding creature whom we left pining over her misfortunes.

Her seat beside her cottage door is desolate. We now see her in the midst of a gay group of merry school girls, quite as cheerful and happy as her companions. She has now reached her fifteenth year, and become a regular inmate of the New York Institution for the Blind. At this period, it is said, commenced the dawn of her mental existence, from which time her intellectual powers have expanded, until her imaginative mind has been enabled to clothe its thoughts in language at once chaste and poetic. No longer under the tender care and ever-vigilant eye of a fond mother, whose anxious solicitude and commiseration for her sightless daughter tended only to render her delicate nature the more sensitive, she was now thrown in the society of those whose latent powers had already begun to unfold to the genial rays of an intellectual day. Soon her slumbering energies were aroused to vigorous activity. Her fondness for poetry soon manifested itself. Some of her first effusions may still be seen in the early reports of the institution. Her first book of poems was published in 1844. For this she realized for herself and mother considerable pecuniary aid. Her last work, entitled "Monterey and other Poems," appeared in 1851. From this we have made the following selections:

VISIT TO A FIXED STAR.

[Suggested on attending a course of lectures delivered at the Broadway Tabernacle, by Professor Mitchell, the celebrated American astronomer.]

'T was night, and by a fountain side,
I stood and mused alone;
Strange objects rose upon my sight,
That were to me unknown.

Mysterious forms fantastic moved,
With slow and measured tread,
Like shadows floating in the air,
Or spectres from the dead.

A goblet from that fountain filled,
How quickly did I drain!
For those who taste its cooling draught
May live the past again.

Then suddenly a meteor glare
Flash'd from the midnight sky;
'Twas gone,—and on immensity
Was riveted mine eye.

Borne upward by a power unseen,
In air I seemed to glide;
Onward—still onward—was my course
A spirit was my guide.

We passed on never-tiring wings
Through boundless realms of space,
Till lost amid those clustering stars
That here we scarce can trace.

Vast suns, with burning satellites,
Burst on my wondering eyes:
Bewildered by their dazzling light,
I gazed in mute surprise.

"Tell me, celestial one," I said,
"If thou mayst be addressed,
Are not the brilliant orbs I see
The dwellings of the blest?

"Can we the utmost limits search?—
The heights of space attain?"
"When ends eternity," he cried,
"And Heaven shall cease to reign."

He spoke, then pointed to a star,
That far beyond us lay;
And swifter than on lightning's wing
We thither bent our way.

In robes of passing loveliness
Was Nature there arrayed,
The air was fragrant with the breath
Of flowers that never fade.

"Spirit," I asked, "can aught of grief
These regions fair molest?
My pinions gladly would I fold,
In this bright land to rest."

'Mortal," he answered, "thou must pass
The portals of the dead;
For sacred are these verdant fields,
Where only spirits tread."

He ceased; then waved me back to earth:
I saw, I heard no more;
I woke as from a pleasing dream;
The mystic spell was o'er.

VOICE OF THE TWILIGHT HOUR.

Voice of the twilight hour!
I list to thy heaven-breathed tone,
In the tender sigh of the closing flower
Or the soft wind's dying moan:
Thou speak'st of the hopes that smil'd
On the bright spring-time of youth,
When a mother knelt, and in language mild,
A lesson, though simple, she taught her child—
'Twas a lesson of artless truth.

Voice of the twilight hour,
How sweet is thy sound to me!
For my soul is entranced by thy soothing power
And its sorrows are lost in thee:
Thou art heard in the trembling strings
Of the harp which the breezes wake;
In the bird, as her farewell note she sings
To the golden hues which the sunset flings
O'er the breast of the silver lake.

Thou speak'st of a brighter land—
Of a far-off region fair,
And thy whispers are soft of a shadowy band,
And I know that the loved are there.
Voice of the twilight hour!
Ere thy heaven-breathed tones depart,
Oh, speak in the sigh of the closing flower,
Or the winds that die in the green-wood bower
Once more to my anxious heart.

Do those we have cherished here
In that land their love forget?
Though their home is a holier, happier sphere
Oh! say, do they guard us yet?

But the twilight answer'd not;
  And a voice from the distant hills
Replied as I stood on that lonely spot:
The friends thou hast cherished forget thee not,
  And they love and they guard thee still.

'Twas the voice of the silent night—
  And the earth and the ocean slept,
And the silent stars with their mellow light
  O'er nature their vigils kept.
And I thought it were bliss to die,
  To fade with the tints of even,
For gladly then would the spirit fly
On its angel wings to the realms on high,
  And meet with the lost in Heaven.

MISS CYNTHIA BULLOCK.

AN AMERICAN AUTHORESS.

'Lo! heaven's bright bow is glad!
Lo! trees and flowers all clad!
In glory bloom!
And shall the immortal sons of God,
Be senseless as the trodden clod,
And darker than the tomb?
No! says God, our sire!
Let souls have holy light within,
Let every form of grief and sin
Now feel its fire!
Truth—truth alone,
Is light, and hope, and life, and power;
Earth's deepest night from this blest hour,
The night of mind be gone!"

Far inadequate is human wisdom, aside from divine revelation, to foster the sacred ties that should bind our race in gentleness together. The arts, sciences, and multifarious schools of philosophy, in which the sages of antiquity won for themselves immortal fame, tended but to magnify the distinction between the lowly and privileged classes, and dry up the vein of sympathy between the opulent and dejected. On Bethlehem's plains, by angelic hosts, was first announced on earth, the advent of humanity's great Benefactor. When 'neath Eden's bowers, our primitive representatives invoked consuming wrath, His potent hand turned aside the stroke of death, and now came to raise the fallen, bind up the broken-hearted, and wipe the tear from the cheek of the disconsolate. His words imparted activity to the maimed, life to the dead, and sight to the blind. The injunctions that fell from his holy lips, attended by grace divine, have gently distilled upon the sterile heart of humanity, like the dews of heaven on the tender grass, and caused it to germ, and bring forth fruit to bless the afflicted. The many brilliant benevolent institutions that gem our land, like stars the ethereal blue, are but emanations from that glorious gospel that shall eventually restore primitive paradise to man.

Though the votaries of learning of every nation, from a high antiquity, held in enthusiastic admiration the inimitable songs of sightless Homer, no institution for the benefit of this class, adorned the plains of Egypt, or crowned the sunny hills of Greece, or reflected the brightness of an Italian sky. It is from the fountain of christianity alone, that flow those benign principles that lead men, at the present day, to supply the want of sight, by means devised by mercy. One of the recipients of such public munificence, in whose soul was poured the light of gladness, is our present authoress. And, like Israel's poet, her lines glow with fervent thanks to God, the bountiful dispenser of temporal as well as spiritual blessings.

It is with pleasure that we ornament the pages of this work, with the name and a few select poems of this distinguished and highly gifted authoress. And we only regret that its design confines us to so small a space, in which to give a sketch of her biography; but hope that ere long she will favor the public with a fuller history of her experience and perigrinations in her world of physical darkness.

For the public munificence and educational opportunities which the blind of this country at present enjoy, we are largely indebted to the efforts of this lady. She was among the small group of sightless children collected at New York, by the benevolent Dr. Akerly, for the purpose of making experiments in the instruction of this class. Her quick perception and readiness in acquiring a knowledge of all the branches of science in which she was trained, and her interesting appearance at the several examinations and exhibitions given before the legistature of our state, greatly aided in moving that body to make provisions for the education of this class, on a more extensive plan; whose example nearly all the sister states of this great republic have nobly imitated. Who can estimate the vast good which her indomitable perseverance has done, in self-culture, and to dispel the mental gloom that so long shrouded all under similar circumstances. Like resistless ocean's tide, it commenced with a small riplet, but will continue to flow on, extend, and rise, until it breaks on the boundless shores of eternity.

Miss Bullock was born at Lyons, Wayne county, New York, March 7th, 1821. There are, perhaps, few deprivations to which our physical organization is subject, that tend, in a greater degree, to weaken our predominant and all-absorbing passion for life, than that under which this infant launched her frail bark on life's tempestuous sea. The earth robed in richest loveliness, tinged with beauty's fairest dyes must ever be to her but a mocking unreality; the luminous worlds that gem the sable curtains of night could have no voice to allure her thoughts heavenward; and the rosy tints of morn, nor the gorgeous drapery of the setting sun, could ever thrill one chord of gladness in her heart; for her captive soul must be barred in a living tomb, until her passage through the icy portals of death.

But the sunshine of parental love and tenderness in which her gentle spirit basked through the early years of childhood, dissipated all the dark gloom that often hovers over such misfortunes, and fostered a spirit of cheerfulness in her heart that has seldom since forsaken her. The current of her days was, however, not long thus gently to glide on. To the kind voice, gentle hand, and well known footsteps of her protecting parent, who supplied, so far as possible, her want of sight, and filled her heart with joy and gratitude, together with the wealth and ease in which her home abounded, she must soon bid adieu forever. While her father was engaged in extensive business, he suddenly died, and his affairs being unsettled, "unprincipled persons took advantage of these unfortunate circumstances, and the mother and her children were left almost destitute; and she was obliged to exert herself to the utmost of her abilities to sustain her little family."

Little Cynthia early manifested great activity of mind, "and when her brothers began to go to school, a loneliness crept over her spirit, to which it had before been a stranger. She felt herself isolated without knowing why, yet took great pleasure in committing to memory the words which fell from the lips of her brothers, as they conned their lessons in the evening. Frequently, after they had ceased reading, would she take the book, and for some time feel its smooth pages. Then might you see a burning tear rolling silently down her young cheeks, as if started by the thought: 'Oh, how delightful thus to learn so much that is beautiful and interesting!' But these thoughts did not long cast their shadow over her childish spirit." The rosy morning tints of a brighter day dawned on her pathway, and a brilliant star of hope arose to adorn the horizon of her soul. The glorious hand of philanthropy, that, in the forenoon of the nineteenth century, commenced strewing her choicest flowers along the pathway of the blind, and ushered into the world of humanity a new era, sought her out, and endowed her with that liberal instruction which her dawning intellect so much craved.

Accordingly, in 1833, when in the thirteenth year of her age, she joined the small, sightless class adverted to in the foregoing. From this diminutive germ, has grown the now proud institution that is an ornament to the city of New York, and that has dispensed such innumerable blessings to the blind. All along its steadily progressive course, Miss Bullock has been a shining light, and when charity convened her noblest sons, to lay the foundation of its present beautiful building, her silvery voice joined in swelling high the anthem of praise to Him who sits enthroned in resplendent glory, and yet has made the poor and afflicted the object of his especial care.

In every age prior to the present, parents looked upon their sightless offspring with scarcely any feelings but of pity and sorrow; their life was viewed as one of dark privation and sadness, and death as a release from misery. Without the means of acquiring knowledge, and not promising to be useful, they were generally kept out of society, and away from the best sources of information. This institution opens a new world to them: they can now enjoy the morning sun and evening shade; they can welcome the return of day as a scene of busy variety, and the repose of evening as a happy rest from labor; the monotony of silent grief is here dispelled, the heaving bosom calmed, and the soul once more enters on a blissful career. They were without hope of participating in the common felicities of life, but they now enter upon their actual possession and enjoyment. Rescued from degradation and mourning, and brought from darkness to light; they begin at once to think correctly, to act consistently, to feel that they are an important, and may be a useful portion of our race. The health, cheerfulness and independence that wait upon honest industry, are secured to them: and even the sweets of happy home to be their own possession, are placed within their reach.

As a teacher in both the literary and musical department of this Institute, Miss Bullock has rendered efficient service. And many are its present friends and patrons, whom her ever ready and highly poetic eloquence on all public occasions has won.

In 1852, she presented herself before the public as an authoress, with a collection of her choicest poems, characterized by a poetic genius, elegance of style, and a knowledge of nature truly surprising in one so young. "She is endowed with the feeling and fancy of a poet, and so answers the classic maxim—a poet is born, not manufactured." As an example of her chaste and happy style, we quote the following lines, addressed to her bird:

Thou call'st me from ambition's dream,
  From thoughts that wear the taint of earth,
From fancy's bright and airy beam,
  To list thy song of artless mirth.

Thy song of mirth, O joyous bird!
  Breaks with Aurora's gushing light,
Is with the sigh of evening heard,
  When vails the sun his radiance bright.

I sometimes deem that thou hast flown
With birds in amaranthine bowers,
And caught their melody of tone
To cheer this lonely world of ours.

Love dwells for thee in every flower,
In fertile vale and gurgling rill;
On zephyr's breath in sorrow's hour,
It sheds a perfume round thee still.

Then call me from ambition's dream,
From thoughts that wear the taint of earth,
From fancy's bright and airy beam—
I love thy song of artless mirth.

Though she loves most to contemplate subjects full of the grand and sublime, she also possesses a lively appreciation of the humorous, as the following lines may serve to show:

FALLING OF THE DINNER-POT.

To all who have an hour to spend,
I'll sing a little song;
Please promise me you will not smile
When told it can't be long.

Of death, of loss of property,
Of blighted hope and love;
Of friends that coil around the heart,
And then deceptive prove!

Ah! there are hues of darker shade,
Reserved for each poor sinner;
But none their withering blast can know,
Who has not lost his dinner.

Seated in social converse sweet,
The hours sped quickly past:
We talked of C. D.'s perjured oath,
His motives first and last.

And as the kitchen door would ope,
Was the olfactory nerve,
Aye, greeted by a savory smell,
Which would as whetstone serve

Of appetite. Tables and chairs,
All in their places stood,
And needed but their occupants,
To make all very good.

What means that loud, tremendous crash
Why startle with affright?
Why stands aghast yon trembling girl,
With lips so ashy white?

Ah, me! my dear, said Mrs. P.,
Ours is a woful lot;
An accident—our careful girl
Upset the dinner-pot!

Yes, there a most delicious stew
Lies strewn along the floor!
I'm sure those boards have never known
Such feasting times before.

Each to the other comfort spoke,
For, from a bounteous store,
An humbler meal the table graced:
We ate and laughed once more.

And all agreed with one accord,
That we'd forget it not,
The day on which our hopes fell down
With that said dinner-pot.

A few other choice selections may not be without interest to the reader:

HOPE.*

I've floated o'er earth on a beam of light,
As the fire-fly shines in the darkest night,
I've kissed the flowers bespangled with dew,
Then soared aloft to my home of blue.
On a golden beam through a fairy bower
I have sought in vain for a fadeless flower;
Its hue must be bright as a seraph's wings,
When he basks in the smile of the King of kings
Its fragrance pure as the light above
That beams from the brow of the God of love.
I sought on that lovely sea-girt shore,
Where science and wisdom were blent of yore,
Where, sportive as birds in their leafy bowers,
Young children were twining the earliest flowers
Yet their sires were groaning with anguish keen,
On each manly cheek was the tear-drop seen,
And lone by that shore, where the Grecian wave
Was dashing its spray, stood a chieftain brave.
His people were slaves, and their galling chain
Was rending his soul. Shall it suffer in vain?
I sought to solace his anguish deep,
And encourage his heart that he should not weep;
And he said, as I whispered: My arm is strong
Unconscious of might, I have wept too long;
My land shall be free as the mountain air,
And the tyrant be crushed in his hideous lair
But his generous soul with revenge grew dark,
And I wept, though I quenched not its kindling spark.
Where the happy were wrapped in their visions of love,
And the sky-lamps were gemming the azure above,

* Written for the anniversary of 1853.

On the downy breath of the sportive breeze,
That murmured all night 'mid the leaf-clad trees,
I was gently borne to a chamber lone,
Where the midnight lamp o'er a scholar shone,
The offspring of genius, whose every thought
With fancy and feeling was richly fraught.
But a dream of ambition was lurking there,
And I turned with a sigh to a scene more fair,
Where the perfume sweet o'er my senses stole:
'Twas the balm of peace to the anguished soul;
It breathed from a flower, a lovely thing
That bloomed in the heart's most sacred spring.
Then the trophy-clad seraphs around me came;
Their harps of glory were sounding its name.
'Twas blessed beneficence, spotless and mild,
And I hailed it immortal with joys undefiled.
In an amaranth wreath, for the brow of the kind,
It is twined by the orphan, the mute, and the blind,
And it blooms ever fair, as the star of even,
Though drooping and sad with the tear-drops of heaven.

THE RETURN.*

All-hallowing memory, holy, blest,
  Comes like the wind-harp's note at even,
Soothing the spirit's sad unrest
  With glimpses of its promised heaven.

Fond moment of terrestrial bliss!
  In fancy's magic mirror bright,
I feel a mother's fervent kiss,
  And hear a father's sweet good night.

* Emotions of a friend, who, after long absence from home, drank the Croton water a few moments before landing at New York.

I've wandered from my boyhood's home,
And stood beneath Italia's skies;
I've trod thy streets, imperial Rome,
And learned how earth-born splendor dies.

In sunny France, 'mid England's bowers,
And Scotland, with its varied view
Of rocky glens and lovely flowers—
Each fairy haunt how well I knew!

And mused o'er Erin's shamrock green,
So precious to each Irish heart,
Till in the faded past were seen
Its glories from the dust to start.

I'm turning from these scenes away
To thee, my boyhood's happy home;
To the fond friends of early day,
Like the lone, wandering dove, I come.

And while I quaff the waters bright,
Dear Croton, of thy crystal stream,
Unnumbered airy dreams of light,
Around my truant fancy beam.

Light of my life art thou to me,
Sweet home, my first and latest star;
I never knew how dear thou'dst be,
Till I had wandered thus afar.

So, sacred Nile, thy sons for thee
Would weep in Cashmere's lovely vale.
Look wildly on Marmora's sea,
Nor heed Arabia's spicy gale.

But sigh for Egypt's pleasant stream,
That washed their sunny land the while;
Day's star of hope, night's dearest dream,
Were the sweet waters of the Nile.

MISS DAPHNE S. GILES.

"With affections warm, intense, refined,
She mingled such calm and holy strength of mind,
That, like heaven's image in the smiling brook,
Celestial peace was pictured in her look."

There is perhaps no manifestation of the human intellect that more conclusively proves its immortality, than our constant discontent with the present, and insatiate reaching forward after objects of desire shrouded in the vista of futurity. Before the budding mind is sufficiently developed to comprehend its responsibility or learn its destiny, the heart is moved forward by an innate impulse, and the pure fancy is impressed with alluring images, natives of a brighter sphere. When in the sunny hours of childhood we sport upon the flowery lawn, sit by the murmuring rill, as it gently meanders along its willowed banks, or chase with fantastic tread the gay butterfly over the rich green meadows, plucking from our path the lily and the wild rose, life seems to us but one scene of charming beauty, unsullied by the snares of sin.

Yet oft from those innocent sports we turn away, our hearts panting for maturer years; and, while glancing to the future, we paint in our youthful ardor all that is delightful and gay. But, alas! as we gently glide along the current of time and emerge into the busy scenes of life, how oft are our fondest hopes blighted, and mountains of sorrow and disappointment appear in view, rearing their summits to the sky, yet glittering with the tears of earthly pilgrims that have passed over before us. Yet who dares murmur at his lot? He who holds in his hands the destiny of individuals as well as nations, has purposes to accomplish. Whatever he decrees in his righteousness, though it at first seems our loss of all, will ultimately prove our highest good. "For my thoughts are not your thoughts, neither are my ways your ways, saith the Lord. For as the heavens are higher than the earth, so are my ways higher than your ways, and my thoughts than your thoughts."

No theme or philosophy devised by ancient or modern sages can administer so sovereign a solace to the afflicted or sorrow-stricken soul as an unshaken confidence in a wise, overruling Providence, and an enlightened faith in the doctrines of the everlasting gospel. On the precious promises beaming from that volume our present authoress has securely rested under all her trying afflictions.

Miss Giles was born at New Haven, Vermont, October 2d, 1812. Of her parentage we can gather no information from either her writings or allusions to her life by other authors. It appears that her former biographers, like ourselves, placed no high estimate on hereditary celebrity, or, feared to commit treason against this age of progression by dragging their readers back over the ruins and rubbish of feudalism and chivalry, to detail the wonderful achievements of her ancestors; but in harmony with the true republican spirit of her own themes, we are content to rest her fame upon the literary and poetic merit of her own productions.

As the years of her youth afford no incidents deserving notice in this connection, we will pass them over to the fourteenth year of her age. At this period, when the mind is just beginning to unfold to the beauties of nature and science, and elating hopes of the future inspire the heart, the blighting hand of disease laid hold upon her, and bowed her tender heart to the sad destiny of having looked upon the variegated colors of creation, the fleecy clouds, the silvery moon, the burnished stars, and the radiant king of day in his meridian splendor, for the last time. The deep sorrow and gloom that must have shrouded her spirits at the time of this melancholy privation, we can justly appreciate, but have no terms to give them utterance. And were all the force of each language, ever spoken by human tongue, concentrated into one short sentence, it would be far inadequate. Her native energies and brilliant intellect were, however, not crushed by this appalling event, nor long suffered to slumber undeveloped. The glorious spirit of the gospel, that in the morning of the nineteenth century has raised up friends to bless every class of suffering humanity, also moved the hearts of philanthropists, (though last of all,) to ameliorate the condition of the blind. In the twenty-second year of her age, while residing at Dexter, Michigan, being informed that books with embossed letters were printed for the blind, she would not rest content until in possession of such (to her) priceless volumes. She has since been enabled to read the sacred oracles, together with other works prepared in this manner, and highly esteems the privilege, though it is by the slow process of feeling out the letters.

In 1839, the refulgent star of the New York Institution for the Blind, that has shed its intellectual light upon so many noble youths, and who in return have become lights of the first magnitude in the literary world, beckoned her to come, and soon her cheerful voice echoed within its spacious halls. Her legitimate residence being in Michigan, and she therefore unable to claim the patronage of our state proffered to all New York pupils, the Baptist society (of which she was a member and ornament) and the directors of the institute, generously offered to defray her expenses while here passing through a course of scientific studies.

There have been episodes in the annals of literature, whose greatest and controlling intellects were the spontaneous productions of nature, and their own unaided efforts. But in an age like the present, when everything in the scope of human reason is so thoroughly theorized and systematized, the world is slow to acknowledge merit, unless tipped by a diploma and honorary medals of some renowned university. But aside from the honors generally awarded to superior knowledge, to secure a literary education and connection with the mighty battery of science that electrifies and binds together the entire enlightened portion of mankind, and thereby keep pace with the spirit of the nineteenth century, is an object claiming the most assiduous attention of every social being.

There is perhaps no institntion in our country more eminently calculated to develop all the essential powers of our nature, than the one of which Miss Giles became a happy inmate, and no effort did she spare to avail herself of all the advantages afforded in its several departments. The student's time is here divided into three parts, and his instruction arranged into three separate classes, intellectual, mechanical, and musical. By means of the first, regular instruction is given in reading, writing, grammar, geography, arithmetic, history, and all other English branches taught at the best schools, together with the Latin and French languages.

The number of books printed in raised characters being as yet very limited, the instruction in this department is principally conducted orally; a system of teaching not inferior to any other, especially where the retentive powers of the pupil are as tenacious as those of the blind. The mechanical operations consist of several trades, in the prosecution of which sight can be most easily dispensed with. This, while it produces something towards the expenses of the institution, is the means of instructing the laborers and learners in branches of industry that will enable them to provide for themselves. Music in every age has been the chief delight and principal pursuit of the blind, and owing to the extreme refinement of their auditory powers, it perhaps affords them higher gratification than any other class of mankind. This science is here taught to great perfection. Almost every instrument of modern use has been introduced, and great proficiency in performance has been attained by students, especially on the piano forte and organ. The vocal department of music has also received efficient attention. In acquiring a knowledge of this branch, but little inconvenience is realized by the pupil from his loss of sight. After receiving a thorough knowledge of its rudiments, all the assistance he requires is the reading of the music until committed to memory, which practice greatly facilitates.

In all the varied exercises and duties of this institution, and the perplexing incidents invariably attending a student's life, Miss Giles sustained herself with commendable ability. In 1841, she bade adieu to the institute, her teachers, and kind benefactors, and returned to her friends in Michigan, with a more exalted and rational idea of life and happiness. We need not the feeling eloquence of a Milton to paint out before the public mind the utility of such institutions for this class of community; we need only advert to the child as it enters the school, borne down with a sense of blindness, and witness the changed condition of the graduate student in the honorable walks of life; happy as if unmindful of the want of sight, his soul filled with the thought that he can always find in labor, support, and in reading, amusement, without painfully depending on the eyesight of others, while in writing he has his circle of communication enlarged until it embraces the world.

When Miss Giles wrote her first poems, it appears to have been far from her intention to present herself before the public in the capacity of an authoress. They were the result of her solitary musings on heavenly themes, while in a measure secluded from society, and were written down for the gratification of those few friends with whom she was daily conversant. Several of these found their way into the public journals, and the favorable notice they attracted induced her to publish from her portfolio a small volume. The approving smile with which an indulgent public received this laudable effort for self-maintenance, and the essential pecuniary aid realized from its sale, induced her more extensively to employ her pen.

Three years subsequent, in 1848, her second work made its appearance, entitled "Female Influence;" and her third publication, entitled "Balm of Gilead," was issued from the press in 1852. Much might be justly said in praise of the chaste, poetic, and highly descriptive style of these productions; but it is not our purpose, in the present work, to bias the minds of our readers in favor of the authors we notice with an elaborate review, but prefer to give a few select extracts.

We copy the following essay on intellectual development from her work entitled "Female Influence," chapter seventh :

"What a striking resemblance there is between a well cultivated garden and the immortal mind! What a living picture is here of the beneficial effects of industry! By industry and cultivation this neat spot is an image of Eden. Here is all that can entertain the eye or regale the smell. Whereas, without cultivation, this sweet garden had been a desolate wilderness. Vile thistles had made it loathsome, and tangling briars inaccessible. Without cultivation, it might have been a nest for serpents, and the horrid haunt of venomous creatures. But the spade and pruning knife, in the hand of industry, have improved it into a sort of terrestrial paradise. How naturally does it lead us to contemplate the advantages which flow from a virtuous education, and the miseries which ensue from the neglect of it! The mind, without early instruction, will, in all probability, become like the 'vineyard of the sluggard,' if left to the propensities of its own depraved will; what can we expect but the luxuriant growth of unruly appetites, which, in time, will break forth in all manner of irregularities? What but that anger, like a prickly thorn, arms the tempter with an untractable moroseness; peevishness, like a stinging nettle, render the conversation irksome and forbidding; avarice, like some choking weed, teach the fingers to gripe, and the hands to oppress; revenge, like some poisonous plant, replete with baneful juices, rankle in the breast, and meditate mischief to its neighbor; while unbridled lusts, like swarms of noisome insects, taint each rising thought, and render 'every imagination of the heart only evil continually?' Such are the usual products of savage nature; such the furniture of the uncultivated soul!

"Whereas, let the mind be put under the 'nurture and admonition of the Lord;' let holy discipline clear the soil: let sacred instruction sow it with the best seed: let skill and vigilance dress the rising shoots, direct the young idea how to spread, the wayvard passions how to move; then what a different tate of the inner man will take place! Charity will breathe her sweets, and hope expand her blossoms; the personal virtues display their graces, and the social ones their fruits; the sentiments become generous, the carriage endearing, the life honorable and useful.

"Oh! that governors of families and masters of schools would watch, with a conscientious solicitude, over the morals of their tender charges. What a pity it is, that the advancing generation should lose these invaluable endowments, through any supineness in their instructors. See, with what assiduity the curious florist attends his little nursery! He visits them early and late, furnishes them with the properest mould; supplies them with seasonable moisture; guards them from the ravages of insects; screens them from the injuries of the weather; marks their springing buds; observes them attentively through their whole progress; and never intermits his anxiety until he beholds them blown into full perfection. And shall a range of painted leaves, which flourish to-day and to-morrow fall to the ground—shall these be tended with more zealous application than the exalted faculties of an immortal soul?

"Yet, trust not in cultivation alone. It is the blessing of the Almighty Husbandman which imparts success to such labors of love. If God 'seal up the bottles of heaven,' and command the clouds to withhold their fatness, the best manured plat becomes a barren desert. And if he restrain the dew of his heavenly benediction, all human endeavors miscarry; the rational plantation languishes; our most pregnant hopes, from youths of the most promising genius, prove abortive. Their root will be as rottenness, and their blossom will go up as dust. Therefore, let parents plant; let tutors water; but let both look up to the Father of spirits for the desired increase. On every side I espy several budding flowers.

"As yet, they are like bales of cloth from the packer's ware-house, each is wrapped within a strong enclosure, and its contents are tied together by the firmest bandages; so that all their beauties lie concealed, and all their sweets locked up. Just such is the niggardly wretch, whose aims are all turned inward, and meanly terminated upon himself; who makes his own private interests or personal pleasures the sole center of his designs, and the scanty circumference of his actions. Ere long the searching beams will open the silken folds, and draw them into a graceful expansion. Then what a lovely blush will glow on their cheeks, and what a balmy odor exhale from their bosoms! So when divine grace shines upon the mind, even the churl becomes bountiful; the heart of stone is taken away, and a heart of flesh, a heart susceptible of the softest, most compassionate emotions, is introduced in its stead O! how sweetly do the social affections dilate themselves under so benign an influence! just like these disclosing gems under the powerful eye of day. The tender regards are no longer confided to a single object, but extend themselves into a generous concern for mankind, and shed liberal refreshments on all within their reach. Arise, then, thou sun of righteousness; arise with healing on thy wings; and transfuse thy gentle but penetrating ray through all our intellectual powers. Enlarge every narrow disposition, and fill us with a diffused benevolence. Make room in our breasts for the whole human race; and teach us to love all our fellow-creatures, for their amiable Creator's sake. May we be pleased with their excellencies, and rejoice in their happiness; but feel their miseries as our own, and, with a brother's sympathy, hasten to relieve them."

The following we give from her "Balm of Gilead:"

THE CAUSE OF TEMPERANCE.

Dear Friend: — As the subject of temperance elicits the attention of every philanthropist, and causes the heart of every lover of human happiness to increase its pulsation, as he views the dark tide of desolation as it has flowed through our country, bearing upon its accursed waves the hopes of the young, and the stay and staff of the aged, the groans and tears of the widow, while the disgraced orphan sends up the piteous cry, "Help! help! save, Lord, or we perish!" shall we, who have long advocated the cause of temperance, be silent? We will not. Let the pulpit and the press, the workshop and the store, the ballot-box and the halls of legislation, be the place where it shall be boldly advocated and defended. I envy not that man—if he is worthy the name of man —that is so steeped in stoicism as to be indifferent to the millions that are falling annually by this fell destroyer—the demon intemperance. It would be far better for the youth to inhale the deadly poison of the upas, than to mingle in the society of one that is so degraded as to defend the manufacturing or vending, or the moderate use of alcohol, save for medicinal purposes. There are even now fathers, in the full glare of light that is poured upon this subject, who will go to their sideboard and cupboard, and, in the presence of four or five young children, take down the bottle—morning, noon, and night, if not oftener—and pour out their dram, smacking their lips, saying to their little ones, It is bad stuff—the most important truth they ever told them, yet their practice giving the lie to their assertion. Oh, the direful influence of such fathers! better deserving the name of monsters. Brandies and wines disgrace the fashionable parties that are given by those that would be respectable, if it did not require too great a sacrifice. In these gatherings the professed follower of Christ is found; forgetful of his covenant vows, he bids God speed to the most infamous practices with which the world was ever cursed. How long, how long, O Lord God Almighty, will the chariot wheels of deliverance delay? Oh, for a full redemption; yea, a speedy deliverance from this soul-destroying evil! It may be asked by some, What is most needed to bring into disuse this beverage? I answer, it is simply decision of character on the part of those that would elevate man in the scale of his moral being, and place him in the sphere God designed him to move in; we should not then see him who had been the center of the fondest hopes, and along whose pathway shone the purest light reflected from the combined virtues of loving sisters, and sainted mothers' fervent prayers, and the earnest entreaties of fathers long since deceased, and that one on whom all these fond hopes centered become almost a putrefied mass, possessing naught of life but the power of endurance, and all of death save the silence of the grave. The inebriate should not be regarded with indifference. No : rather let us rally to the rescue, and from the vortex of intemperance snatch the wretched victims who are constantly being engulphed, as in a lake of molten fire. There are scenes, revolting to humanity, constantly coming under our observation, consequent on the legal toleration extended to the venders of distilled liquors. Moral suasion has seized the monster, and the strong arm of organized bodies has endeavored to bind him, but has only succeeded in part. Now, what shall we do? Shall we still refuse to have it become a political question, and keep it from our ballot-box and our halls of legislation, where it could at once be shorn of its strength? Let the champions of temperance stand undaunted on the stormy battlements of this great reform, which is calculated to blot out from the world the foulest stain that ever disgraced humanity.

The most skilled artist has failed in his attempts to delineate upon canvas the wretchedness of the inebriate's family. For such a task his pencil lies broken before him; and the combined eloquence of thousands, in their most graphic descriptions, have failed to portray their woes. Ah, who can describe with language, or illustrate with metaphor, the havoc that intemperance has made among mankind?

In executing a descriptive scene of its abominations, methinks the acute conceptions of fancy, and the loftiest flights of the imagination, would be inadequate to the task. Could we change the mighty ocean to paint, transform every stick into a brush, make every man an artist, every star a scaffold, and the outstretched, boundless sky a canvas; could we take the dismal clouds for shade, the frightful lightning's awful element for tinge, the midnight darkness for drapery of gloom; could we use the doleful winds for sighs, the countless drops of rain for tears, the broken music of the howling storm for wails, and shrieks, and cries, the earthquake's violent shock for agonizing pains, and the long, loud, rumbling thunder for piteous, dying groans; and could we, with pious Joshua, command the glowing sun to stand still in the west, and the full, blushing moon in the distant east, and there wait, while laboring artists dash the amazing horrors of intemperance on the expanded sheet, to delineate all its loathsome, horrible, and everlasting effects, would quite exhaust the ocean, wear out every instrument, tire every artist, and more than fill heaven's immeasurable blue from pole to pole.

MISS ALICE HOLMES,

AN AMERICAN AUTHORESS.

"Oh! who would cherish life,
And cling unto this heavy clog of clay,
Love this rude world of strife,
Where glooms and tempests cloud the fairest day."

Alice Holmes was born in the county of Norfolk, England, February, 1821. Her father, an enterprising mechanic, maintained himself and family by the fruits of his industry, in his own country, until, drawn into the broad current of emigration that has wafted Europe's millions to our shores, he embarked with his effects and family to seek a home and fortune in the New World. Bound for New York, the vessel set sail in April, 1830, and landed off quarantine in the harbor of its destination, on the 19th of June following. On their passage, to the terrors of a long voyage, tempestuous winds, rolling billows, and those inconveniences usually realized in crowded ships, were added the horrors of disease. That most loathsome of all maladies, small-pox, made its appearance among the passengers, and among its subjects was the little Alice, having just then entered upon her ninth summer. When the passengers disembarked.

the fell disease was still upon her; but she was permitted to behold the beauties of the New World, a scene, whose anticipation had filled their hearts with raptures of delight, raised their drooping spirits on the boisterous ocean, and influenced them to leave dear friends and country, with no hope of ever communing with them again. But, alas! it was the little sufferer's last view of the green earth, land of promise, clear blue sky, and glorious sunlight, which painted upon her memory an abiding image of beauty. She was taken to the city hospital, and when medical skill had broken the fetters of disease, it was found that her sight was irrecoverably lost. Her parents, immediately subsequent to landing, took up their residence in Jersey City. Though her young and gentle spirit had not yet advanced far enough on life's rugged journey, fully to realize the greatness of her loss, yet sad and lonely must have been her condition at this time. For she was a stranger in a strange land, and having not yet learned to substitute other senses for that she had lost, in communicating with the physical world, and thus beguile her misfortune, the long monotonous hours and days passed heavily away. Oft did her thoughts mount on pinions of fancy, and wing their way over the star-lit Atlantic to her native cot, and hold sweet converse with her little schoolmates, and the scenes of her childhood, now more bright and loving than ever.

To these prospects, she adverts in the following simple, yet graphic lines:

"Farewell to the cottage, the garden and flowers,
Where oft in my childhood passed frolicsome hours;
Farewell to the meadow, the brook and the trees,
Where the music of birds is borne on the breeze;
Farewell to the lane, the green hillside and glen,
Whose paths I have trodden again and again;
Farewell, dear companions, so joyous and gay;
For, alas! I must go away, far away."

In January, 1837, through the generosity of a friend of whom she speaks in the most glowing terms of gratitude, Alice became a pupil of the New York Institution for the Blind. And by virtue of an act passed by the New Jersey legislature, in the ensuing year, providing for the sightless youths in that state who chose to enter the New York Institute, she was enabled to prosecute her studies there five years longer. By this public munificence, she received a thorough knowledge of all the scientific branches, included in an English education. While at this, one of the noblest monuments of human benevolence, daily acquiring additional rays of intellectual light, that dispel the heavy gloom of ignorance, and open to the soul pure and inexhaustible fountains of happiness, and associating with those young hearts whom a like affliction rendered tenderly sympathetic and kind, her years glided pleasantly away, leaving no room for despondency. There is, perhaps, no period in life, of which we retain such pleasant recollections, or around whose scenes cluster more hallowed associations, than that of our school-days. Free from the sordid cares and perplexities of life, the ambitious student views, in his future field of triumph, rich garlands of fame awarded him by applauding multitudes, and beholds, in imagination, his name high on the scroll of fame, as a hero and benefactor of his race. Though these hopes often vanish in maturer years, like dew-drops before the morning sun, they form an oasis on life's dreary desert, around which our thoughts love to linger in darker hours.

Miss Holmes left the Institute at the expiration of her term, in 1844, and returned to her friends in Jersey City, where she has since resided. Her emotions, at this time, she has expressed in the following lines, written on the occasion:

"Adieu, adieu, my long-loved home,
  Where genial spirits dwell,
For I must bid thy hearth and halls,
  This day a sad farewell.
Thy vesper-bell will peal at eve,
  But not, alas! for me;
For I shall be alone and sad,
  Far, far away from thee!

"Adieu, adieu, companions dear,
  My sisters, brothers, friends;
This day completes my stay with you,
  This day our union ends.
But oh! how can I, can I bear
  To hear the death-like knell,
That bids me tear my heart away
  From those I love so well?

"Adieu, adieu to morning walks,
  Along the Hudson's side,
Where oft among the rocks we heard
  The music of the tide:

And wanderings at twilight hour,
  Through grove, by hill and stream,
That I have ever fondly prized,
  But dearer now they seem."

By her needle and other handiwork, she has since earned for herself a respectable livelihood, and has only turned her attention to poetry in her leisure hours, to avert the dark shadows of gloom that might otherwise have mantled her spirit. After repeated solicitations of friends, she consented to publish a small collection of her poems, which made its appearance in 1849. For this work, she claims neither literary nor poetic merit; but modestly expresses the hope that a good intention may atone for many faults. The lowly rank which she claims for her verses, is, no doubt, their proper one in the scale of refined literature; we could, however, mention a catalogue of rhymers, in full possession of sight, who have found less favor with the muses than this modest authoress; and yet they flourish their rusty pens, and rack their conceited brains over subjects of the greatest magnitude, with an air of importance, as if by the ancient Britons' theory of transmigration, they possessed the soul of Byron, Shakspeare, or Milton. Such presumption makes faults intolerable; but true modesty in an author, like juvenile inexperience, moves us rather to apologize than censure. We will, however, allow our readers to judge for themselves, respecting the poetic merits of Miss Holmes, from the few following extracts:

FAITHFUL LOVE.

The clear evening sky was mantled in blue,
And flow'rets that slept were covered with dew;
Laden with perfume, a soft summer breeze
Came floating along through whispering trees;
Enthroned above, the fair queen of night
Was tinging the sea with silvery light,
And bright gleaming stars that circled her brow,
Glanced down amazed on the beauties below.
'Neath ocean's calm breast, its billows and waves
Had sunk to repose in the coral caves:
Nature seemed praising in silence her Lord,
Who gave to her birth by power of His word.
Such was the fair evening, so lonely and still,
When by the side of a clear mountain rill,
'Neath an old oak's boughs that were waving there,
A maiden breathed for her lover a prayer;
For hither had been their chosen retreat,
At still even-tide, when fond lovers meet.
Now lonely each night she knelt by that stream,
Whose murmurings low seemed charmed with her theme.
As softly she spoke, in tones sweet and clear,
One might have fancied a seraph was near.
While her hands were clasped on her snow-white breast,
A small golden heart to her own was pressed,
Which she had received as a parting pledge,
'Neath the old oak tree at that streamlet's edge.
Solemn and pure was the prayer of love,
That rose from her heart to the throne above,
For his safe return, who was dearer far
Than the morning sun or evening star.

His duty was now in a distant land,
To hazard his life with a noble band,
In the toils of war he was called to share,
And a soldier's part for his country bear.
A tear-drop rolled from her soft blue eye,
As upward she gazed at the starlit sky,

Watching perchance some angel's flight
That bore on his wings her request each night;
For her's was the prayer of faith and of love,
That ever finds grace in that world above.
Though heaven may please awhile to delay
The favor that's sought from day to day,
Still it hearkens and hears, and will answer give,
To such as by faith its bounties receive.
And so did it prove with that maiden fair,
Whose pure faith banished all gloom and despair.

So, at the same hour, the next even-tide,
There knelt by her one that called her his bride,
Who had hastened from war to fulfill his vow,
While victory's wreath was fresh on his brow.
And, hand joined in hand, by that mountain stream,
They sat to rehearse love's long-cherished dream·
And hovering round came angels of light,
Soft whispering joy, then winging their flight.
The bliss of that hour was dear to each heart,
That love had entwined, now never to part.

A SOLILOQUY.

My harp is on the willow hung;
  To me the morning brings no light·
No ray of sun or moon I see,
  But one unchanging night.

I cannot view those gem-like stars,
  That sparkle in the ethereal skies;
Nor trace the clouds with golden fringe,
  That o'er the sunset rise.

Nor gaze upon the blooming flowers,
  That make the face of nature gay;
Nor watch the ocean's sparkling waves,
  Where dancing sunbeams play.

BEAUTIES OF THE BLIND.

To me the variegated earth,
  Would seem one dark, unbroken plain,
If, in my heart, I had not hid
  Bright visions that oft come again,

For I through nine fair summers passed,
  With scarce a cloud to shade my way,
And loved the face of nature more,
  With each returning day.

But ere a tenth had fully come,
  My gladsome heart was wrapt in gloom,
Lo! I was banished from the light,
  Condemned to a living tomb,—

Where even Hope's fair star grows dim,
  With clouds that o'er my spirit rise,
And hide the gleams of holy light,
  Imparted from the skies.

But oh! I will with patience bear
  A grief which none can feel or know,
But those for whom it is ordained,
  By him who wills it so.

And faith, not light shall be my guide
  To Canaan's fair, celestial shore,
Where faith is lost in perfect sight,
  And darkness is no more.

ON MORNING.

Oh, sweet is the dawning hour,
  When dews like holy incense rise,
And waft to God, on mystic wings,
  Earth's morning sacrifice.

And fair Aurora tints
  The azure sky with golden light,
And chases far the sable clouds,
  That vail the world in night.

And angels bright, that nightly watch,
  While earth reposing lies.
Spreading their pure celestial wings,
  Mount swiftly to the skies.

Or rosy twilight fades
  Before the gorgeous king of day,
Who from the east rejoicing comes
  In glorious array.

And gentle zephyrs kiss
  Dew-drops from the blushing flowers,
That waking shed their odors sweet,
  Through fields and summer bowers.

And on the ocean's wave
  Sunbeams like golden shadows gleam,
And laughing breezes catch the spray
  That leaps from mountain stream.

And to the huntsman's horn,
  The echoing rocks and hills reply,
And beasts of prey that nightly prowl,
  Like falcons swift go by.

And insect voices greet,
  With songs of praise the waking day
And feathered songsters warble sweet,
  To God their morning lay.

And man from sweet repose,
  Joyful again to see the light,
Goes forth to toil with cheerful heart,
  Till day gives place to night.

O sweet and hallowed time,
  Let thy peaceful influence rest
On all the hours that shall succeed
  To this that thou hast blessed.

ACHIEVEMENTS OF THE BLIND IN THE LEARNED PROFESSIONS.

SERIES I.—SECTION I.

PROGRESS IN THE SCIENCES.

Having given in the preceding pages a somewhat detailed account of a sufficient number of authors, and extracts from their writings, to establish the literary character of the blind, we next proceed to notice in a more summary manner, the success of this class in the scientific pursuits. As the hydrographical chart points out to the mariner a safe course over the trackless ocean, and national history affords to the legislator the experience of past ages, so the biographies of those who have risen against every tide of opposition from a lowly station in life to one of honor and distinction, serve in a powerful manner to stimulate others to grapple with similar difficulties. Whatever may be the impediments in our course, if we have the assurance that others, under like circumstances, have surmounted them, and arrived in triumph at the mark to which we aspire, the bugbear of impossibility is removed, and the timid heart, gathering courage, moves forward, cheered by the way-

J

marks of predecessors. But more especially is this true of the blind, than any other class of mankind.

All the higher institutions of learning, with their experimenting laboratories, improvements in the arts, and an application of natural agents to the multifarious labor-saving machineries that have transformed the civilized world into one spacious bee-hive, these are all especially adapted to the seeing. And the blind must still depend upon their own experience, and that of their predecessors, to force from society and nature the means by which to supply their daily wants, and to exercise their genius in the arts and higher pursuits of knowledge. The examples we shall give in these series are so diversified, (we are happy to say,) as to furnish every blind youth with a pattern or example, into whatever worthy pursuit his genius or taste may incline him.

The first notable character under this head of which history informs us, is DIODOTUS, a stoic philosopher, who lived about one hundred years B. C. He was the preceptor of Cicero, the Roman orator, in Greek literature and geometry, and for many years his intimate friend. He was ever assiduous in the study of philosophy, and eminently successful as a teacher of geometry; a thing, says Cicero, which one would think scarcely possible for a blind man to do, yet would he direct his pupils where every line was to be drawn just as exactly as if he had the use of his eyes.

Another Roman, named AUFIDIUS BASSUS, who lost

his sight in early youth, was famous in his time for attainments in philosophy, geometry, and knowledge of general literature. He was also the author of an excellent Greek history.

But antiquity can boast of no greater genius than Didymus, of Alexandria, who flourished in the fourth century. This distinguished man, who lost his sight at four years of age, is known to us principally as a theological writer. But we are informed by his pupil, St. Jerome, that he also distinguished himself at the school of Alexandria, in every department of science then conceived to constitute the whole field of human learning. He was so great a proficient in theology that he was chosen to, and long filled, the chair in the famous divinity school at Alexandria. His high reputation secured for him many scholars, some of whom are known as among the most distinguished writers of that period. He was the author of numerous works, a catalogue of which is preserved in the writings of St. Jerome. His treatise on the Holy Spirit (a Latin translation of which only remains) is said to be the best ever possessed by the Christian world. He died in 398, aged eighty-five years. So great was his fame abroad, that St. Anthony (excited by the same curiosity that moved the queen of Shebah to visit Solomon) came from the desert to satisfy himself concerning the wisdom and sanctity of this famous philosopher, who being informed by Didymus in answer to his questions, that he deplored his deprivation, notwithstanding his attainments, the saint was much surprised, and marveled that so wise a man should lament the loss of a faculty, "which we only possess" (as he chose to express it) "in common with the gnats and ants."

James Shegkins, a native of Shrandorf, in Wirtemburg, who lived in the latter part of the sixteenth century, seems to have been a character more after the taste of Anthony. This learned German, having lost his sight in early life, was so little sensible of his privation, that he refused to be couched by an oculist who assured him that the operation would prove successful, in order, as he said, not to be obliged to see many things that might appear odious and ridiculous —a decision not altogether absurd for one whose taste and habits of life had been so thoroughly assimilated to his condition, and who had found such unbounded resources of pleasure in ranging the fields of science by methods of his own invention. He taught philosophy and medicine with eminent success at Tubengen, for a term of about thirteen years. He died in 1587, leaving many treatises on different subjects in philosophy, medicine, and controversy.

To the preceding we may add that of the Count de Hagan, who was born in the beginning of the seventeenth century. Having entered the army at the early age of twelve years, he lost his left eye at seventeen; he still, however, pursued his profession with unabated ardor, and distinguished himself by many acts of brilliant courage. At last, when about to be sent into Portugal with the rank of field-marshal, he was seized with an illness which deprived him of sight in his remaining eye, in the thirty-eighth year of his age. He had always been attached to mathematics, and his misfortune being no impediment in the pursuit of this science, he now earnestly devoted himself to the study of geometry, with a view to improve the system of fortification, on which subject he wrote an interesting and important work. During a period of twenty years, subsequent to his blindness, he gave to the world a variety of publications, among the most important of which may be mentioned Geometrical Theorems and Astronomical Tables. He was also the author of a rare book called "An Historical and Geographical account of the River Amazon," which is remarkable as containing a chart, asserted to have been made by himself, after he became blind.

The study of mathematics seems in every enlightened age to have occupied the most ingenious and master minds, and no science has revealed to the world more essential facts, or opened more sublime fields of contemplation. In the development of this sublime branch of human learning, the blind may claim, we think without arrogance, a full share of honor. In all the annals of self-educated and ingenious characters, there is none more justly claiming our admiration than Dr. NICHOLAS SAUNDERSON, who we shall next briefly notice.

This great man was born at Thurlston, in Yorkshire, in 1682, and when but twelve months of age he was totally deprived of sight by small-pox. Early evincing promising abilities, he was sent to the free school at Pennistone, where he soon distinguished himself by his proficiency in Greek and Latin. This enabled him to become acquainted with the works of Euclid, Archimedes, and Diophantes, which he afterward diligently studied in their originals. His father being unable to afford him the pecuniary means requisite for the prosecution of his studies at a university, Dr. Nettleton, and Richard West, Esq., who were great lovers of mathematics, having noticed the uncommon genius of young Saunderson in this science, gave him instruction in algebra and geometry. His friends discovering his clear and perspicuous manner of communicating his ideas, suggested the propriety of his attending the University of Cambrige, as a teacher of mathematics, to which his own inclination strongly led him. Accordingly, in 1707, when in the twenty-fifth year of his age, he made his appearance in that university under the protection of a friend, one of the fellows of Christ's College. That society with great generosity immediately allotted him a chamber, admitted him to the use of their library, and gave him every other accommodation in their power for the prosecution of his studies.

Mr. Whiston, successor to Sir Isaac Newton in the Lucasian professorship of mathematics in that university, instead of manifesting jealousy of one whom a less generous mind might not unnaturally have regarded as a rival, sought in every way to encourage

Mr. Saunderson in his undertaking. While thus engaged in explaining the principles of the Newtonian philosophy with astonishing success, he became acquainted with its illustrious author.* And when Mr. Whiston was removed from his chair, Sir Isaac Newton exerted his utmost influence to obtain the vacant situation for Saunderson. Accordingly the crown issued a mandate conferring upon him the degree of Master of Arts, as a necessary preliminary to his election.

On his inauguration, he delivered a Latin address with extraordinary taste and elegance. From this time he applied himself closely to the reading of lectures, and gave up his whole time to his pupils. He shortly afterward married the daughter of Rev. Mr. Dickens, by whom he had a son and a daughter. When George II. visited the college, in 1728, among other tokens of marked respect, Saunderson was, by the king's command, created Doctor of Laws, and was admitted a member of the Royal Society, in 1736. He died on the 19th of April, 1739, aged fifty-seven years. Notwithstanding his almost unparalleled assiduity in the studies of his professorship, he found time to prepare several works on algebra, and one on fluxions, which, together with the works of Euler,

* Saunderson commenced his prelections with Newton's optics. "The subject itself which he thus chose, independently of the manner in which he treated it, was well calculated to attract notice, few things seeming at first view more extraordinary than that a man, who had been blind almost from his birth, should be able to explain the phenomena and expound the doctrines of light."

will ever stand as lasting monuments of the perseverance and genius of the blind.

It may seem unjust to some of our readers to introduce Euler in this connection, from the fact that he acquired his knowledge of the sciences, and much of his fame previous to his deprivation. But it must be remembered that the principal object of this work is to demonstrate that a want of sight alone does neither preclude the acquisition of knowledge, nor, after acquired, its practical exercise in any of the higher branches of science. The unremitting and successful labors of this great man, after his blindness, tend strikingly to illustrate how little genius or the progress of mind is depending on mere outward or physical circumstances.

Leonard Euler who flourished in the early part of the eighteenth century, after numerous brilliant achievements in the science of mathematics, lost his sight from excessive application, in the fifty-ninth year of his age, while professor of mathematics at St. Petersburg. While in this condition, he published his famous work, "Elements of Algebra," which has been translated into every European language. Shortly after this he was elected a foreign member of the Parisian Academy of Science, and an academical prize was adjudged to three of his memoirs, concerning the inequalities in the motions of the planets. The two prize questions proposed by the same academy for 1770 and 1772, were designed to obtain from the labors of astronomers a more perfect theory of the moon. Euler, assisted by his eldest son, was a competitor for these prizes, and obtained them both.

His writings are so numerous that a mere catalogue of them would fill several of these pages. They are preserved by the royal societies of London, Berlin, Paris, Vienna, and Stockholm, of all of which he was a member. Among the numerous and elaborate productions of his genius, subsequent to loss of sight, was his "New Theory of the Moon's Motions," with its accompanying tables, which has been deemed by astronomers, in exactness of computation, one of the most remarkable achievements of the human intellect. His brilliant career was terminated by apoplexy while amusing himself at tea with one of his grand-children, in 1783, in the seventy-sixth year of his age.

Another illustrious character in the annals of privation, with whose name we are happy to ornament the pages of this work, is that of John Gough. This distinguished philosopher and mathematician was the son of a glover, of Kendal, and lost his sight by small-pox, in 1752, before he had completed his third year. When six years of age, he commenced the study of English grammar, at a school in his native town, and when about twelve years of age, under the care of a proficient teacher, he made rapid progress in the languages, natural philosophy, and classic literature. The science of zoology was one for which he almost from infancy manifested great partiality, and he now began to enlarge his knowledge of organic bodies, by

extending his researches from the animal to the vegetable kingdom. By devoting to botanical pursuits all the time he could spare from the regular studies of the school, he soon became enabled to classify, with great accuracy, all the plants which came under his notice.

As a substitute for the eye, in discriminating between the finer species, he used the tip of his tongue, which he applied to their several parts, while he readily recognized ordinary plants by the touch of his fingers. So perfect a knowledge did he acquire of this science, and so tenacious was his memory, that at one time, near the close of his life, when a rare plant was put into his hands, he immediately called it by its proper name, observing that he never met with but one specimen of it previously, and that was fifty years ago.

Mr. Gough's attention was first turned to experimental philosophy, in the year 1772, and by studying with characteristic assiduity the works of Mr. Boyle, he soon obtained a knowledge of the specific gravity of fluids, hydrostatics, and pneumatics. Some time subsequent he entered upon the study of mathematics, under a celebrated instructor at Mungriodale. Here he not only acquired a taste for this science, but laid the foundation of those high attainments which subsequently entitled him to a place among the most distinguished mathematicians of his age. Of his success in after life, as a teacher of philosophy and mathematics, we have the most abundant proof. For

among the limited number of his pupils, an unusual proportion became eminent in those sciences; among which occur the names of Whewell, afterward tutor of Trinity College; Mr. Dawes, tutor of Downing College; Mr. Gaskin, of Jesus College, and Mr. King, tutor of Queen's College, one of the most distinguished mathematicians of his age; and the eminent philosopher, John Dalton, president of the Manchester Philosophical Society, was also four or five years under his instruction. Mr. Gough was actively engaged as a teacher, and in his usual philosophic investigations to the close of the year 1823, when declining powers began to be visible to his friends. He died July 27th, 1825, in the sixty-eighth year of his age. His numerous essays published in the memoirs of the "Manchester Literary and Philosophical Societies," have been highly valued by the most competent judges; and are said to contain decisive evidence of the acuteness of his intellect and accuracy of knowledge in almost every department of science.

Dr. Henry Moyes, who was the wonder and admiration of every country he visited, like the subject of the foregoing sketch, lost his sight when but three years of age. He was the first person of his class who ventured to conduct experiments in chemistry, in connection with lectures upon that science.

After leaving college, he commenced a series of lectures on the "Theory and Practice of Music," at Edinburgh; but not meeting with sufficient encouragement, he next turned his attention to natural and experimental philosophy, which presented an extensive field for the exercise of his talents. His lectures were always of the most interesting character, and his audiences large and respectable. Being of a restless disposition, and fond of traveling, he left Scotland in 1779, for England, and from thence sailed for the United States, where he took his degree from one of her colleges. In the summer of 1785 he made a tour of the Union, and was everywhere courteously received by the lovers of science.

The following paragraph respecting him appeared in one of our public journals of that day: "The celebrated Dr. Moyes, though blind, delivered a lecture upon optics, in which he delineated the properties of light and shade, and also gave an astonishing illustration of the power of touch. A highly polished plate of steel was presented to him, with the stroke of an etching tool so minutely engraved on it, that it was invisible to the naked eye, and only discoverable by a powerful magnifying glass; with his fingers, he discovered the extent and measured the length of the line. Dr. Moyes informed us, that, being overturned in a stage-coach one dark, rainy evening, in England, the carriage and four horses thrown into a ditch, the passengers and driver, with two eyes apiece, were obliged to apply to him who had no eyes, for assistance in extricating the horses. 'As for me,' said he, 'after I had recovered from the astonishment of the fall, and discovered that I had escaped unhurt, I was quite at home in the dark ditch.

The inversion of the order of things was amusing. I, that was obliged to be led about like a child, in the glaring sun, was now directing eight persons to pull here and haul there, with all the dexterity and activity of a man-of-war's boatswain.'"

After Dr. Moyes returned to his native land he visited Ireland, and was there received with the respect due to his great merit. When his desire for traveling was satiated, he settled at Manchester, with the view there to spend the remainder of his days. Here he had access to numerous and well selected libraries, and was elected a member of the Manchester Philosophical Society. He enriched its collection by several valuable papers on chemistry, and many other branches of physical science.

This extraordinary man, after spending a studious life of fifty-seven years, during which he acquired a thorough knowledge of the ancient languages, music, algebra, geometry, chemistry, mechanics, optics, astronomy, and other departments of natural science, paid the debt of nature August 10th, 1807.

ALEXANDER DAVIDSON, cotemporary with Dr. Moyes, who had lost his sight before the completion of his seventh year, stimulated by the success of the latter, entered upon a similar career. The parents of young Davidson, not willing to allow the calamity which thus early befel their son to crush the fond hopes which his precocity had inspired, continued sending him to the school in his native village, (Dalkeith, Scotland,) where, under the instruction of a kind teacher, together with the assistance of a lad, he proceeded through the Latin classics, committing to memory the text of each author, as well as the arrangement of syntax and the vernacular translation.

Laborious and unceasing were the toils he had thus to undergo, but his powers seemed to expand in a degree proportioned to the burden they had to sustain. He soon, however, began to experience an ample reward for all his labors, in the access which they gave him to the finest models of literature and taste, to examples of the most fascinating creations of the imagination, to the most delicate application of the powers of language, and to the exhibition of common objects, through the splendid medium with which genius alone can invest them.

On leaving this school, he entered the Edinburgh University, where he became a favorite pupil of the learned Dugald Stewart. His studies during this course were conducted with a view to prepare him for the ministry; but having passed through all the trials and exercises prerequisite to taking orders, warm debates arose among the judges, (perhaps as blind morally as Davidson was physically,) whether his misfortune did not altogether disqualify him for an active charge. Their decision being unfavorable, he turned his attention to natural philosophy and chemistry, under the instruction of Dr. Black, a celebrated chemist. Mr. Davidson commenced his career as a public lecturer, in Edinburgh, where his previous high reputation as a college student drew around him many friends. From thence he made a tour of Scotland, delivering a course of lectures in each village and city he visited, with remarkable ability and success. He invented a very important apparatus for relieving mining pits of their fire-damp, or carbonic acid gas. Dr. Davidson was twice married, and both ladies aided him in his experiments, with a neatness and grace that excited general admiration.

Death closed the labors of this amiable and accomplished philosopher in the autumn of 1826.

To these great names we may add, without descending in the scale of merit, that of our own Nelson, professor of classics in Rutger's College, New Jersey. We find a sketch of this eminent and accomplished scholar in the memoirs of Rev. Dr. Griffin, and as we possess no additional facts concerning him, we give from it the following brief extract:

"The life of Mr. Nelson was a striking exemplification of that resolution which conquers fortune. Total blindness, after a long and gradual advance, came upon him about his twentieth year, when terminating his college course. It found him poor, and left him, to all appearance, both penniless and wretched, with two sisters to maintain; without money, without friends, without a profession, and without sight. Under such an accumulation of griefs, most minds would have sunk, but with him it was otherwise; at all times proud and resolute, his spirit rose at once into what might well be termed a fierceness, and independence, and he resolved within himself to be indebted for support to no exertions but his own. His classical education, which, owing to his feeble vision, had been necessarily imperfect, he now determined to complete, and immediately entered upon the apparently hopeless task, with a view to fit himself as a teacher of youth. He instructed his sisters in the pronunciation of Greek and Latin, and employed one or the other constantly in the task of reading aloud to him the classics usually taught in the schools.

"A naturally faithful memory, spurred on by such strong excitement, performed its oft-repeated miracles, and in a space of time incredibly short, he became master of their contents even to the minutest points of critical reading. In illustration of this, the author remembers on one occasion, that a dispute having arisen between Mr. Nelson and the classical professor of the college, as to the construction of a passage in Virgil, from which his students were reciting, the professor appealed to the circumstance of a comma in the sentence, as conclusive of the question. 'True,' said Mr. Nelson, coloring with strong emotion, 'but permit me to observe,' said he, turning his sightless eyeballs towards the book he held in his hand, 'that, in my *Heyne's* edition it is a colon, and not a comma.'

"At this period a gentleman, who accidentally became acquainted with his history, in a feeling somewhat between pity and confidence, placed his two sons under his charge, with a view to enable him to try the experiment of teaching. A few months' trial was sufficient; he then fearlessly appeared before the public, and at once challenged a comparison with the best established classical schools in the city. The novelty and boldness of the attempt attracted general attention; the lofty confidence he displayed in himself excited respect; and soon his untiring assiduity, his real knowledge, and a burning zeal, which, knowing no bounds in his own devotion to his scholars, awakened somewhat of a corresponding spirit in their minds, completed the conquest. His reputation spread daily; scholars flocked to him in crowds; competition sunk before him; and in the course of a few years he found himself in the enjoyment of an income superior to that of any college patronage in the United States, with to him the infinitely higher gratification of having risen above the pity of the world, and fought his own blind way to honorable independence. Nor was this all; he had succeeded in placing classical education on higher ground than any of his predecessors or cotemporaries had done, and he felt proud to think that he was, in some measure, a benefactor to that college which, a few years before, he had entered in poverty and quitted in blindness."

When we reflect upon a list of characters like the foregoing, who have elicited light from darkness, and become ornaments to their nation and age, we cannot but feel more reconciled to our lot, and inspired with the glorious thought that, notwithstanding our privation, life is yet what we make it. Whatever may be the obstacles opposed to our progress, so long as perseverance and enterprise can triumph over them, none but the timid and pusillanimous should fear or sink in despair. Science and religion, the unalloyed and inexhaustible fountains of human happiness, lie still within our reach, inviting as the fruits of Paradise.

SECTION II.

DIVINES, LAWYERS AND PHYSICIANS.

As ministers of the gospel, the blind have in every age and branch of the christian church received but little encouragement, if they have not always been indiscriminately rejected. Davidson, notwithstanding his fine talents and thorough preparation, could not obtain clerical credentials; and Blacklock was driven from his charge by popular prejudice, after a regular installment. Yet, with all these discouragements, love to God, and an ardent desire to see humanity rescued from the thralldom of sin and misery, have constrained many of our order to become able and efficient laborers in Christ's moral vineyard. We would not, however, urge claims to a sphere to which the Lord himself will call those "of whom he hath need;" but should the all-wise Creator and controller of the universe call one deprived of natural vision, that he might "see and tell of things invisible to mortal sight," we cannot comprehend by what authority he is prevented from exercising the ministerial functions.

We are aware, that under the law of Moses, blindness was a disqualification for the priestly office; but as the wholeness of that order, as well as the unblemishedness of the victims sacrificed, were only typical of the coming Messiah's moral and physical perfection, that clause of the law can certainly (we think) have no bearing on the ministry under the new dispensation, from which types and shadows have disappeared. Jehovah spoke to his people by the mouth of Teresias and Phineas, blind prophets of old, and we can see no reason why the same privation should prevent holy men, at the present day, from preaching the truths of the everlasting gospel.

Rev. John Traughton, of the seventeenth century, one of the most able and devoted advocates of the Puritan faith, was blind from the fourth year of his age. This eminent divine received his rudimentary instruction at the free school at Coventry, his native place, and in 1655 entered a student of St. John's College, Oxford, of which he became a fellow, and there took the degree of Bachelor of Arts. But on the restoration of Charles II. he was expelled from fellowship on account of his Puritan faith. Soon after this, he removed to Bicester, where he read academical lectures to young men, and occasionally preached in private, whereby he obtained a comfortable subsistence.

Upon the issuing of his majesty's declaration for

the toleration of religion, dated March 15th, 1671, Rev. Mr. Traughton was one of the four Bachelors of Divinity sent by his sect, to establish preaching in the city of Oxford. So great was his learning, piety, and moderation, that he not only drew large numbers of college students as auditors to his chapel, who were fascinated by his eloquence, but maintained an amicable correspondence with many of the best conformable clergy until his death, which occurred in 1681, in the forty-fourth year of his age. His funeral discourse was preached by Rev. Mr. James, master of the free school at Woodstock, who was also blind. Traughton wrote several books; nothing, however, but their titles are now extant: "The Protestant Doctrine of Justification by Faith only, vindicated;" "Popery the Grand Apostacy;" "An Apology for the Nonconformists;" and "A Letter to a Friend, touching God's Providence."

William Jamieson, D. D., and professor of history at the Glasgow University, also spent the greater part of his life in preaching the gospel, with so much success that historians have ranked him among the first of the Scotch clergy.

He was educated at the University of Glasgow, and, after taking his degree, was there for some time employed in reading lectures upon civil and ecclesiastical history. He was also earnestly and ably engaged in the Episcopal controversy, which, during the latter part of the seventeenth century, formed a distinguished feature in the church history of Scotland.

His numerous works on this subject have been highly valued, and are said to bear marks of astonishing erudition. From the numerous complimentary notices which his cotemporary writers have given him, we select the following from Crawford's history of that country:

"Near the house of Berochan, and within the barony, was born the learned Mr. William Jamieson, preacher of the gospel, and also professor of history in the University of Glasgow, who was a miracle of learning, considering he was deprived of the sense of sight from his birth, and his works afford sufficient proof of his being a very able scholar."

The chastening hand of affliction, in every form, always tends to curb our selfish natures, subdue the heart, and render us more alive to the meek and gentle spirit of the gospel. We might give numerous examples of blind preachers' melting pathos, but only insert the following on account of its somewhat extraordinary character: "Dr. GUYSE, who was suddenly deprived of sight, while in prayer before the sermon, preserved sufficient self-command to lay aside his notes, and deliver his discourse extempore. But after service, while being led through the chapel, he was heard to lament the sudden loss of sight, when a good old lady accosted him with the following congratulations: "God be praised that your sight is gone; I think I never heard you preach so powerful a sermon in my life. Now we shall have no more notes. I wish, for my own part, that the

Lord had taken away your eye-sight twenty years ago, for your ministry would have been more useful by twenty degrees."

From an English writer we copy the following interesting account of a blind clergyman, which serves forcibly to illustrate the degree of independence that one, under this misfortune, may acquire by undaunted courage and perseverance:

"In my rambles last summer," says the writer from whom this account is taken, "on the borders of Wales, I found myself one morning alone on the banks of the beautiful river Wye, without a servant or a guide. I had to ford the river at a place where, according to the instructions given me at the nearest hamlet, if I diverged ever so little from the marks which the rippling of the current made as it passed over a ledge of rocks, I should sink twice the depth of myself and horse. While I stood hesitating on the margin, viewing attentively the course of the ford, a person passed me on the canter, and the next instant I saw him plunge into the river; presuming on his acquaintance with the passage, I immediately and closely followed his steps. As soon as we had gained the opposite bank, I accosted him with thanks for the benefit of his guidance; but what was my astonishment, when, bursting into a hearty laugh, he observed, that my confidence would have been less had I known that I had been following a blind guide! The manner of the man, as well as the fact, attracted my curiosity. To my expressions of surprise at his venturing to cross the river alone, he answered, that he and the horse he rode had done the same thing every Sunday morning for the last five years; but that, in reality, this was not the most perilous part of his weekly peregrination as I should be convinced, if my way led over the mountain before us. My journey had no object but pleasure; I therefore resolved to attach myself to my extraordinary companion, and soon learned, in our chat, as we wound up the steep mountain's side, that he was a clergyman; and of that class which is the disgrace of our ecclesiastical establishment; I mean the county curates, who exist upon the liberal stipend of thirty, twenty, and sometimes fifteen pounds a year! This gentleman, aged sixty, had, about thirty years before, been engaged in the curacy to which he was now traveling, and though it was at the distance of eight long Welch miles from the place of his residence, such was the respect of his flock towards him, that, at the commencement of his calamity, rather than part with him, they sent regularly, every Sunday morning, a deputation to guide their old pastor on his way. The road, besides crossing the river we had just passed, led over a craggy mountain, on whose top innumerable and uncertain bogs were constantly forming, but which, nevertheless, by the instinct of his Welch pony, this blind man has actually crossed alone for the last five years, having so long dismissed the assistance of guides.

"While our talk beguiled the way, we insensibly

arrived within sight of his village church, which was seated in a deep and narrow vale. As I looked down upon it, the bright verdure of the meadows, which were here and there chequered with patches of yel low corn; the moving herd of cattle; the rich foliage of the groves of oak, hanging irregularly over its sides; the white houses of the inhabitants, which sprinkled every corner of this peaceful retreat; and, above all, the inhabitants themselves, assembled in their best attire, round their place of worship: all this gay scene, rushing at once on the view, struck my senses and imagination more forcibly than I can express.

"As we entered the church-yard, the respectful 'how do you do?' of the young, the hearty shakes of the old, and the familiar gambols of the children, showed how their old pastor reigned in the hearts of all. After some refreshment at the nearest house, we went to the church, where my veteran priest read the prayers, psalms, and chapters of the day, and then preached a sermon, in a manner that could have made no one advert to his loss of sight. At dinner, which it seems that four of the most substantial farmers of the vale provide in turn, he related the progress of his increased powers of memory. For the first year, he attempted only the prayers and sermons, the best reader of the parish making it a pride to officiate for him in the psalms and chapters; he next undertook the labor of learning these by heart, and, at present, by continual repetition, there is not a psalm or chapter, of the more than two hundred appointed for the Sunday service, that he is not perfect in. He told me, also, that, having in his little school two sons of his own, intended for the university, he has, by hearing them continually, committed the greatest part of Homer and Virgil to memory."

The Rev. Doctors BLACKLOCK and LUCAS would also properly come under this head; but they have been disposed of more at length in another part of this volume.

Rev. EDWARD STOKES, who zealously preached the gospel for a term of fifty years, was born in 1705, and exchanged this for a brighter world, at Blaby, in Leicestershire, 1796, at the good old age of ninety-three. When in his ninth year, while at school, an accidental discharge of a pistol totally destroyed his sight. He, however, continued his studies with pleasing success, until he took his degree of Master of Arts at the university, soon after which he was admitted into holy orders, and appointed a parish minister in Leicestershire. With the assistance of a person to read the lessons, he performed all the service of the church; and few pastors were ever more beloved by their people than this benevolent and devoted man.

In the legal profession, we have but few names of our order to record. Whether the divine denunciation, "Woe unto you, lawyers," or conscientious scruples have deterred them from this pursuit, we are not prepared to decide. It is quite certain, however, that it is not the obstacles which a want of sight imposes; for, to encounter and overcome difficulties, seems to have uniformly afforded the blind a fruitful source of pleasure.

Dr. NICHOLAS BACON, a celebrated advocate at the council of Brabant, who was deprived of sight in childhood, encouraged by the example of one Nicasius de Vourde, born blind, who lived near the close of the fifteenth century, and who, after distinguishing himself in his studies at the University of Louvain, had taken his degree of D. D. in that of Cologne, himself resolved to make the same attempt. "But his friends," says Wilson, "treated his intention with ridicule, and even the professors themselves were not far from the same sentiment; for they admitted him into their schools, rather under the impression that he might amuse them, than that they should be able to communicate much information to him. He had the good fortune, however, contrary to their expectations, to obtain the first place among his fellow-students. They then said, that such rapid advances might be made in the preliminary branches of education, but that they would soon be effectually checked in studies of a more profound nature. This opinion, it seems, was reiterated through the whole range of his pursuits, and when, in the course of academical learning, it became necessary to study the art of poetry, it was declared by the general voice, that all was over, and that at length he had reached his *ne plus ultra;* but, here, likewise, he disproved their prejudices, and taught them the immense difference between blindness of the intellect, and blindness of the bodily organs. After continuing his studies in classics and philosophy for two years longer, he applied himself to law, and took his degree in that science at Brussels." During the long and extensive practice of his profession, he had the good fortune, almost invariably, to terminate the suits in which he engaged, to the entire satisfaction of his clients.

Sir John Fielding, who became blind in youth, acted in the capacity of justice, in Westminster, with great energy and sagacity for many years. So prompt and assiduous was he in the execution of the law, that the name of blind Fielding, it is said, was a terror to evil doers. He was also an active and benevolent promoter of the Marine Society; was knighted in 1761, and died at Brompton, in 1780. Sir John published various tracts on the penal code, and was the author of a miscellaneous publication, entitled, "Universal Mentor."

For one destitute of sight to enter upon the practice of medicine, may to some, at first, appear preposterous; but when the comparative facilities of the blind and seeing in this field of usefulness are rightly viewed, this impression may in some degree be removed. By the eye, it is true, the physician learns the attitude of his patient, the expression of the countenance, the state of the tongue, and the color of the skin; and these signs often indicate the nature of the disorder. How, then, can a blind man be a good physician? We answer: he may acquire a correct knowledge of all these signs, with the exception of the color of the skin, by the sense of touch; and this sense being in him more acute and refined, he is perhaps able to judge more correctly of the state and condition of the skin, which is considered a matter of great importance in the practice of this profession. External diseases, particularly cutaneous, are seldom attended with danger, and are chiefly distinguished by the eye; internal complaints, on the other hand, which are very numerous and more dangerous, are frequently discovered by the sense of feeling; and, as a blind physician has the advantage of a more acute sense of touch, he is able to form a very correct opinion of the seat and nature of these complaints.

HUGH JAMES, M. D., followed his profession for many years with eminent success, after he was totally deprived of sight. This distinguished physician was born at St. Bee's, in Cumberland, 1771. After having passed through a thorough course of medical study, he graduated at Edinburgh, in 1803, and settled at Carlisle as a practicing physician. Several years previous to this, his sight had been much impaired by severe inflammation in the head, and in the winter of 1806, he became totally blind. But, instead of allowing this misfortune to frustrate all his plans of future usefulness, he continued the practice of medicine with so much assiduity and skill, that, after his death, the people of Carlisle erected to his memory a monument, with the following inscription·

"To the memory of Hugh James, M. D., who practiced physic with eminent skill for many years, in this city. Providence largely recompensed the loss of sight in early life, with talents which raised him to distinguished reputation in his profession, and more abundantly blessed him with a disposition ever prompt to succor poverty and pain. The study of his art, which showed him the weakness and uncertainty of life, taught him to meditate deeply on the works of God, and animated his faith in a merciful Redeemer. He died the 20th of September, 1817, in the forty-fifth year of his age, and was interred in the parish church of Arthuret."

In the summary notices comprised in this series, of those eminent blind, who must ever be cheering as well as guiding stars to their order, we have uniformly omitted a description of the various methods and apparatuses employed by them in the study of the different sciences; as they could be of no service at present, save to gratify the curious. In the institutions for the education of this class, established in almost every state of our Union, as well as those of Europe, vastly improved and simplified apparatuses are introduced, answering as perfect substitutes in every department of science, for those commonly used in schools for the seeing. But, notwithstanding the educational facilities which all the blind at present possess, none have attained to that celebrity which our predecessors enjoyed, when no institutions of this kind were known. This, we think, cannot be so much attributable to comparative talent, as to the limited and inadequate course of study, within the pale of these establishments. Where these institutions exist, the public expects that they shall do the work of educating the blind, and consequently the colleges and universities, in which our eminent predecessors were admitted, and where they received the high intellectual training that enabled them to rise above their misfortune, are, in a great measure, closed against us. Until the blind student's course of study is raised to a level with those pursued at our best colleges, he is unable to move successfully in the sphere whence he draws his highest happiness, and in which he can be most useful to himself, and society. In the world of thought and idea is his most congenial realm. Here in the broad field of scientific research, he needs no guide; but walks with unfaltering tread, and with the torch of reason explores the darkest vaults of nature's archives; then climbs on the chain of universal laws, to distant worlds, and weighs in the balance of calculation vast systems plunged in the depth of space.

We would not be understood, however, to depreciate the philanthropic hand that has placed within our reach, as a class, the common branches of education; but would only beg leave to remark, that all has not been done for the blind that can be accomplished, or that we have reason to expect at the hands of our government, and christian philanthropists. We implore those, whose generous hearts have been enlisted in our behalf, to put within our reach a finished college education; such as many who have the use of their eyes, and all other natural faculties, enjoy at the expense of government. Here is yet a field open that will richly repay, in human happiness, the labors of public or private munificence; for it imparts sight to the blind. Showers of emotional sympathy we have on every side; but stern experience has taught us, that these will neither fill an empty stomach, nor satisfy the cravings of an immortal mind; but, on the contrary, unless accompanied by well-directed christian benevolence, they serve only to awaken in our bosoms smouldering emotions of sorrow, which we would fain forever suppress. Nothing can be more cruel and inconsistent, than for persons who would commiserate our misfortune, to point out its darkest phase, and draw before our imagination a panorama of all the fascinating beauties hid from our view, painted in the most extravagant colors. Such compassion can but aggravate our wounds, and move us to murmur against an irrevocable providence. Even under this affliction, life is not without its charms. So multifarious and boundless are the resources of human happiness, that by the loss of natural sight, new and more glorious scenes of contemplation break upon our spiritual vision. With a lively hope soon to be disencumbered from the imperfections of sense, and forever roam through the regions of fadeless beauty, we endure our lot with patience, and can say, in the language of the poet:

"He doeth all things well." The great Milton, who under a depression of spirits, lamented his loss of sight in the most pathetic strains, said, in moments of cooler reflection: "It is not, however, miserable to be blind: he only is miserable who cannot acquiesce in his blindness with fortitude. And why should I repine at a calamity which every man's mind ought to be so prepared and disciplined as to be able, on the contingency of its happening, to undergo with patience a calamity to which man, by the condition of his nature, is liable, and which I know to have been the lot of some of the greatest and the best of my species?"

ACHIEVEMENTS OF THE BLIND IN THE INDUSTRIAL PURSUITS.

SERIES II.—SECTION I.

MECHANICS.

THERE is, perhaps, no calling in which it may become necessary for us to act, where sight is so necessary, as in the manual labor pursuits. In rude stages of society, when mechanical operations were all performed by hand, it may have been more possible for a blind person, in some branches, to compete with the seeing. But in an age like the present, when steam and other natural agents, have usurped the place of muscular power, and the manufacture of all articles of profit is monopolized by large capitalists, this possibility seems almost entirely to have vanished. The facility with which a seeing person will manufacture articles by the aid of machinery, from which those without sight have been entirely excluded, appears to have left this class of laborers utterly without a hope of gaining even a livelihood. But it seems to us that with a little kindly aid, this inequality might, in a great measure, be remedied. That the blind have sufficient ingenuity, and can also acquire the requisite knowledge of any mechanical pursuit, necessary to success, will not be questioned by any one, in the least acquainted with their history.

But, in any branch requiring the use of numerous tools, change of position, and bringing together many parts into one whole, they must necessarily lose more time, in feeling over their work, selecting, using and replacing their implements, than one who has his eyes. Here, then, arises their only inability to compete with other laborers. Facility is what they have lost, and not skill. It seems to us that, in those manufacturing establishments where labor is so divided among the operatives, that each person has but one distinct part of the whole to perform, and where no change of position is requisite, the blind might perform some portions of the process with but little or no inconvenience. Should manufacturing establishments of this kind be erected, in connection with our Institutions, where machinery would facilitate labor, we think, with the aid of a few seeing persons to perform the most difficult parts, a more profitable and honorable operation might be conducted, than in the few simple trades at present selected for, and taught to, the blind. Complex mechanism seems never to have frightened them, but on the other hand, when left to their own inclination in this respect, they have almost uniformly selected those pursuits in which great ingenuity and delicacy of perception were most indispensable.

William Huntly, a native of Barnstaple, in Devon, who was born blind, spent the principal portion of his life in watch and clock making. His father seems to have possessed great skill in this business, and brought up his son to the same craft. He was considered by the inhabitants of his native place, a very superior hand in his profession, especially in repairing musical clocks and watches. It is said that he seldom met with any difficulty, even in the most complicated cases; and it often occurred that when others failed in repairing a clock or watch, Huntly found no trouble in discovering the nature of the malady, and presently administered the proper nostrum. Had not our own experience and observation taught us to what an astonishing degree the sense of touch may be cultivated, the idea of making it supply the place of the eye, and a powerful magnifying glass, (which is generally used by jewelers,) might, to us, as well as to others, seem preposterous. Besides, these facts will appear still more reconcilable, when it is remembered that Huntly lived in the days of huge wooden clocks, and watches about the size of a Moravian biscuit.

Neither is he the only blind person who turned his attention to this art. WILLIAM KENNEDY, who became sightless in childhood, had the reputation of being one of the best clock builders, both common and musical, of his time. This mechanical genius was a native of Tanderagee, Armagh, and lived in the latter part of the seventeenth century. When a boy, he was master builder and projector for all the children in his native town, nor did maturer years relax his desire to engage in useful employments.

When at the age of thirteen, having been sent to Armagh for the purpose of receiving lessons in music, and while there, residing with a cabinet maker, his mechanical propensities were newly awakened, and he soon made himself acquainted with the tools of his host, and the manner of working them. Although this more congenial employment occupied much of his time, he also made a very satisfactory progress in music; but, on his return home, his first care was to procure tools, with which he fabricated many articles of household furniture. He also constructed Irish bagpipes of a very improved patent, together with other wind and stringed instruments; and so perfect was his knowledge in this art, that he was, by a sort of common consent, elected repairer and builder-general, for the entire musical order, over a large section of country. In the alternate occupations of clock and cabinet making, building looms, with their various tacklings, and his other mechanical accomplishments, he maintained and raised a large and respectable family.

Another genius of the same kind, not altogether without fame, was THOMAS WILSON, a native of Dumfries, who lost his sight in very early infancy. His intuitive fondness for mechanical pursuits, early enticed him to gain a knowledge of the wood-turning trade, in which occupation he spent most of his life. So well did he succeed in this business, that his rolling-pins and potatoe-mashers gained great reputation among the good wives of both town and country; and in making tinsmiths' mallets, lint-breaks, and hucksters' stands, honest Tom was acknowledged on every side to be without a rival. He also made a lathe suited to his purpose, and the numerous tools which this business requires, he had so arranged that he could take from his shelf any one he might need, without the least difficulty.

It is related of Cæsar, the ambitious Roman, that, on passing through a small country village one day, in company with some of his courtiers, he turned to one of them, and said, "Believe me, I had rather be the first man in this small town, than the second in Rome." If Wilson was inspired with any such desires of superiority, he had the good fortune to have them early gratified; for, in addition to the honor arising from his mechanical genius, he was elected principal, not of a college or university, for why should he have his peace of mind disturbed by the impertinent trickery of mischievous students?—but principal of the high situation of bell-ringer in the mid-steeple of Dumfries. And to prove to all future generations that a blind man can be true to high situations, as well as any other man, he died at his post, in the mid-steeple, at the age of seventy-five years, and the sixty-third year of his bell-ringership. He was respected and beloved during the whole of his life, by his fellow-citizens, and all who knew him. It appears that he was never married, but lived the enviable life of a bachelor, doing his own cooking, making his own bed, raising his own potatoes, and living, in every respect, a freeman.

John Kay, of Glasgow, was engaged at the carpenter and joiner trade for a number of years, though he lost his sight through the accidental discharge of a musket, when but nine years of age. His skill in the use of edge tools was so complete that he gave his work as perfect a finish as the most skillful of his fellow-tradesmen. He also worked in mahogany and other sorts of fine wood, and made various kinds of furniture. But the most valuable labors of Kay's life, and those that endeared him most to his friends and the church, were directed towards the spiritual and intellectual elevation of the youth. As a teacher and promoter of Sabbath schools, distributer of tracts, and an humble and assiduous disciple of Christ, his influence will long be felt in the villages and country of Scotland. He died December 16th, 1809, in the thirty-second year of his age.

In this connection we may also notice Bagero, the blind carpenter and joiner of Western New York. This enterprising man, who was sightless from infancy, has gemmed the counties of Livingston and Steuben with beautiful cottages, finished in the most elegant style.

It seems that there are but few mechanical departments in which sight may not be dispensed with, as the following example may serve to show: Macguire, the family tailor of Mr. McDonald, of Clan ronald, Invernesshire, totally lost his sight fifteen years before his death. Yet he continued to work for the family as before, not indeed with the same expedition, but with equal correctness. It is well known how difficult it is to make a Tartan dress, because every stripe and color (of which there are many) must fit each other with mathematical exactness; yet from this material he made an entire suit for his master's brother, with as much precision as he could have done before he lost his sight.

DAVID MAPES, who lost the use of his eyes, after having learned the trade of wagon making, continued in that pursuit with nearly the same success as before, and is at present earning a very respectable livelihood at Angelica, New York.

It has been remarked, that those who lose their sight in mature years, never succeed in learning a new trade. But even to this rule we must offer an exception. NATHANIEL PRICE, who became blind from severe cold, while on a voyage to America, after his return betook himself to the employment of binding books. It seems that he had no previous knowledge of this art, as his former occupation was that of a bookseller. Yet it is recorded that he bound books in the very first style. Several specimens of his skill are in the English libraries of the curious, among which is an elegantly bound quarto bible, in the library of the Duke of Marlborough, at Sion-hill, in Oxfordshire. Mr. Price also gave vent to his ingenuity in the manufacture of his clothes, which he made, from the shoes on his feet to the hat on his head.

We shall now proceed to notice a few characters, who, it seems, rose to greater proficiency in the mechanical department than any adverted to in the foregoing. One of these is JOSEPH STRONG, a native of Carlisle, who lost his sight at the age of four years. He early exhibited an inventive and mechanical genius, in the construction of a curious fiddle, bell-harp, hautboy, and other musical instruments; and at the age of fifteen his great ambition was to build an organ, on which he had learned to play. In order to gain a more perfect knowledge of its several parts and their combinations, he was anxious to examine that in the cathedral of Carlisle. For this purpose he concealed himself one afternoon in that place, and when the congregation had retired and the gates were shut, he proceeded to the organ loft, and examined every part of the instrument. He was thus occupied till about midnight, when, having satisfied himself respecting its general construction, he began to try the tone of the different stops and the proportion they bore to each other. This experiment, however, could not be conducted as silently as the business which had before engaged his attention; the neighborhood was alarmed, and various were the conjectures as to the cause of the nocturnal music, as spiritual manifestations were then unknown. But at length some persons mustered courage sufficient to go and see what was the matter, and Joseph was found playing the organ. The next day he was sent for by the dean, who, after reprimanding him for the method he had taken to gratify his curiosity, gave him permission to play whenever he pleased.

He now set about building his first organ, which, after its completion, he sold, and it is now in possession of a gentleman in Dublin, who preserves it as a curiosity. After receiving some instruction in this art at London, he built a second organ for his own use, and afterward constructed a third, with great perfection, which he sold to a gentleman in the Isle of Man. Mr. Strong was married at the age of twenty-five, and had several children. His house was elegantly furnished, yet it contained but few articles, either of utility or ornament, that were not of his own construction. He died at Carlisle, in March, 1798, in his sixty-sixth year.

The acquirements of WILLIAM TALBOT were so numerous and diversified, that it is difficult to determine in which of his accomplishments he most excelled. As we have reserved for our next series a sufficient number of musicians (among whom he might claim an eminent rank) to prove the capacity of our order for that profession we shall mainly speak of his mechanical attainments. He was born near Roscrea, in Tipperary, in the year 1781, and lost his sight from small-pox at four years of age. Afterwards his family removed to the seaside, at a place near Waterford, where young Talbot soon began to evince a taste for mechanics, in the construction of miniature wind-mills and water-wheels, and in fitting up small ships and boats, with every rope and appendage as exactly formed as in those of a larger scale.

At the age of seventeen he became acquainted with a captain in the navy, and was finally persuaded to go with him to sea. In the four years of his seafaring life, during which time he visited many parts of the world, he became so thoroughly acquainted with the ship that he could readily go aloft among any part of its tacklings, and was frequently seen ascending to the mast-head with the dexterity of an experienced seaman. But the alternate smooth and billowed breast of the ocean had not sufficient variety to satisfy his nature, and in 1803 he again set his foot upon the turf of green Erin. He soon after married at Limerick, and resorted to the exercise of his bagpipes, on which he was a perfect performer, and to mechanical ingenuity, as means of support.

About this time he commenced building an organ, and admirably succeeded, without the least assistance. Soon after completing this instrument, he moved to the city of Cork, where he purchased an organ, for the purpose of making himself better acquainted with its mechanism. After dissecting and examining all its parts minutely, he built a second instrument of this kind, of a superior tone and finish. In this way Mr. Talbot maintained a large family in respectability and comfort.

Among these sons of Jubal, we must not omit our

own John Hellick, a native of Northampton county, Pennsylvania, who lived at the beginning of the present century, and lost his sight in youth. Among the many fine musical instruments which this man constructed, without the least assistance, was an organ that would have reflected credit upon any workman skilled in this art, and in possession of perfect sight.

These examples must prove beyond a shadow of doubt, to every reflecting mind, that as perfect a knowledge of form and structure can be obtained by the sense of touch as by that of sight. They seem, also, to indicate that the blind derive as much pleasure from the exercise of their ingenuity as any other class of men, since a genius is always more impelled to labor from a desire to give tangible form to his inventions, or ideal images, than by the real value of the article when completed.

But perhaps the most complete triumph of tactual perfection over want of sight, that history records, is to be found in the artistic skill of John Gonelli, sometimes called Gambasio, from the place of his birth in Tuscany. This remarkable person lost his sight at the age of twenty, and after having been in this condition about ten years, he first manifested a taste for sculpture. His first work in this art, was to imitate a marble figure, representing Cosmo de Medici, which he formed of clay, and rendered a strikingly perfect likeness of the original. His talent for statuary soon developed itself to such a degree that the Grand Duke Ferdinand, of Tuscany, sent him to Rome to model a statue of Pope Urban VIII., which he completed to the entire satisfaction of his patron. It is supposed that this is the same famous blind sculptor whom Roger de Piles met with in the Justinian palace, where he was modeling, in clay, a figure of Minerva. It is related that the Duke of Bracciano, who had seen him at work, doubted much that he was completely blind, and in order to set the matter at rest, he caused the artist to model his head in a dark cellar. It proved a striking likeness. Some, however, objecting that the duke's beard, which was of patriarchial amplitude, had made the operation of producing a seeming likeness too easy, the artist offered to model one of the duke's daughters, which he accordingly did; and this also proved an admirable likeness. Among his numerous other works is a marble statue of Charles I., of England, said to be finely finished. So far as this art pertains to the form and contour of a statue, it is not more difficult for a blind person to pursue, than others adverted to in this section. But to engrave upon a marble statue that intangible, life-like expression, in which mainly consists the individual similitude, is altogether extraordinary, and must be regarded as the climax of tactual attainments.

SECTION II.

MISCELLANEOUS OCCUPATIONS.

WHATEVER serves to illustrate a condition to which by the vicissitudes of life every person is exposed, cannot fail to awaken interest in the public mind. In view of this fact, we shall devote this section to the notice of such characters who, on account of their various pursuits, would not admit of regular classification, yet whose honorable attainments may afford interest to the general reader, and many valu able hints to our class.

Among these may be mentioned WIMPRECHT, the bookseller of Augsburgh, who was sightless from birth, yet by his energy and perseverance secured a good education, and is at present maintaining a large family in respectability and comfort, from the profits of his thriving business. His stock usually consists of about eight or nine thousand volumes, which he frequently reviews with no other assistance than his intelligent wife. His honesty, obliging deportment, and general acquaintance with books, have secured for him a large and profitable business.

We are informed of another blind person, who is the proprietor of a "music store," at Plymouth, England, and by this employment, together with the teaching of music, has placed himself in very independent circumstances.

It is evident that our class is by no means exempt

from the law of necessity, imposed upon Adam by the divine declaration, viz, "In the sweat of thy face shalt thou eat bread." Yet it is perhaps worthy of remark, that few among us have engaged in the cultivation of the ground, as a means of support. For this we can assign no better reason than has already been hinted, viz, that the greatest inconvenience attendant on the lack of sight in the industrial pursuits, is the inability to transport ourselves with facility from place to place, and this difficulty is perhaps most felt in farming. Yet as proof that even this branch of business is not altogether beyond our reach, we record the name of JOHN HALL, brother of one of the present writers, who has been successfully engaged for several years in agricultural pursuits, notwithstanding his lack of sight from birth, and is at present an able and respectable farmer in the state of Ohio. Nor are his labors confined (as some may suppose) to the mere supervision or management of his farm; there are really but few kinds of labor in which he cannot engage with nearly as much dexterity as though he possessed perfect sight. The work of preparing his ground for seed, sowing, dragging, &c., is of course performed by his hired man; but in harvest time John is at his post, and can perform, as he chooses to express it, as big a day's work as the next man. He has yet scarcely passed the meridian of life, has an amiable and affectionate companion, and two rosy, bright-eyed boys, who seem to have inherited the enterprising spirit of their father, bu' not his misfortune.

In all the labors and engagements of life, heroic courage is one of the most essential virtues. No matter how favorable may be the circumstances at the outset, before any great enterprise is terminated, we always find occasion to call this principle into requisition. Swift says that "blindness is an inducement to courage, because it hides from us the danger which is before us." How far the dean may be right in his conjectures, we shall not here endeavor to determine.

But to illustrate that lack of sight does not intimidate or disqualify us for great encounters, even when dangers are most apparent, we record the name and a few adventures of ZISCA, the Bohemian reformer. This distinguished patriot was a native of Bohemia. His real name was John de Trocznow, but in the course of his military services he lost his left eye, from which circumstance he was called Zisca, that word, in the Bohemian language, signifying one-eyed. He served for some time in the Danish and Polish armies, but on the conclusion of the wars he returned to his native country. The Council of Constance, which had then assembled (1414) for the purpose of rooting heresy out of the churches, and at whose command John Huss and Jerome of Prague, were burned at the stake, sent terror and consternation throughout Bohemia, and its cruel and unjust decrees filled the public mind with horror and indigna tion. The people at last became exceedingly exasperated against the pope and the emperor, on account of their cruelties, and were obliged to take up arms in defense of their lives, and chose Zisca as their general, who soon found himself at the head of forty thousand patriots. But at the siege of Ruby, while viewing a part of the works on which he intended an assault, an arrow from the enemy struck him in his remaining eye, and when extricated tore out the eye with it. This accident caused his whole devoted army to mourn; for, while under the gleaming of their general's sword, triumphant victory awaited them in every contest.

He was carried to Prague by his weeping soldiers, and his life was for some time despaired of. After much pain and suffering, however, he recovered, but with no other hope before him than of spending the remainder of his days in total blindness. But, like Sampson of old, he drew more dreadful destruction upon the heads of his enemies, after this misfortune, than he before had done. His friends were surprised to hear him talk, after his recovery, of setting out for the army, and did all in their power to dissuade him, but he remained fixed in his resolutions. "I have yet," said he, "my blood to shed for the liberties of Bohemia. She is enslaved; her sons are deprived of their natural rights, and are the victims of a system of spiritual tyranny as degrading to the character of man as it is destructive of every moral principle; therefore, Bohemia must and shall be free." True to the magnanimity of soul that characterized his eventful life, he again presented himself to the army, a few months after his privation, and was hailed with loud and joyful acclamations, by a soldiery whom his presence ever inspired with invincible courage.

When the news came to the Emperor Sigismond, that Zisca had again taken the field, he called a convention of all the states in his empire, at Nuremburgh, and entreated them, for the sake of their sovereign, for the honor of their empire, and for the cause of their religion, to put themselves in arms. His harangue had its desired effect; proper measures were concerted, and the assembly broke up with a unanimous resolution to make this audacious rebel feel the full weight of the empire. Accordingly, the news came to Zisca that two large armies were in readiness to march against him, one composed of confederate Germans, under the Marquis of Brandenburgh, the Archbishop of Mentz, Count Palatine of the Rhine, and other princes; the other of Hungarians and Silesians, under the emperor himself. The former was to invade Bohemia on the west, the latter on the east; they were to meet in the center, and, as they expressed it, crush this handful of vexatious sectaries between them. But it appears that the blind reformer was not to be frightened by threats nor imperial armaments. He knew that his army could not cope in number with those of his enemies, but with the firm conviction that every soldier was ready to lay down his life for his country, and that the God of hosts smiled with approbation upon his cause, he placed himself in readiness to meet the shock.

After some delay the emperor entered Bohemia at the head of his army, the flower of which was fifteen thousand Hungarians, deemed at that time the best cavalry in Europe, and led by a Florentine officer of great experience, and the infantry, which consisted of twenty-five thousand men, were equally fine, and well commanded. This force spread terror throughout all the east of Bohemia. Wherever Sigismond marched, the magistrates laid their keys at his feet, and were treated with severity or favor, according as they were well or ill affected towards his cause. His bold career was, however, presently checked. As soon as the news of the emperor's devastation reached Zisca, he put his army in motion, and rapidly advanced towards the enemy. On the 13th of January, 1422, the two armies met on a large plain, near Kamnitz. Sigismond took great care in the selection of his ground, and in the arrangement of his army, and was elated with the hope of crushing this hitherto invincible chief, who could neither be terrified by mandates nor conquered by arms. No general paid less regard to the circumstances of time and place than Zisca. He seldom desired more than to come up with his adversary; the impetuosity and heroism of his troops supplied the rest.

But on this occasion, when the liberties of his country and the interests of the reform depended upon the result of the engagement, all necessary preparations were made with circumspection and care. When the two armies were drawn up in battle array, Zisca appeared in the center of his front line, guarded or rather conducted by a horseman on each side, armed with a poleax. His troops having sung a hymn with determined coolness, drew their swords, and waited for the signal. Zisca stood not long in view of the enemy, and when his officers had informed him that the ranks were well closed, he waved his sabre over his head, which was the signal of battle, and never was there an onset more mighty and irresistible. As dash a thousand waves against the rock-bound shore, so Zisca rolled his steel-fronted legions upon the foe. The imperial infantry hardly made a stand, and in the space of a few minutes they were disordered beyond a possibility of being rallied. The cavalry made a desperate effort to maintain the field, but finding themselves unsupported, they wheeled round and fled upon the spur. Thus was the extensive plain, as far as the eye could reach, suddenly overspread with disorder, the pursuers and the pursued mingling together, in one indistinct mass of waving confusion; here and there might be seen a few parties endeavoring to unite, but they were broken as soon as formed. The routed army fled toward the confines of Moravia, the patriots, without intermission, galling their rear. The river Igla, which was then frozen, opposed their flight, and here new disasters befel them. The bridge being immediately choked, and the enemy pressing furiously on, many of the infantry and the whole body of cavalry attempted the river; the ice gave way, and not fewer than two thousand were swallowed up in the water. Here Zisca sheathed his sword, and returned in triumph to Tabore, laden with all the trophies which the most complete victory could give.

But the heroic reformer's labors had not yet ended. The emperor, exasperated by his defeat, raised new and immense armies, which he sent against Zisca in the following spring, and with which he determined to root heresy out of his dominions. With this view, he placed the Marquis Misnia at the head of a considerable body of Saxons, who were to penetrate by the way of Upper Saxony, while he himself, at the head of another army, should enter Moravia, on the side of Hungary. But the blind general, determined that his country should not be enslaved while he had strength to wield a sword, gathered his brave army, and laid siege to Ausig, a strong town situated on the Elbe. When he had reduced the place to its last extremity, the marquis appeared at the head of an immense army, and offered him battle. His maxim being never to decline fighting, he accepted the challenge, though he had many difficulties to encounter. An engagement ensued, in which the Saxons were utterly routed, leaving no less than nine thousand of their number dead on the field. By this victory, Ausig, with all its surrounding country, fell into the hands of Zisca.

The other branch of the imperial army, under the

command of Sigismond, meeting the same fate, the emperor was obliged, after having carried on the unprovoked contest for a number of years, to sue for peace. Our blind hero having taken up arms only to secure peace, he was glad for an opportunity to lay them down. No ambitious thirst for power inspired his breast. When his grateful countrymen requested him to accept the crown of Bohemia, as a reward for his eminent services, he respectfully declined. "While you find me of service to your designs," said the disinterested chief, you may freely command both my counsels and my sword, but I will never accept any established authority; on the contrary, my most earnest advice to you is, when the perverseness of your enemies allows you peace, to trust yourselves no longer in the hands of kings, but to form yourselves into a republic, which species of government only can secure your liberties."

After a few couriers had passed between them, a place of congress was appointed, and Zisca, attended by the principal officers of his army, set out to meet the emperor. But the reformer lived not to put a finishing hand to this treaty. In passing through a part of the country where a contagious epidemic was prevailing, he was seized by the infection, and died on the 6th of October, 1424, at a time when all his labors were ended, and his great purposes almost completed.

The remains of this great man were deposited in the church at Craslow, in Bohemia, where a monument was erected to his memory, with an inscription to this purport: "Here lies John Zisca, who, having defended his country against the encroachments of papal tyranny, rests in this hallowed place, in despite of the pope."

In the daring courage of JOHN, the blind king of Bohemia, who fell in the famous battle of Cressy, we have another illustration of the fact that sight is not always a requisite to valor. This king, who had been blind for many years, anxious to know how the battle proceeded, was led forward during the heat of the engagement, and when the clang of arms fell upon his ear, he turned to his lords, and said: "Gentlemen, you are men, my companions and friends in this expedition; I only now desire this last piece of service from you, that you would bring me forward so near to these Englishmen that I may deal among them one good stroke with my sword." They all said they would obey him to the death, and lest by any extremity they should be separated from him, they all, with one consent, tied the reins of their horses one to another, and so attended their royal master into battle. There this valiant old hero had his desire, and came boldly up to the Prince of Wales, and gave more than one, four or five good strokes, and fought courageously, as also did all his lords, and others about him; but they engaged themselves so far that they were all slain, and next day found dead about the body of their king, and their horses' bridles tied together.

Perhaps the most complete triumph of mental energy over physical circumstances which the history of man affords, is exhibited in the career of JOHN METCALF. We have reserved the summary of his novel adventures for the conclusion of this paper, for the reason that his attainments were so various, and many of them so peculiar to himself, that he seems decidedly an odd link in the chain. Metcalf was born in 1717, at Knaresborough, Yorkshire, and lost his sight at six years of age. This disability did not, however, prevent him from joining boys of his own age in their juvenile pranks of taking birds' nests and robbing orchards, and, as his father kept horses, he learned to ride, and soon became a good horseman. At the age of thirteen he was taught music, an accomplishment which he afterward turned to great utility, being employed for several years as chief player at the assemblies of Harrowgate. Here he was a favorite of the visiting nobility and gentry. In this employment he passed his evenings, and the mornings he spent in cock-fighting, hunting, and coursing.

At the age of twenty-one Metcalf was extremely robust, six feet one inch and a half in height, possessed a peculiar archness of disposition, with an uncommon flow of spirits, and though his conduct was long marked by a variety of mischievous tricks, yet he afterward planned and brought to perfection several schemes, both of private and public utility. Indeed, there are but few fields of enterprise in which he was not engaged, and what was most strange, he usually selected those in which sight appears most essential. He kept chaises at Knaresborough for public accommodation, and ran a stage between that place and York, which he drove himself. In 1745, he enlisted as musician in the army; later, largely engaged in contraband importation of Scottish goods, and subsequently became an extensive projector and builder of public roads.

Dr. Bew, who was personally acquainted with Metcalf, in his account of him, says: "This man passed the younger part of his life as a wagoner, and occasionally as a guide in intricate roads during the night, or when the tracks were covered with snow. Strange as this may appear to those who can see, the employment he has since undertaken is still more extraordinary; it is one of the last to which we would suppose a blind man would ever turn his attention. His present occupation is that of projector and surveyor of highways in difficult and mountainous parts. With the assistance, only, of a long staff, I have several times met this man traversing the roads, ascending precipices, exploring valleys, and investigating their several extents, forms and situations, so as to answer his designs in the best manner. The plans which he designs, and the estimates he makes, are done in a method peculiar to himself, and which he cannot well convey the meaning of to others. His abilities in this respect, are, nevertheless, so great, that he finds constant employment. Most of the roads over the peaks in Derbyshire have been altered by his directions, particularly those in the vicinity of Buxton; and he is at this time constructing a new one between Winslow and Congleton, with a view to open a communication to the great London road, without being obliged to pass over the mountains." Mr. Bew adds in a note, "Since this paper was written, I have met this blind projector of roads, who was alone, as usual, and among other conversation, I made some inquiries concerning this new road. It was really astonishing to hear with what accuracy he described the courses, and the nature of the different soils through which it was conducted. Having mentioned to him a boggy piece of ground it passed through, he observed that 'that was the only place he had doubts concerning; and that he was apprehensive they had, contrary to his directions, been too sparing of their materials.'"

"Among the numerous roads which Metcalf contracted to make, was part of the Manchester road, from Blackmoor to Standish Foot. As it was not marked out, the surveyor, contrary to expectation, took it over deep marshes, out of which it was the opinion of the trustees, that it would be necessary to dig the earth till they came to a solid bottom. This plan appeared to Metcalf extremely tedious and expensive, and liable to other disadvantages; he therefore argued the point privately with the surveyor, and several other gentlemen, but they were all immoveable in their former opinion. Metcalf attended their next meeting, and addressed them in the following manner: Gentlemen, I propose to make the road over the marshes after my own plan, and if it does not answer, I will be at the expense of making it over again, after yours." To this proposal they assented. Having engaged to complete nine miles in ten months, he began in six different parts, nearly four hundred men being employed. One of the places was peat, and Standish Common was a deep bog, over which it was thought impracticable to make any road. Here he cast it fourteen yards wide, raising it in a circular form, and the water, which, in many places, ran across the road, was carried off by drains; but he found the greatest difficulty in conveying stones to the spot, on account of the softness of the ground. Those who passed that way to Huddersfield Market, were not sparing in their censure of the undertaking, and even doubted whether it would ever be completed. Having, however, leveled the piece to the end, he ordered his men to collect heather or ling, and bind it in round bundles, which they could span with their hands; these were placed close together, and another row laid over them, upon which they were well pressed down, and covered with stone and gravel. This piece being about half a mile in length, when completed, was so remarkably fine, that any person might have gone over it in winter unshod, without being wet; and, though other parts of the road soon wanted repairing, this needed none for twelve years."

A few anecdotes of his early adventures may not be without interest to the reader.

When about the age of fourteen, Metcalf, with some other young men, expressed a great desire for a day's sport; and knowing that Mr. Woodburn, the master of the Knaresborough pack of hounds, had often lent them to Metcalf for the same purpose, they doubted not of the success of his application. On the evening before the appointed day, Metcalf went, flushed with hope, to Mr. Woodburn, requesting him to lend the pack for the next day. This was a favor out of his power to grant, having to meet Squire Trapps with the hounds, next morning, upon Scoton Moor, for the purpose of entering some young fox-hounds. Chagrined at this, Metcalf debated with himself whether the disappointment should fall on Mr. Woodburn's friends, or his own: determining that it should not be the lot of the latter, he arose, the next morning, before daybreak, and crossed the high bridge, near which he had the advantage of the joint echoes of the old castle and Belmont-wood. He had brought with him an extraordinarily good hound of his own, and taking him by the ears, made him give mouth very loudly, himself giving some halloos at the same time. This device had so good an effect that, in a few minutes, he had nine couples about him, as the hounds were kept by various people about the shambles, and were suffered to lie unkenneled. Mounting his horse, away he rode with the dogs, to Harrowgate, where he met his friends, ready mounted, and in high spirits. Some of them proposed going to Bilton-wood, near Knaresborough, but this was opposed by Metcalf, who preferred the moor; in fact, he was apprehensive of being followed by Mr. Woodburn, and wished to be farther from Knaresborough, on that account. Pursuant to his advice, they drew the moor at the distance of five miles, when they started a hare, killed her after a fine chase, and immediately put up another: just at this moment came up Mr. Woodburn, very angry, threatening to send Metcalf to the house of correction, and his passion rising to the utmost, he rode up with an intention to horsewhip him, which Metcalf prevented by galloping out of his reach. Mr. Woodburn then endeavored to call off the hounds, but Metcalf, knowing the fleetness of his own horse, ventured within speaking, though not within whipping distance of him, and begged that he would not spoil them by taking them off, and that he was sure that they would (as they actually did) kill in a very short time. Metcalf soon found that Mr. Woodburn's anger had begun to abate, and, going nearer to him, pleaded a misunderstanding of his plan, which, he said, he thought had been fixed for the day after. The apology succeeded with this good-natured gentleman, who, giving the hare to Metcalf, desired he would accompany him to Scoton Moor, whither, though late, he would go, rather than wholly disappoint Mr. Trapps. Metcalf proposed to his friend to cross the river Nid at Holm Bottom; and Mr.

Woodburn not being acquainted with the ford, he again undertook the office of guide, and leading the way, they soon arrived at Scoton Moor, where Mr. Trapps and his company had waited for them several hours. Mr. Woodburn explained the cause of the delay, and being now able to participate in the joke, the affair ended very agreeably.

Our young hero, also frequented the hippodromes at York, and other places. At the races, he commonly rode in among the crowd, and was often successful in his bets, in which he was, however, assisted by several gentlemen, to whom he was known. Having once matched one of his horses to run three miles for a considerable wager, and the parties agreeing each to ride his own horse, they set up posts at certain distances on the Forest Moor, describing a circle of one mile, having, consequently, to go three times round the course. Under the idea that Metcalf would be unable to keep the course, great odds were laid against him, but his ingenuity furnished him with an expedient in this dilemma. He procured some bells, and placing a man with one at each post, was enabled by the ringing to judge when to turn; by this contrivance, and the superior speed of his horse, he came in winner amidst the applauses of all present, except those who had betted against him.

We also give place to the following account of his marriage: At the Royal Oak, (an inn,) where Metcalf was in the habit of spending his evenings, after the season at Harrowgate, he attracted the notice of Miss Benson, the landlady's daughter, whose constant attention and kindness soon inspired him with a reciprocal affection; knowing, however, that her mother would oppose their union, various successful devices were employed to conceal their mutual partiality and frequent meetings. An event, however, occurred, which obliged Metcalf to quit not only the object of his attachment, but likewise that part of the country. During his absence, a Mr. Dickenson had paid his addresses to Miss Benson, and now urged his suit with such ardor, that the banns were published, and the wedding-day appointed, to the no small mortification of Metcalf, who thought himself secure of her affections. But, though he loved her tenderly, his pride prevented him from manifesting his feelings, or attempting to prevent the match. On the day preceding that on which the nuptials were to be celebrated, Metcalf, riding past the Royal Oak, was accosted with, "One wants to speak with you." He immediately turned toward the stables of the Oak, and there, to his joy and surprise, he found the object of his love, who had sent her mother's servant to call him. After some explanation, an elopement was resolved upon, which Metcalf, with the assistance of a friend, effected that night, and the next morning they were united. The confusion of his rival, who had provided an entertainment for two hundred people, may easily be imagined. Mrs. Benson, enraged at her daughter's conduct, refused either to see her or give up her clothes nor was she reconciled until the baptism of her second child, on which occasion she stood sponsor for it, and presented Metcalf with his wife's fortune. It now became a matter of wonder that she should have preferred a blind man to Dickenson, she being as handsome a woman as any in the country. A lady having asked her why she refused so many good offers for Blind Jack, she answered, "Because I could not be happy without him." And being more particularly questioned, she replied, "His actions are so singular, and his spirit so manly and enterprising, that I could not help liking him."

ACHIEVEMENTS OF THE BLIND IN POETRY AND MUSIC.

SERIES III.—SECTION I.

SOME EXPLANATION OF THE METHOD BY WHICH THE BORN BLIND GAIN A KNOWLEDGE OF THE EXTENSION, MAGNITUDE AND APPEARANCE OF DISTANT OBJECTS.

It is not difficult to understand how it is that the obstacles which imperfect sight throws in the way of blacksmithing, painting, or anatomical investigations, are no impediments to the study of music, or even to very superior attainments in it, both as an art and a science. But we confess it is not so easy to perceive how it happens that some persons, denied the blessings of sight from birth, can describe scenes so graphically that even a connoisseur of natural scenery could not detect their condition; or how, indeed, they can form any notion of objects as they must appear to the eye from a distance, of the nature of light itself, of the indescribable glory of the sun, moon, and stars, and much less of those peculiarly pleasurable sensations which the blending of light and shade, and contrast of colors produce.

It is not wonderful that those who regard sight as the grand avenue to the mind, and who through this entrance receive most of their impressions from without, are slow to believe that so many fields of enterprise, and rich subjects for contemplation, are open to the blind. How, say they, can one whose ideas of extent and superficial area can be gathered only from the distance within his reach, or the space of ground over which he may have traveled, form any adequate conception of the magnitude of a mountain, or picture to himself a vast landscape, diversified with groves, meadows, sunny hill-sides, winding streams, with plains and grazing flocks, and here and there isolated trees, at distinct though irregular distances from each other? That the born blind do possess this imaginative power, and even the ability to form new combinations from isolated ideas, is clearly shown in their writings.

The following descriptive lines gathered from the poems of Blacklock, by Spence, his critical reviewer, may serve to demonstrate this fact:

"Mild gleams the purple evening o'er the plain."

"Ye vales, which to the raptured eye,
  Disclosed the flowery pride of May;
Ye circling hills, whose summits high,
  Blushed with the morning's earliest ray."

"Let long-lived pansies here their scents bestow,
The violets languish and the roses glow;
In yellow glory let the crocus shine—
Narcissus here his love-sick head recline;
Here hyacinths in purple sweetness rise,
And tulips tinged with beauty's fairest dyes."

"On rising ground, the prospect to command,
Untinged with smoke, where vernal breezes blow,
In rural neatness let thy cottage stand;
Here wave a wood, and there a river flow."

"Oft on the glassy stream, with raptured eyes,
Surveys her form in mimic sweetness rise;
Oft as the waters, pleased, reflect her face,
Adjusts her locks, and heightens every grace."

"Oft while the sun
Darts boundless glory through the expanse of heaven,
A gloom of congregated vapors rise;
Than night more dreadful in his blackest shroud,
And o'er the face of things incumbent hang,
Portending tempest; till the source of day
Again asserts the empire of the sky,
And o'er the blotted scene of nature throws
A keener splendor."

The idiosyncrasies of the blind, or those traits of the mind which the want of sight from birth has uniformly developed, have long furnished the seeing with curious subjects of metaphysical speculation. Many strange conjectures have been hazarded, and some very happy conclusions arrived at; but as yet, we think they have not received sufficient attention from the blind themselves. In view of this fact, we have ventured to offer, in this connection, a few remarks, as the result of our united experience. Not that we fancy ourselves equal to the task of explaining to the seeing what, to ourselves, is mysterious, but we are persuaded that many of the manifestations of mind that seem peculiar only to our class, may be accounted for, on as strictly philosophical principles as though they had been developed by a full use of all the senses.

Our first inquiry is, then, by what means are those faculties of the mind which perceive physical objects, and contemplate and retain facts concerning them, developed? We answer, by the very impression which those objects produce upon the mind through the external senses. The conversion of these impressions or shadows of the external world, into its own nature, not only affords it healthful exercise, but increases its capacity for the reception of facts. Knowledge is its aliment; and the senses are so many mouths through which it receives its food. But, it may be asked, what if sight, that medium through which the mind can take cognizance of so large a field of objects at the same time, be obstructed from birth; will not the powers of the mind lie dormant? Certainly not, for every essential fact relative to the nature or properties of outward objects, would reach the mind through the other senses or channels of communication, although they might not come robed in such gorgeous colors. A pill may possess medicinal properties, whether it is sugared or not. Delicious fruits are as inviting to the blind man's taste, as gratifying to his appetite, and quite as salutary in their effect upon the system, as though he could behold the bright, rich colors with which nature has painted them.

Color, it should be remembered, is nature's dress, and not nature's self. No one will contend that beautiful colors are essential to the existence of bodies. Correct ideas of every terrestrial object might have been presented to the mind without them. To illustrate this more clearly: a certain quantity of nutritious food is requisite to the support of our animal nature. Now, this aliment may be introduced directly into the stomach without the ordinary process of mastication, and produce the same salutary effect. Indeed, all food might be prepared for the immediate action of this organ, by artificial means. But, in order to afford us greater enjoyments than those of simply answering nature's demand, the God of nature has given us the sense of taste. Yet, had he denied us this source of pleasure, we can conceive how life might have been perpetuated, and all the physical powers naturally developed.

We come now briefly to notice the superior advantages which some of the senses possess over sight, the degree of cultivation of which they are susceptible, and the manner in which they can be made to perform nearly all the functions of the visual organ. This is a large subject, and so thickly enveloped in the mist of metaphysical science, that scarce a ray from our feeble light can be expected to reach it. But darkness to the blind has no terrors. In the first place, then, we remark that, to the eye alone, the common properties of bodies, namely, hardness, density, elasticity, etc., are not cognizable. To the sense of touch, only, are they appreciable. For example: Glass is a hard, dense and brittle body, but independent of the sense of touch, the eye could never have perceived this fact. Indeed, our knowledge of the physical world must have been very limited and superficial, had the Creator endowed us with no other organ of sense than this. Shadows would have been thought as real as the objects by which they were cast. Images reflected from polished surfaces, would have lived and moved, and in short, life would have been even less than a shadowy dream, a beautiful panorama, with neither soul nor substance.

Of all the senses, that of sight is the most liable to delusive impressions. Ocular illusions are common, but who ever heard of a tactual illusion. Spectres, hobgoblins, and every chimera of the imagination of which it is possible to conceive, have frightened and deceived the timid, in every age of the world. But who was ever terrified at the sudden appearance of a tangible ghost? An untutored infant reaches after its toy, while the object desired is, perhaps, some feet from it. It grasps at a sunbeam, or its own image in a mirror, and cries with vexation and disappointment because it cannot possess itself of the beautiful objects. We confess it might be difficult to determine whether these deceptive appearances are attributable to the infant's undisciplined vision, or to the undeveloped state of its mental perceptions, were it not that numerous instances are recorded of persons having been restored to sight, at a mature age, who had lost all recollection of objects as they appear to the eye. To several of these persons, all objects at first appeared at a uniform distance from the eye, although differing greatly in form and magnitude. But what is most surprising, they were wholly unable to recognize familiar objects, until they had first been submitted to the sense of touch, when the eye immediately became satisfied as to their identity. Hence, we are led to infer that to the child, all bodies at first appear at a uniform distance, and perhaps inverted, but that this delusion vanishes when it comes to examine them by the sense of touch ; that it learns to calculate relative distance by comparative magnitude ; that there is nothing in the nature of reflected light, or in the images which it forms upon the retina, by which the mind can determine absolute distance or magnitude ; and that these facts, like most others, can only be reached through the efficient aid of the other organs of sense.

But how, then, it may be asked, does the blind child, whose means of perception do not seem to extend much beyond the reach of his arms, gain any adequate idea of figure, extent, elevation or magnitude? By modes, of course, somewhat differing from those used by the seeing, yet always productive of the same results. But, as these modes may not, at first, appear to the reader, we shall notice a few of them, as the result of the experience of one of the present writers, who, it will be remembered, has been deprived of sight from birth :

I fancy that the entire form or contour of bodies, may be discovered by the eye at a single glance, by the contrast of light and shade, or in other words, by contrasting their particular colors, with the light medium which surrounds them. But by the sense of touch, shape is more gradually communicated. For instance: A large body is presented to me. By passing my fingers over its several parts, retaining in memory a complete idea of each, as they are presented to the mind by the sense of touch, until the entire surface has been carefully examined, the imagination at once combines each ideal proportion, and presents to my view a perfect image of the object. Not by contrast of color, since this property of bodies, it will be remembered, is never perceptible to the touch. But by contrasting, in memory, the density of the object with the rare medium or space which surrounds it. In this way, I can picture to myself without color, (if I choose,) groups of distinct objects of various shapes, with smooth or rough surfaces, in motion or at rest, and can change their relation to each other at will, both in position and distance.

Of course, it will not be expected that, at this period of life, I retain any distinct recollections of the first impressions which tangible objects produced upon my mind. I suppose, however, their peculiar forms and diversified surfaces afforded me sources of great amusement, and, perhaps, created quite as many pleasurable sensations, as the same variety of bright and beautiful colors would have done. And even at the present time, I take a strange and indescribable delight in passing my hands gently over highly polished surfaces, especially if they are curved or undulating. Hard, rough surfaces, like those of sand-paper and unpolished metal, are extremely disagreeable to the touch. Angular figures, with fuzzy, glutinous, or adhesive surfaces, excite in the blind feelings of disgust, kindred, perhaps, to those experienced by the seeing, when the eye falls upon grim and dingy colored objects; while spherical bodies, with soft, smooth, or glossy exteriors, never fail to create the most pleasing sensations and impart ideas of fascinating beauty. Consequently, with these qualities, and sweet sounds, we associate our conceptions of beautiful colors.

"To those who see," says a distinguished writer, "a scarlet color signifies an unknown quality in bodies, that makes to the eye the appearance with which we are well acquainted. The blind man has not this appearance as the sign of that particular quality in bodies; but he can conceive the eye to be variously affected by different colors, as the nose is by different smells, or the ear by different sounds. Thus he can conceive scarlet to be different from blue, as the sound of a trumpet is different from that of a drum: or as the smell of an orange is from that of an apple." As regards our mode of inferring how different colors must appear to the eye, the writer is essentially correct. We do, indeed, fancy a sort of analogy to exist between the sensations which light and color produce upon the eye, and those which sounds produce upon the ear. With almost every property of bodies that may address itself to our hearing, smelling, taste, etc., we associate, as we have before remarked, some ideal quality of color. But what is most singular, these qualities seem to have a separate existence in the imagination, and may be formed by fancy into new and various combinations, as may be seen in the highly colored lines above quoted.

Much more might yet be said in explanation of the methods by which we are enabled to gain a knowledge of extent by the effect of distant sounds upon the ear, and of height and magnitude, by multiplying many times in imagination, the size and elevation of bodies commensurate with our means of perception. But as we have nearly exhausted the space allotted to us in this section, and perhaps the patience of the reader, we shall proceed briefly to notice, in conclusion, a few more favorites of the muses. The most ancient of these, and perhaps the first in merit, is HENRY the Minstrel, more commonly called Blind Harry. This poet was born in 1361, and lost his sight in infancy. He was the author of a historical poem, in ten books, narrating the achievements of Sir William Wallace. This poem continued for several centuries, to be in great repute, but afterwards sunk into neglect, until very lately, when it was recovered from obscurity, and a very neat and correct edition was published at Perth, under the inspection and patronage of the Earl of Buchan. As an example of the author's style, we subjoin the following, which is, perhaps, one of the most lively, and animated descriptions in the whole poem. It is frequently remarked that those who have never seen, should not attempt descriptive verse. If facts can reach the mind by no other entrance than the eye, and if color is the only stuff out of which poets' dreams are made, then, perhaps, it may be true that the blind can neither feel deeply nor describe naturally. But whether our author succeeds in giving this scene its true coloring or not, we leave our read ers to judge:

Now Bigger's plains with armed men are crown'd,
And shining lances glitter all around;
The sounding horn and clarion all conspire
To raise the soldier's breast, and kindle up his fire.
So Triton, when, at Neptune's high command,
He heaves the swelling surge above the land;
When with full breath, he bids the tempest roar,
And dash the sounding billows to the shore;
His angry waves the wrinkled seas deform,
They rise, they rave, and blacken to the storm,
Each eager soldier seized his ready shield,
Drew the fierce blade and strode along the field;
The black'ning wings extend from left to right,
Condense the war and gather to the fight!
Now rose the battle,—there the warriors tend,
A thousand deaths on thousand wings ascend;
Swords, spears and shields, in mixed confusion glow;
The field is swept, and lessens at each blow.
Wallace's helm, distinguished from afar,
Tempests the field, and floats amid the war;
Imperious death attends upon the sword,
And certain conquest waits her destined lord!
Wallace beheld his fainting squadron yield,
And various slaughter spread along the field;
Furious he hastes and heaves his orbid shield,

Resolved in arms to meet his enemy;
Before his spear they run, they rush, they fly
And now in equal battle met the foes,—
Long lasts the combat, and resound their blows
Their dreadful falchions brandishing on high,
In wary circles heighten to the sky.
Now all is death and wounds; the crimson plain
Floats round in blood, and groans beneath its slain;
Promiscuous crowds one common ruin share,
And death alone employs the wasteful war;
They trembling fly, by conquering Scots opprest,
And the broad ranks of battle lie defaced;
A false usurper sinks in every foe,
And liberty returns with every blow!

JOHN GOWER, another ancient poet, who flourished in the latter part of the fourteenth century, and died in 1402, deserves a place in this series. He lost his sight, it appears, at an advanced period in life, but from what cause we are not informed. Some have supposed from imbecility of age; but this does not appear probable, from the fact that after his misfortune he wrote several of his best Latin and English poems.

There is nothing more certain than the uncertainty of human events; nor is there a greater disability than human inertness, or a want of power to break away from the sinking wreck of condemned projects, and to bear up manfully against the tide of reverses and disappointments, until a foothold can be gained on safer and more feasible plans. Failures are the creatures of error and mismanagement, and not of fatuitous misfortune. The only way to battle successfully with natural difficulties, is to meet the ills of life with fortitude, and if obliged to yield a desired point, to rally all the energies in another quarter of the field. Nor is triumph over difficulty the only achievement; the true moral hero is able to endure as well as contend.

Another encouraging example of the power of resolve over physical circumstances, is exhibited in the life of Dr. M. CLANCY, a dramatic poet, who flourished in the beginning of the eighteenth century. He was born in the county of Clare, Ireland, and was deprived of sight in 1737, by a severe cold, and was thus rendered incapable of following his profession as a physician. As the doctor in his earlier days had evinced a fondness for scribbling verse, he was advised by some friends to try his success as an author, and supposing the theater was open alike to all, his first attempt was in the dramatic line. His first piece was a comedy, called the "Sharper," which was acted five times at the theater in Smock-alley, Dublin, and obtained for him the notice of Dean Swift. The dean having critically read a copy of this play, which had been secretly placed upon his table, was so highly pleased with it that, on learning the circumstances of its author, he immediately dispatched the following:

"TO DR. CLANCY:

"*Sir*,—Some friend of mine lent me a comedy, which, I was told, was written by you. I read it carefully and with much pleasure, on account both of the characters and the moral. I have no interest with the people of the play-house, else I would gladly recommend it to them. I send you a small present, in such gold as will not give you trouble to change, for I much pity your loss of sight, which, if it had pleased God to let you enjoy, your other talents might have been your honest support, and had eased you of your present confinement.

"I am, sir, your well-wishing friend,
"and humble servant,
"JONATHAN SWIFT.

"Deanery House, Christmasday, 1737."

In the year 1746, he received a sum of money for performing the part of Tiresias, the blind prophet, in "Œdipus," which was acted for his benefit at Drury Lane theater. He afterward settled at Kilkenny, where he was for some time connected with a Latin school. Clancy was the author of three dramatic pieces, and also of a Latin poem, called "Templum Veneris, sive Amorum Rhapsodiæ." From the following fragment, found among the papers of Mrs. Pilkington, we conclude the stream which most embittered our author's life did not spring from want of sight, but from the climax of domestic misery — a scolding wife.

"Hapless Clancy! grieve no more,
Socrates was plagued before;
Though o'ercast, thy visual ray
Meets no more the light of day,

Yet even here is comfort had,
Good prevailing over bad.
Now thou canst no more behold
The grim aspect of thy scold;
Oh! what raptures wouldst thou find,
Wert thou deaf as well as blind."

A German, named John Pheffel, a native of Colmar, who lost his sight in youth, wrote several volumes of poetry, consisting chiefly of fables, which were published in 1791. He also established in his native town a military school, to which youths of the best families in Germany were sent to be educated. He died in 1809, in the seventy-third year of his age.

Miss Anna Williams, who came to London in 1730, with her father, a Welch surgeon, lost her sight from cataract, in the thirty-fourth year of her age. This disheartening calamity did not strip life of all its attractions, nor crush every hope of future usefulness, but seemed rather to give new zest to intellectual pursuits. Her world was now one of thought, and every bright creation of fancy seemed more glorious in contrast with the dark world without. In 1746, after six years of blindness, she published a translation from the French of Le Bleterie's "Life of the Emperor Julian," and twenty years after she appeared again as an authoress, of a volume entitled, "Miscellanies in Prose and Verse." Her fine literary attainments recommended her to the notice of Dr. Johnson, in whose house she lived for several years, and died in 1783, at the age of seventy-seven.

We have also before us a miscellaneous collection

of prose and verse, yet in manuscript, from the pen of O. Hewitt, late deceased, who was an intimate friend and classmate of the present writers.

> "We thank thee, Lord, that in each stricken heart,
> The radiant star of hope doth brightly shine;
> And while we weep that thus we early part,
> We bless the chast'ning hand, for it is thine;
> We know thy mercy, Lord—thy righteous ways,
> And while we mourn, we praise."

Hewitt was born 1827, in Tioga county, New York, and lost his sight in infancy. He entered the Institution for the Blind at New York in 1839, and, after a term of six years, graduated with the highest honors of that institute. He died, from pulmonary consumption, June 10th, 1852, in the twenty-fifth year of his age. We cannot but feel a deep regret for his early death, in common with the numerous and admiring friends which his kindness, generosity, and promising genius had endeared to him. But from the deep rooted and unaffected piety that characterized his life, we are encouraged to hope that his immortal spirit has winged its flight to realms of unclouded day. "And there shall be no night there; and they need no candle, neither light of the sun; for the Lord God giveth them light: and they shall reign for ever and ever." His manuscripts, from which we subjoin the following short poem, as a specimen of the author's style, have fallen into the hands of a relative, who appreciates the r value, and they will, it is hoped, ere long find thei way to the press.

REFLECTIONS ON VISITING THE RESIDENCE OF A DECEASED FRIEND.

I entered that lone dwelling, all was still;
No sound of joy or mirth was heard along
Those now deserted halls, but silence deep
Reigned there, in all its solemnity.
But each familiar thing, so dear to me
In other days, remains unchanged by time;
Like living sentinels they ever stand
To speak to me of the departed dead.
But where is she, whose tones of gladness oft
Echoed so joyously through these lone walls?
Gone, never to return, or cheer again
The hearts that sigh in vain for scenes long fled.
And must it be, that other feet shall tread
The spot still sacred to her memory?
Be, as she oft has been, the pride and joy
Of those that gather round the social board?
No, though ye revel still in smiles, and though
In mirth and joy the livelong night may pass,
Sad thoughts of other days will sometimes come,
To cast a shadow o'er your brightest joys.
'Tis strange, though true, those we have held most dear,
Wither and die, touched by the icy hand
Of death; and o'er their slow but sure decay
Grieve as if all that we most prize on earth
With that loved form had perished in an hour:
And yet, we soon forget that they have been,
Forget that they to us were ever dear;
That yesterday they mingled in the dance,
To-day are slumbering cold in death's embrace.
Again I entered that once loved abode;
But other forms and other scenes were there,
And I, of all that vast assembled crowd,
Am now a stranger where was once my home.
Oh, it is sad, that time should ever bring
Such fearful changes to so fair a spot—

That one who once was gladly welcomed there
Should stand alone by all forgotten now.
But I can bear it, though the sacred past
Be full of sadness—yet 'tis sweet to know
That those I loved have slumbered in the grave,
And buried friendship in oblivion deep,
Ere yet its holy flame had ceased to burn
Or dimmed its brightness by the flight of years.

In arranging these characters, we have usually treated them in order of time; but after the completion of this article, we found, on looking over our list of authors, that we had omitted the name of EDWARD RUSHTON, whose abilities as a writer justly entitle him to a place among the poets, as the extract subjoined will show.

He was a native of Liverpool, and lost his sight in 1774, in his nineteenth year, while on a slaving voy age to the coast of Africa. It is, however, due to his memory to record, that when he beheld the horrors of this disgraceful traffic, he expressed his sentiments in very strong and pointed language, with the boldness and integrity which characterized his every action; and though in a subordinate situation, he went so far that it was thought necessary to threaten him with the irons if he did not desist.

The first occupation worthy of note in which he engaged after his return to England, was the editing of a newspaper called the "Herald." But finding his views too liberal and magnanimous for the times, and the engagement not very lucrative, he exchanged it for that of a bookseller, a branch of business more congen al with his habits and taste than any other that presented itself. A few years subsequent to the loss of his sight, he had married, and now his capital consisted of a wife, five children, and thirty guineas. But by incessant toil and frugal management, he soon rendered his circumstances more easy, and found time to indulge his fondness for reading, and to exercise his talents in composition. With the exception of two letters on the subject of negro slavery, one addressed to President Washington, and the other to Thomas Paine, his productions are all in verse. As a poet, he seems to have possessed considerable merit. Throughout all his writings the reader is charmed with the display of rich and glowing imagination, and a lively conception of the beautiful. His poems, which first appeared in the periodicals of the day, were afterwards collected by his friends, and compiled in one volume, at London, in 1814.

FROM HIS LASS OF LIVERPOOL.

Where cocoas lift their tufted heads,
And orange blossoms scent the breeze,
Her charms the wild mulatto spreads,
And moves with soft and wanton ease.
And I have seen her witching wiles,
And I have kept my bosom cool,
For how could I forget thy smiles,
Oh lovely lass of Liverpool?

The softest tints the conch displays,
  The cheek of her I love outvies;
And the sea breeze midst burning rays,
  Is not more cheering than her eyes.
Dark as the petrel is her hair,
  And Sam, who calls me love-sick fool,
Ne'er saw a tropic bird more fair
  Than my sweet lass of Liverpool

SECTION II.

BLIND MUSICIANS.

There is a world to which night brings no gloom, no sadness, no impediments; fills no yawning chasm, and hides from the traveler no pitfall. It is the world of sound. Silence is its night, the only darkness of which the blind have any knowledge. In it every attribute of nature has a voice; the beautiful, the grand, the sublime, have each a language, and to one whose heart is in tune, every sound has a peculiar significance. In the voice of the flood, the thunder and the earthquake, Omnipotence is heard, and deeper and stronger emotions seem to agitate the feelings, than those which are awakened by the appearance of the dashing water, the gathering storm, the sweeping tempest, or the lightning's flash. Sound fills the soul, while light fills the eye only. The brightest glance that morning ever threw over this beautiful earth, was but a reflected beam of heaven's ineffable glory; but sound is a living echo of that voice that spake and the world stood fast, that commanded and holy stars came forth from the depths of night. "As the visible world, with all its pleasing varieties of form, its endless combinations, and beautiful blendings of light and shade, is to the soul that is permitted to look out upon it, and feel its refining, nay, its regenerating influences, so is the world of sound to him who is denied the contemplation of these beauties." "In the varied stream of warbling melody," as it winds its way in graceful meanderings to the deep recesses of his soul, "or of rich and boundless harmony, as it swells and rolls its pompous tide around him," he finds a solace and a compensation for the absent joys of sight.

Consequently, the educated blind musician becomes enthusiastic in his admiration of the science and art of music. Secluded ever from the joys of vision, he seeks for consolation here. Oft, in the pensive musings of his active mind, when lonely and retired, he contemplates the excellence of music, and seeks the sources of its powerful charms. He runs through the nice gradations and minute divisions of its scale, and fancies an unlimited extent, in gravity and acuteness, beyond the reach of all perception; thence he traverses the rich and devious maze of combinations which result from harmony, and all its complicated evolutions—the soft and loud, the mingling light and shade of music—the swelling and decreasing tones, which form the aerial tracery and fading tints of just perspective—all are to him the body, color, strength and outline, which compose the vivid picture his imagination has created. He ponders next upon the various sounds produced in nature, from the soft and balmy whisper of the vernal breeze to the loud pealings of the deep-toned thunder, heard amid the wailings of the fiercely raging storm. Lost in the tumult of his strong emotions, he exclaims, "What is there in the wide creation so sublime, magnificent, or beautiful, as sound?"

In the lives of those eminent blind, who have in different ages distinguished themselves in the science and practice of music, the truth and justice of the foregoing remarks are fully exemplified. Franciscus Salinas, professor of music at the University of Salamanca, and created Abbot of St. Pauciato della Rocca Salignas, in the kingdom of Naples, by Pope Paul IV., was one of the most remarkable musical geniuses of which any age can boast. He was the author of an elaborate treatise, in seven books, on his favorite science, under the title of "De Musica," which held a preëminence for many centuries, and was, perhaps, one of the most profound and erudite works ever produced on this subject, in any language or country. Franciscus Salinas was born in the year 1513. His blindness from birth probably early lead him to the study of music, and during his youth nearly the whole of his time was employed in singing and playing the organ. When but a lad, he acquired a knowledge of the Latin language, from a young lady, to whom he gave lessons in music in return. Encouraged by his rapid attainments, his parents sent him to the University of Salamanca, where he applied himself assiduously and with astonishing success to the study of the Greek language, philosophy and the arts. After leaving the university, his genius recommended him to the favorable notice of Archbishop Compostella, afterward made cardinal, whom Salinas accompanied to Rome, where he spent thirty years in studying the works of Boetias and the writings of the ancient Greek harmonicians. He afterward returned to Spain, where he was invited to the professorship of music in his own university, on a liberal salary. He died in 1590, at the advanced age of seventy-seven, leaving behind him many excellent musical compositions, together with the valuable productions above alluded to.

In the sixteenth century, when the tender influence of music seemed for a time to warm into action the nobler impulses of men's natures, and to cause springs of feeling to gush anew from hearts long calloused with vice and cruelty, flourished Caspar Crumbhorn, who was blind from the third year of his age. He composed several pieces of music in parts, and performed, with such superior taste and skill, on both the flute and violin, that he won the favor and patronage of Augustus, elector of Saxony. But, preferring his native Silesia to every other country, he returned thither, and was appointed organist of the church of St. Peter and St. Paul, in the city of Lignitz, and likewise had the chief direction of the musical college in that place. He died there on the 11th of June, 1621.

Cotemporaneous with Crumbhorn lived MARTIN PESENTI, a native of Venice, who was blind from birth. He was a distinguished composer, both of vocal and instrumental music.

One of the more modern musicians, if not the first among the blind in point of talent, was JOHN STANLEY, the celebrated English organist and composer. who was born in 1713, and lost his sight when but two years of age, from a fall on a marble hearth. In early youth his friends placed him under a musical master, but more from a desire to amuse him than a hope of his excelling in the art. But so rapid was his progress, that, at the age of eleven, he obtained the situation of organist at All-Hallows, and in 1726, at the age of thirteen, was elected organist of St. Andrew's, Holborn, in preference to a great number of candidates. In 1734 the Benchers of the Inner Temple elected him one of their organists; and the last two situations he retained until his death. Few professors have spent a more active life in every branch of their art than this extraordinary musician; who was not only a most neat, pleasing, and accurate performer, but an agreeable composer and successful teacher. Besides several voluntaries for the organ, he was the author of two oratorios — "Jeptha," written in 1757, and "Zimri," which was performed at Covent Garden, during the first season of Mr. Stanley's management of the oratorios there. He also composed the music to an ode, performed at Drury Lane, and set music to a dramatic pastoral, entitled "Arcadia, or the Shepherd's Wedding," which was played at the same theater. After the death of the great master, Handel, (who was himself blind for several years before his decease,) Stanley, in conjunction with Smith, undertook the management of the oratorios during Lent, and after Mr. Smith retired, he carried them on in connection with Mr. Lindsley, till within two years of his death, which took place on the 19th of May, 1786. On the 27th, his remains were interred in the new burial-ground of St. Andrew's, and on the following Sunday, instead of the usual voluntary, a solemn dirge was performed, and, after service, "I know that my Redeemer liveth," was given with great effect upon that organ at which the deceased had for so many years presided.

In proof of his masterly management of the organ, it is related by one of his biographers, that when at the performance of one of Handel's Te Deums, on finding the organ a semitone too sharp for the other instruments, Stanley, without the least premeditation, transposed the whole piece; "and this, with as much facility and address," adds the writer, "as any person could have done, possessed of sight." The ready transposition of harmony so intricate as the composition of Handel, alluded to, from the key of two sharps to that of seven, certainly proved Stanley to be a competent master of the instrument, and exhibited a degree of skill, power of concentration, and celerity of thought, truly surprising. Nor would it have been less wonderful had he possessed perfect sight; for what had sight at all to do with the matter? Music is addressed to the ear, and not to the eye; nor could two of the brightest eyes that ever prototyped crotchets and quavers have rendered him any material aid. True, the relative length, pitch, and power of musical sounds are all represented by signs or characters addressed to the eye, by which the most difficult composition may be read almost at a glance. But in the transposition of a piece committed to memory, the presence of these must tend rather to distract than to aid.

One of the most brilliant and interesting performers in the concerts at Paris, during the season of 1784, was Mademoiselle PARADIS, of Vienna, who lost her sight in the third year of her age, from excessive fear. Her friends, it appears, had placed her, at a very tender age, under proficient instructors, and when but eleven years old, she was able to accompany herself on the organ in a "Stabat Mater," of which she sung a part at St. Augustin's church, in the presence of the empress queen, who was so touched with her performance and interesting appearance, that she settled a pension on her for life. After completing her musical education, she, in company with her mother, visited the principal courts and cities of Germany, France, and England, where her talents never failed to engage the admiration of musicians, and the respect and patronage of the royal families.

Dennis Hampson, the blind bard of Magilligan, also deserves a place in this series; but more, perhaps, on account of his abstemious habits and remarkable longevity than true musical taste. He was born in 1697, and died at the advanced age of one hundred and ten years. Hampson lost his sight from small-pox, at the age of three years, and spent most of his life as a traveling bard. He was present at the great meeting of harpers, at Belfast, and his performance was pronounced by the amateurs of Irish music, the best example of true bardic style. In later years, adverting to the occasion, he said, with an honest feeling of self-love, "When I played the old tunes, not another of the harpers would play after me."

The following lines were carved on his time-nibbled harp:

In the time of Noah I was green,
After his flood I have not been seen
Until seventeen hundred and two, I was found
By Corman Kelly, under ground;
He raised me up to that degree,
Queen of music they call me.

The following lines on Hampson's death, which appeared in the Belfast Magazine, in 1808, serve to show how fondly his memory was cherished in the hearts of his countrymen:

The fame of the brave shall no longer be sounded,
The last of our bards now sleeps cold in the grave;
Magilligan's rocks, where his lays have resounded,
Frown dark at the ocean and spurn at the wave.

For Hampson, no more shall thy soul-touching finger
  Steal sweet o'er the strings, and wild melody pour;
No more near thy hut shall the villagers linger,
  While strains from thy harp warble soft round the shore.

No more thy harp swells with enraptured emotion,
  Thy wild gleams of fancy forever are fled;
No longer thy minstrelsy charms the rude ocean,
  That rolls near the green turf that pillows thy head.

Yet vigor and youth with bright visions had fired thee,
  And rose buds of health have blown bright on thy cheek
The songs of the sweet bards of Erin inspired thee,
  And urged thee to wander, bright laurels to seek.

Yes, oft hast thou sung of our kings crowned with glory,
  Or, sighing, repeated the lover's fond lay;
And oft hast thou sung of the bards famed in story,
  Whose wild notes of rapture have long passed away.

Thy grave shall be screened from the blast and the billow,
  Around it a fence shall posterity raise;
Erin's children shall wet with tears thy cold pillow,
  Her youth shall lament thee and carol thy praise.

Francis Linley, who lived near the close of the eighteenth century, though blind from his nativity, was a most excellent performer on the organ. Nor were his abilities confined alone to the science of music. He was a charming companion, a very acute reasoner, and well acquainted with the works of the most eminent authors, ancient and modern. Having completed his musical studies under Dr. Miller, of Doncaster, he went to London, and was the successful candidate, among seventeen competitors, for the situation of organist of Pentonville chapel, and soon after married a blind lady of large fortune. This latter step, however, we by no means approbate, nor do we record it as a worthy example to be followed by other blind persons. True, the afflicted feel for each other a deeper and more enduring sympathy than the mere appearance of misfortune can possibly awaken in others. But the loss of sight begets, in some degree, a physical dependence upon those who possess it. And although a seeing companion may not at once anticipate every want, her highest happiness may be found in guiding the footsteps of her sightless husband, and receiving in return his love and confidence. We have nowhere contended that eyes may be entirely dispensed with in human society; but as there are more eyes than brains in the world, a few of the former may (we think) be dismissed without creating scism among the members of the body politic. Subsequent to the event adverted to, having lost a large portion of his property through the treachery of a friend, Linley came to the United States, where his performances soon brought him into favorable notice. He died at Doncaster, shortly after his return to England, September 13th, 1800, in the twenty-ninth year of his age.

William Clemantshaw, organist of the parish church in Wakefield, Yorkshire, which situation he held for upwards of forty years, lost his sight in youth. He died in 1822, and the following significant epitaph, composed by himself, was inscribed on his tomb-stone:

"Now, like an organ robbed of pipes and breath,
Its keys and stops all useless made by death;
Though mute and motionless, in ruins laid,
Yet, when rebuilt by more than mortal aid,
This instrument, new voic'd and tun'd, shall raise.
To God, its builder, hymns of endless praise."

To this list we might add a large number of American blind, who have received thorough instruction in the science of music at our several state institutions, and are at present engaged as successful teachers and organists throughout the Union. But as the most of these are still young in reputation, we leave them for a future enlarged edition of this work. Perhaps one of the most eminent of this number is Professor R. Elder, graduate of the New York Institution for the Blind, who has held for several years the situation as organist in the Sixteenth-street Baptist Church, New York city, and is acknowledged the second best performer on that instrument in the metropolis. He is emphatically a true musical genius; and, notwithstanding his blindness from childhood, his pleasing address and gentlemanly deportment have secured for him extensive patronage as a teacher of the piano forte.

LEMUEL ROCKWELL.

To distinguish man from the lower animals he has sometimes been denominated the tool-using animal. By this is meant, that instead of following the instincts of his nature, he is governed by a higher law of necessity, and he is not only an intellectual, but an inventive creature. Indeed, method is the grand lever of the human mind. It is emphatically the tool of thought. Put diligence at the long arm, and let genius direct her labors, and there are but few obstacles, even in the blind man's path, that may not be thrown aside. Another example of mental triumph over physical condition, or in other words, of natural defects overcome by perseverance and proper discipline, may be seen in the life and successes of Lemuel Rockwell, an American musician.

> His birth was hail'd by those spirits of song,
>   Who dance in the torrent's foam,
> Or glide with soft music the streamlets along,
>   Or leap from the fountain's home.
> Mingling forever their silvery notes,
>   As from harps with moonbeams strung,
> With the dashing flood or breeze that floats
>   The shady trees among.

In compliance with our request, Mr. Rockwell has kindly furnished us with a brief sketch of his life, comprising some of the most important and interesting events of his early history, and clearly demonstrating a fact which we have all along sought to establish, viz: that helplessness and inactivity is not a necessary sequence of blindness—that the lack of sight is only a physical defect, and does not presuppose mental deficiency, or a want of capacity for knowledge—and that there are but few of the active pursuits of life, in which this class of persons may not engage with a confident hope of success. It seems to have been Mr. Rockwell's maxim, never to hang up the fiddle while a string remains unbroken. Never abandon a favorite project while hope sheds a ray into the future, or at least until defeat is inevitable; never desert hope until she has first deserted you, has been the theme of his life's song. May it find an echo in every aspiring heart.

In Mr. Rockwell we recognize the true American hero. Entirely independent of the special provision made by this and several other of the sister states, for the education of the blind, he has raised himself by his own industry and perseverance, from a very humble station in life, to one of honor and usefulness. The complete victory he has achieved over the difficulties consequent on blindness—his proficiency in thorough bass, and success as a teacher of vocal and instrumental music—it is hoped may serve as an incentive to greater exertions on the part of the blind, generally, and to convince those who still entertain doubts whether the blind can or cannot teach music, that what has been realized in Mr. Rockwell's experience, might be true in almost every other instance, were it not for public prejudice. Why refuse this class of musicians what you do not deny to others, whom nature has more highly favored, at least the benefit of an experiment? We speak with candor and earnestness, because it has been our misfortune to experience some strong opposition in this particular branch. It seems most astonishing that, notwithstanding the ability of the blind as teachers of music has been proved in so many instances, and acknowledged by so many eminent masters of the art; that, regardless of all that has been done by philanthropists in instituting schools for the education of this class, in order to fit them for a high and useful station in life; that, notwithstanding all this, there are some who still persist in thinking that the lack of sight totally incapacitates a man for any branch of business. To aspire to any of the professions, or even to the art of piano forte tuning, is in their opinion an unpardonable presumption. They cannot, it seems, understand how it is, that one who is unable to distinguish by actual contrast of color the form of the characters which represent sounds, should have any knowledge of the nature or properties of sounds themselves, or the relation they sustain to each other, in pitch, power, or duration. We are pleased with the manner in which Mr. Rockwell has presented this subject, and we trust our readers will find it equally interesting and instructive.

"I have not the vanity," says Mr. Rockwell, "to suppose that a life spent like mine, in poverty and comparative obscurity, a life whose details comprise little of thrilling adventures or remarkable achievement, can furnish any considerable amount of material that will be of much interest to the general reader; nevertheless, in compliance with your request, I submit the following statements, as comprising in the main an account of the leading circumstances and influences to which I am indebted for the little I have achieved, or hereafter may accomplish.

"I was born October 9th, 1817, in the town of Simsbury, Hartford county, Connecticut. Very early in my infancy my parents became apprehensive, from indications that could not elude parental vigilance, that I was laboring under some marked peculiarity or infirmity, either mental or physical, and they were not long in identifying it as total blindness. Those who have watched over the cradle of a new-born infant, observing, with that tender interest which parental affection only can inspire, every indication having the slightest bearing upon the question of its present development or future prospects, will imagine the feeling of my parents on being forced to this most unwelcome conclusion—the more unwelcome, from their present and prospective poverty. I must, in all probability, be dependent for a subsistence, either on my own exertions, or on public or private charity. As for the former, it was difficult for them to conceive how any one enveloped in total darkness should be able to grope his way to any department of useful enterprise; and, as for the latter, everybody feels the truth, as well as the poetry, of Thomas Hood's exclamation —

> 'Alas for the rarity
> Of christian charity
> Under the sun.'

"The key to the little I have attained in the way of general knowledge, will, I apprehend, be found in the fact that my father was an ardent lover of scientific and literary pursuits, and devoted to them more time and attention than the generality of men in his circumstances would have thought it prudent to spare from their ordinary vocations. He delighted in reading to his family, and especially to me, knowing, as he did, that all my knowledge of books must be acquired by hearing them read by others. Not being able to join, to any considerable extent, in the industrial or recreative employments of other children, I had time to hear, and to digest what I heard, so that what I lost in not being able to read for myself was, in a measure, made up to me in the fact that I had leisure to hear and to think.

"When I was in my sixth year, I was sent, or rather permitted, to go to school with my elder brother, and from that time onward, I continued to go to school about as regularly as children in general do, till I was some fifteen years old. During this time, I acquired a tolerable familiarity with the contents of Webster's Old Spelling Book, the historical portions of the New Testament, and Murray's English Reader, as much so, at least, with the book last mentioned, as my limited understanding, and the mumbling, drawling, inarticulate style of school-boy reading in those days, would permit. I also acquired a tolerable knowledge of English grammar, in which Kirkham was my principal text book. To this, if I add Comstock's Philosophy, except so much of it as relates to optics, you will have about the extent of my school attainments.

"In August, 1825, we removed to the town of Southport, Chemung county, New York, some three or four miles from the now large and flourishing village of Elmira; since which time I have resided almost exclusively in Western New York. What I have stated before in reference to my father's connection with my early intellectual development, is preëminently applicable to my musical education. It was under his instruction, almost exclusively, that I acquired a knowledge of the fundamental principles of music. I did not proceed to learn the principles of musical science from a knowledge of the written characters, which are presented to the eye, but from musical sounds themselves, which are addressed to the ear. On the contrary, I had a pretty thorough knowledge of the scale and its various transpositions, through the different major and minor keys, before I knew anything of the staff, clefs, flats, sharps and naturals, which are merely the modes of representing the pitch of sounds to the eye. I knew, also, that musical sounds, as it respects their length or duration, bore certain definite proportions to each other, which I could easily analyze in my mind before I knew anything of the mode of representing them to the eye, by the different forms of whole notes, half-notes, &c., and I probably never should have troubled myself to learn the written characters, but for the necessity of being able to explain them in teaching them to others. The acquisition, however, was of great service to me. For, besides the advantage of being able to explain the written characters, the knowledge of them enabled me to learn musical composition, by hearing the written characters described, one by one, by those who, though they might not be able to sing or play, had acquired that least of all musical attainments, the knowledge of the names and forms of the written characters. A large share of the music which I now retain in memory, and much that I have forgotten, was learned in this way. I subjoin an illustration of this mode of reading music: This tune, says my reader, has B flat for its signature; the rhythmic sign is 4-4; the first note of the soprano is a half-note on the letter F, followed by a bar; the next is a quarter on A; next two quarters on C; next a quarter on D, followed by a bar; then a half on C, and a quarter on A. I need not pursue the illustration farther. The reader familiar with the tune may have discovered that I have given orally the first strain of the well-known Missionary Hymn.

"I never attended a music school of any kind until I was fifteen years of age; and here I must indulge my vanity so far as to state a circumstance which will illustrate the progress which my teacher and I had made, respectively, in musical science, premising that he was a young man just making his first attempt at teaching. Having occasion to sing a tune, which was written in the key of E flat, he directed me to give, on my flute, the letter E. What is the signature, I inquired. Three flats, replied the teacher. Then, said I, the key is E flat. I then explained to him the difference between the keys of E and E flat. He understood it, but said it was something he never thought of before. He had been accustomed, like many that I have since met with, to regard and treat the signature of four sharps and three flats, as indicating, for all practical purposes, one and the same thing. I had never heard anything which even pretended to choir singing, till the winter above mentioned. The only examples of vocal performance I had heard, except at my father's fireside, were at Methodist meetings, in an old school-house, and at camp-meetings, and the like.

"In the autumn of 1833, just as I was entering my eighteenth year, I went to the town of Independence, Allegany county, New York, for the purpose of spending a few weeks in the family of a brother who was residing there. At this time, I could play very well, for a country lad, on the fife and flute, and a little on the violin, and had as good a voice for singing as boys at that age are apt to have, and knew a good many tunes, and could sing them by syllables, or by note, as it was then called; and I could talk learnedly, for a blind boy, about scales, keys, major and minor modes, modulations, etc. etc. On the whole, I suppose I was considered by the good people of that place as a sort of musical prodigy. Under the circumstances, it occurred to me that now was my time to realize what had been a favorite scheme with me for a long time, namely, to become a music teacher. I had attended two singing schools, and watched the movements of the teachers, as well as a blind boy could, but I had not been able to discover anything in their mode of conducting singing schools which I could not learn to imitate.

"The maxim that a prophet is not without honor save in his own country, was now in my favor. I was some sixty miles from home, in a community where there was but little musical knowledge ; success would immortalize, and failure was a bug-bear, which could not, for the moment, obtrude itself upon my sanguine mind. I broached my plan to one or two leading men in the place, who seemed to regard it with favor. A meeting was called, a subscription was circulated, and in process of time, I was duly invested with the labors and responsibilities of a country singing master.

"The time for the commencement of the school was

appointed, and now, for the first time, the difficulties of my position began to stare me in the face. I had now, for the first time, to perplex myself with those little, vexatious details which relate to written music, such, for instance, as the mode of applying the letters to the staff, as indicated by the different clefs. The form of the different kinds of notes, and rests, flats, sharps and naturals, slurs, pauses and staccato marks, and numerous other matters, for which I had heretofore had no use, must all be minutely investigated A thousand little difficulties, real and imaginary pressed upon my mind with such force as to drive me almost to despair. Had it not been for the earnest remonstrances of my brother and his wife, I believe I should have abandoned the undertaking. I felt sure I could not succeed, and should involve not only myself, but the friends whose efforts had been instrumental in bringing me to my present position, in disgrace and mortification. My friends, however, cheered me on, and assisted me in preparing for my work, and on the whole, I have reason to believe that I gave very good satisfaction. It was fortunate for my new enterprise that I had to deal with a plain, hospitable set of people, who were prepared to make the best of whatever was good, and overlook imperfections.

"I have been thus minute in detailing these circumstances, because this was my first entrance upon the life of a singing teacher. From that time, onward, I have taught from one to six classes of vocal music every winter.

"In the summer of 1837, I was made acquainted with the Pestilozzian, or inductive system of teaching, as explained in the Boston Academy Manual. This, together with the black-board, which, though not a part of the system, was strongly recommended in connection with it, was of great service to me in the business of teaching. I could not, of course, write my own lessons on the black-board, but any person who knew the form of different kinds of notes, could easily do so with little practice. The greatest obstacle that I have had to encounter in teaching singing classes in country villages, has been the difficulty of transporting myself from place to place, and this is the reason why, while teachers around me have taught, in some instances, from seven to ten classes per week, I have been, for the most part, restricted to from two to four.

"Between the years 1837 and 1844, I have taught one or more classes in the following places, namely: Elmira, Southport, Laurenceville, (Pennsylvania,) Lindsley, Addison, Painted Post, Corning, Pike, Centreville, Hume, Rushford, Arcade, Sardinia, Franklinville, and Castile. I have attended nearly all the courses of lectures given by Messrs. Mason and Webb at Rochester.

"In 1844, and while I was there, for the purpose of attending their second course, Mr. James Murray, (teacher and leader in the choir of the Brick Church, with whom I had had some previous acquaintance,) proposed to me to stay and try my fortune in that city. He reminded me of the difficulties I labored under in the country, and thought it probable that I might obtain a situation as leader in one of the choirs of the city, which, together with juvenile and adult classes, might be as useful to others, and if not more profitable to myself, much less perplexing and laborious, than my operations in the country. He furthermore proffered me his assistance in obtaining business, and as the first step toward the accomplishment of his object, laid my case before Mr. Mason, who, in turn, manifested a lively interest in the matter, and, in conjunction with Messrs. Webb, Root, and Johnson, kindly furnished me the accompanying certificate. I spent several weeks in Rochester without employment, but at length an opening presented itself. Through the influence of Mr. Murray, I was chosen as leader of the choir of the Washington-street Presbyterian church. In this situation, I continued for more than four years, without interruption.

It was during this time that I took up in good earnest the study of the piano forte, under the instruction of Mr. George Dutton, junior. I had previously had a good deal of hap-hazard practice on the piano, but had never, till this time, taken up anything like a systematic course of piano forte study. Here, as in vocal music, I was obliged to commit everything to memory, by hearing the written characters named one by one. At the end of six months after I commenced this study, I had played through Hunten's entire work, besides some other miscellaneous matter. I continued my practice under the direction of Mr. Dutton, for nearly three years. I was influenced in taking up the piano, chiefly by the desire of learning to play the organ. I soon found, however, that by the time I had gone over enough ground to be a good organist, I should also be a pianist. The result of my four and a half years' residence in Rochester has been the adoption of piano forte teaching, as my leading occupation, while my old business of teaching vocal music has become comparatively secondary.

I left Rochester, April, 1849, since which time, I have resided, at different periods, in the villages of Almond, Rushford, Springville and Olean, giving in struction to individuals and classes, both in vocal and instrumental music. On the fourth day of March, 1850, I was united in marriage to Miss Mary Van Scoter, a native of the town of Burns, Allegany county, New York, and daughter of Elias Van Scoter, one of the oldest inhabitants of that town. Our union has been crowned with a little son and daughter, and I may add, for the benefit of those interested in such matters, that neither of them inherits, in the slightest degree, the paternal misfortune.

The blind have in general the natural feelings and social sentiments of human nature in full vigor; and yet, a cold, mercenary world would impose on them, indiscriminately, the chilling destiny of perpetual celibacy; because it lacks the magnanimity to reach forth a brother's helping hand, to aid them in winning for themselves and families that support which their own efforts, in many instances, would obtain for them, or even, as sometimes happens, to let them alone and leave them to work out the problem of life, untrammeled by impertinent interference. I know of men in whose way I never laid a straw, who, having assumed, *a priori*, that it is impossible for a person without eyesight to succeed in any department of useful enterprise, so far from rendering that assistance which would have cost them nothing, and would have been invaluable to me, have manifested a disposition to throw obstacles in my way, by diverting patronage to other channels, not because they had anything against me personally, as they have sometimes been kind enough to say, but in order, as I am obliged to believe, to demonstrate to the world the wisdom of their premature decision, even though at the risk of blighting all my prospects, and involving my family in hopeless poverty and dependence.

Such men remind one of the ancient prophet, who burned with indignation against divine clemency and forbearance, because those benign attributes were exercised for the preservation of a guilty but repentant city, at the apparent expense of his credibility as a prophet. But these, thank Heaven, are some of the dark phases of human nature—the exceptions, not the rule—and it would ill become me, the almost daily recipient of human kindness, to indulge in anything that should even have the appearance of indiscriminate censure or wholesale animadversion. But such instances of illiberality as those above indicated, though rare, are now and then to be met with, as my own experience painfully demonstrates.

But the inquiry is often made, not only by the captious and narrow-minded, but by those who would fain hear an answer consonant with the aspirations of the philanthropic heart—What is there within the whole range of human effort, which is fairly within the reach of the blind? I will not here stop to discuss their relative fitness or unfitness for the different departments of industrial and professional enterprise; but, with your permission, I beg leave to devote a few sentences to the question as to the influence of blindness as a disqualification for that particular branch of effort in which I am, and have been for so many years, engaged.

Can the blind teach music? Many persons seem to have imbibed the impression, that the most that the blind can do in the way of imparting musical instruction, is to teach their pupils by rote such musical compositions or tunes as they have learned themselves in the same way; that, not being able, from the nature of the case, to read and understand the musical characters for themselves, they cannot of course be expected to teach them to others. Such persons forget or overlook the principles adverted to by Mr. Mason, in the paper heretofore referred to, viz: that music is addressed to the ear. The knowledge of those characters which are addressed to the eye, and which constitute the visible symbols or signs by which musical relations are represented to the sense of sight, forms in reality but a small part (we might, indeed, say almost no part) of the science of music. Their relation to it may be illustrated by that of the alphabet to the science of language. The eye alone, it is true, can take cognizance of the forms of the letters, but beyond this, everything relating to the nature and power of letters, and their various arrangements and combinations in forming syllables and words, as well as everything else relating to the structure of language, is addressed primarily to the ear, or per haps more properly comprehended by the mind.

If this view of the subject be correct, it will follow as a natural inference, that the principal qualification in a music teacher must be a correct and cultivated musical ear, and a mind familiar with the nature and various relations of musical sounds; and in the case of instrumental music, an acquaint ance with the genius of the particular instrument intended to be taught. It will scarcely be contended, that these conditions cannot be met in the case of the blind. I am far from assuming that blindness is not in itself a real disadvantage, but then so are numerous other things that very successful teachers have to encounter, as for instance, the want of a knowledge of the language in which instruction is attempted to be communicated. And in vocal music, the want of compass, clearness, fullness, flexibility, or any other of those qualities which go to constitute a good voice for singing. All these, and many more disadvantages that might be named, have been successfully met and overcome by teachers of music, who have, in spite of them, enrolled their names high on the list of fame.

I should hardly be justified, perhaps, in adverting to my own experience in this connection, and yet were the names of Oliva, Shaw, Lana, and others, (who, in spite of blindness, have distinguished themselves in this department,) blotted from the page of history, still I should have the consolation of knowing that if substantial attainments in the science and practice of music are of any value to mankind, I have not lived and labored in vain.

ACCOMPANYING TESTIMONIALS.

Mr. Lemuel Rockwell has been known to me for a little more than a year past. He has attended the lectures given to teachers of music in this place the present year, and also last year. I feel certain that he has a very thorough and accurate knowledge of music, and also that his taste and style of performance are highly creditable to him. Notwithstanding his want of sight, I believe him to be well qualified to teach singing schools; indeed, this is not saying quite enough, for if I am not very much in error, he is in an extraordinary degree qualified for such teaching. I have not any doubt but that, as a teacher, he will make himself uncommonly useful, and I feel as if I could cordially recommend him to societies or communities in want of a teacher of a singing school. Let not the fact that he is blind prevent his being employed. Music is addressed to the ear—and it is this that is to be principally cultivated, (together with the voice,) in singing. Many teachers fail from the very fact that they rest satisfied with an explanation of those signs addressed to the eye, while they neglect the things signified in sounds addressed to the ear. I might say much more, but this must suffice. Try Mr. Rockwell, and you will soon know the rest.

LOWEL MASON, of Boston.

Rochester, N. Y., Sept. 19th, 1844.

This is also fully and cheerfully endorsed by Professors WEBB, JOHNSON, and ROOT.

COLLECTED POEMS,

BY L. V. HALL, AND OTHER BLIND AUTHORS.

FROM THE REMINISCENCES OF UNCLE TOBY,

PURPORTING TO HAVE BEEN FOUND AMONG THE PAPERS OF A DECEASED RELATIVE.

One sultry eve in summer time
I sauntered forth to make some rhyme
Upon the moon, or some fair thing
About which poets love to sing:
The stars looked down but wondrous shy.
As if they half suspected I
Had come to sing, as oft I'd done,
My tributes to some favored one,
That chanced to glimmer softly out,
Or twinkle o'er some favorite spot,
Where it might shed its golden light
Upon her silken couch, 'twas right;—
But now the bard could find no theme,
Nor could his muse suggest a scheme.
The nightingale had caught a cold,
And the owl laughed hoarser than of old,
As if he saw my silly plight,
And scorned my mission; well he might,
For truly now I'd lost the vein,
Or sadder still, had racked my brain,
Or crazed it, in a fruitless quest
Of something that might stand the test
Of critics, when my purse should fail,
Since merit, then, can naught avail.

The dust will fill a critic's eye,
So through it he cannot descry
The grossest error, right! 'twill do!
While all assumes a golden hue,
The author has a lofty soul,
He's paid me well, I must extol
His wit, his genius, perfect rhyme,
What imagery! sublime! sublime!
Enough, we turn from this digression,
For lo! the bard has got possession
Of one stray thought, that chanced to crawl
From some dark corner in his skull,
Where, dormant, it perhaps had lain
For years, as seeds their germs retain.
As torpid flies, from rubbish creep,
When spring awakens from their sleep
The insect tribes, the croaking frogs,
And lizards in a thousand quags:
And with her warm sweet breath, inspires
Their little hearts to strange desires,
The bees to buzz among the flowers,
The birds, to test their vocal powers,
By warbling sweetest melody,
From early morn till twilight gray
Steals softly down the flowery vales,
Till milkmaids, with their flowing pails,
Come singing home their evening song,
As merrily they trip along:
While frogdom, from her ugly throats
Contributes such discordant notes,
That e'en the screech-owl turns away
Ashamed of nature's orchestra.
No matter, he shall not defeat
My aim, my simile's complete.
And thus had genius fancy taught,
To break the chrysalis of thought,
To mould it with a sculptor's skill,
In forms that best might please her will;

To give it life and buoyancy,
And powers of such fecundity,
That little thoughts, from embryo,
Came forth and like the fungus grew.
Thus did one straggling thought inspire
The bard with such poetic fire,
That from his ventilated bonnet
Escaped this rare ethereal sonnet:

Through fate's kaleidoscope I see,
That what has been, again may be.
This world is like a dinner pot,
Filled with water boiling hot:
Each atom near the heated sides
Expands, and to the surface glides,
While those which float upon the top,
Are cooled, and to the bottom drop.

But soon they kiss the heated metal,
And soon expand, while from the kettle
Clouds of mist in air ascend,
And so on till the boiling end.
While clouds of mist in air ascend,
And so on till the boiling end.
So on till the boiling end,
And so on till the boiling end.

Nor is the circle yet complete,
Its perimeter does not yet meet.
The air is like an onion formed
Of strata, ever cooled and warmed,
In regions so unequally.
That watery vapor thus set free,
Is soon condensed, soon falls in rain,
But only to be boiled again.

My song had ceased; but my well-tun'd lyre still rung,
As the dying cadence to the passing breeze it flung:
Faintly once more it caught the closing strain,
And trembled with the echo—boiled again.
My song had ceased; the cypress gravely bent
His leaf-crowned head, in token of assent;
The cedars nodded, but the giant oak
In silent awe stood motionless, as broke
From many a deep ravine and rocky dell,
The deathless theme my lyre had learned so well;—
Till every string, now wakening to the strain,
Murmured as died the echo—boil'd again.
The winds were sighing softly through the trees,
As though they had conspired to raise a breeze,
Among some distant clouds, that lowering, hung
Above the mountain peaks that tow'ring flung
Their long dark shadows o'er the grassy plain,
That lengthen'd as the fading moonlight waned.
Amazed I stood, and bent my listening ear
To catch the last faint sound that lingered near,
When, horrible to tell! from some lone dell,
Broke on the midnight air a fiercer yell,
Than ever burst from Satan's marshal'd hosts,
E'en when through space they scourg'd the shiv'ring ghosts.
With knotted chords of fire, full of stings,
With twisted tails of comets, and other things.
As when from thundering Etna burts on high
A flood of liquid fire to the sky,
Piercing its sable shroud with fury driven,
As if the burning shaft were aimed at heaven,
To vent the rage that long had been repressed,
Deep beneath old ocean's heaving breast.
So rose this tide of sound to upper air,
And with the spirits of song who hover there,
Claimed equal fellowship by right of birth,
Since all are creatures of the bards of earth.
Prepost'rous claim! most impudent! as well
Might some infectious, foul and putrid smell,

Reeking from the pest-house, breathing death
On all who feel its pestilential breath,
Claim sweet communion with those spices rare,
That, dewy wing'd, float on the ev'ning air
From many a Persian bower, where hand in hand,
The cinnamon and jessamine sighing, stand
Like lovers, side by side, while at their feet,
On beds of silken moss, sleep violets sweet.
Nor was I at a loss to guess the source
From whence arose a laugh, so crack'd and coarse,
A scream so strange and wild that night drew back
And made the long deep shadow still more black.
The hills once more reëchoed with the sound,
The giant oak, with awe no less profound,
Stood motionless: the lofty cedars bow'd,
And e'en my lyre in concert breathed aloud,
In unison with echo's fickle voice,
That may alike with asses and poets rejoice.
With sick disgust I turned, and soon retraced
The path that led to so unhallowed a place:
But breathing at every step a malediction
On my long-eared competitor—sore affliction!
To see my star of hope so soon eclipsed,
To find the cup of joy dashed from my lips,
Ere from its sparkling brim I scarce had quaffed
One drop of its intoxicating draught.
To hear the voice of praise so soon retire,
To feel my bosom heave with mad'ning ire,
To snuff the breeze of favor but to find
It ever changing, fickle as the wind.
Nay more: the fates had never haply crowned
My efforts with success, but ever frowned,—
And frowning, turned away contemptuously;
Aye, sometimes cursed the half fledg'd progeny,
That patience with assiduous care had brought,
And nurtured from the overa of thought.
Mysterious fate! in what portentous cloud
That rose at life's first dawn didst thou enshroud

Forever in silent gloom my destiny,
And shall this cloud forever obscure life's day?
Shall evening gather o'er me when I'm old,
With all its dusky shadows drear and cold,
And not one star to light my lonely way
Upon the unknown deep of Eternity?
Shall age come tott'ring on with feeble tread,
With furrowed brow, with bow'd and hoary head,
And the dim eye turn once more to view the past,
And the heart grow sick and faint, as the chilling blast
Of disappointment sweeps o'er the sadden'd soul,
When memory fain would die, shall I be old?
Shall youth go forth uncheck'd 'mid the frowns of Heaven,
Unblessed by those who should have counsel given,
Unloved, unwept, by those who should have known
How the young soul lives in affection's tone?
And can the world, with all its pomp and pride,
Its cold and hollow hearts, fill up this void?
My boyhood dreams are past! their visions fled!
And the brightest flowers of hope are crushed and dead.
The thunder's voice, and the wild bleak wind that moans
Through the forests deep, are to me affection's tones.
Ah, yes; e'en now yon ocean's beating surge
Hath hollowed my grave, and sung my funeral dirge;
And on my ear hath died the passing knell,—
Rocks, mountains, streams, and home, farewell! farewell!
Farewell! the echo cried, as the dark sea spread
Its troubled waters o'er my aching head:
And the wild waves moaned, as their sparkling crest I clave,
A requiem o'er the heart-sick poet's grave.
Strange sights: strange sounds; the world seemed all on fire;
A comet's torch had lit the parched air,
Nor would the bold intruder e'er retire,
Till he had scorched each false philosopher.
The stars like meteors fell from the flaming sky,
And hissing, seemed to lick the ocean dry.
Old night, affrighted, spread her sable wings,
Unable to behold such dreadful things.

Centuries passed; the seasons went and came,
Nor did the earth e'er vegetate again.
The conflagration o'er, grim night returned,
Save where volcanic fires dimly burn'd;
And hovering, brooded darkly over earth,
The same chaotic mass that gave her birth.
Silence once more returned, with all her brood
Of timid nymphs, to earth's vast solitude.
And now the question rose, is this a dream?
Or are these things now what they really seem?
And as I thought, returning reason spoke,
And I once more to consciousness awoke.
When, lo! to my surprise, my tortured brain
Had pictured for a dark, deep sea, a field of grain.
And from a wall of stone about four feet high,
I had headlong plunged in a field of waving rye.
The screech-owl laughed outright, as the braying ass
Proclaimed the poet's drowned. Alas! alas!
False echo caught the lie ere it had died,
And with a thousand tongues the rocks replied.
Till e'en my lyre, deserted on the grass,
Murmured with regret, alas! alas!
Strange fate, thought I, the circle did not meet,
The boiling process is not yet complete.
The numbered sands of life had not run out;
The die was not yet cast; the fates, no doubt,
Have yet reserved for me a loftier theme,
Than ever circled in a Dante's dream.
A nobler end is mine: the smallest rock,
Dropped in the sea, communicates a shock
To every inert atom, from side to side
Extends its bounds and elevates the tide.
The ugliest toad that nature e'er gave birth,
Need only hop to move this pondrous earth.
And may not I some magic lever find,
Of modern workmanship, to move mankind?
The smallest mountain stream that winds along
Through deepest solitude, mingling its song

Of wildest joy with nature's symphony,
Contributes its mite to swell the bright blue sea:
Though from obscurity darkly it rose,
Now through the merry sunshine sparkling it flows,
Laughing as it leaps from rocky height,
Or moaning in the depths of chasm'd night,
Down, down it madly rushes from rocky ledge,
Till far across the plains, through heath and hedge,
It gurgles on, and gurgling evermore,
Till lost amid the sea's tumultuous roar.
Inexorable fate! the frailest flower
That blooms to fade and wither in an hour,
That smiles unseen, unloved to pass away,
Secures the object of its destiny!
Yet men there are who never seem to find
The humble end to which they were design'd;
Ambitious aspirants for power and fame,
But die at last, and leave what? scarce a name.
Others there are, though much less worthy, found,
Whom nature with her choicest gifts hath crowned.
Prodigies indeed, yet the world must own,
That fame ne'er epitaphed a more reckless drone.
More pets hath fate, though less supremely blest,
Those who on the arm of fortune rest
Content, if with earth's countless bounties fed,
With pockets filled 'tis true, but empty head.
But here must end the theme of my moonstruck song,
For the ox must hear my voice at tho plow ere long;
The nightingale hath flown, the owl is gone,
And the first red light of morn begins to dawn.

Trol la! trol la! away to the plow!
  Both happy and free is a farmer's son;
He earns his own bread by the sweat of his brow,
  And lives at his ease when his toil is done.
By honest industry he has gained his wealth,
And lives for his friends as well as himself.
    Trol la! trol la! sing merrily
    A farmer's life is the life for me!

With the lowing ox, and the bleating flocks,
With horses and swine his land he stocks;
Of useful books has a rich supply,
And his garners are filled with corn and rye.
In the cool green glade he sleeps in the shade,
But dreams of none but a farmer's maid.
  Trol la! trol la! sing merily!
  A farmer's life is the life for me;
  Trol la! trol la! both happy and free
  Is a farmer's life, 'tis the life for me.

But why this ecstacy, this overflow,
This thrill of soul? the poet does not know.
Of the field of rye he has lost all recollection,
Sufficeth that he's made a resurrection;
And sauntering listless homeward, luckily strayed
Beneath the window of his dairy-maid;
And as the lark her song to the free air flings,
The lover tunes his lyre, and thus he sings·

Sweet Lizzie, awake! 'tis early dawn,
  The golden eyes of morn
Are peeping in o'er flow'ry lawn,
  And fields of waving corn.
The eastern hills with rosy light
  Are blushing through the trees,
And odors sweet from roses bright,
  Float on the morning breeze.

Yet, dim are morning's eyes to thine,
  And pale her rosy light,
To the blushes on thy cheek divine,
  And thy neck so lily white.
Then Lizzie awake! the dew-drops bright
  Are sparkling on each tree,
And a garland of roses red and white,
  Have I wreathed in beauty to thee.

TERESA OR THE PEASANT MOTHER.

I traced a river from the deep, dark wood,
To where it meets old ocean's darker flood,
Through all its windings down the mountain side,
I watched it as it leaped through chasms wide,
Through ravines dark and deep I hear it roar,
And now from craggy heights its torrents pour,
Foaming and dashing in its onward course,
The firmest rock it breaks with giant force;
Hurling far below in deafening sound
Each fragment, till the mountain caves resound.
Still on it flows, not like the jaded steed,
In bloody conflict forced to stay his speed,
But o'er the distant plains and mossy green,
Through fruitful vales, its shining path is seen.
High on the summit of a lofty mount,
There rose in grandeur wild a crystal fount;
Around dense groves of spruce and cedar stood,
To shade the cradle of the infant flood;
The holly bush and fir their branches spread,
But not a single floweret reared its head
Above the mossy rocks, that rudely lay
Around the fountain, glittering with its spray.
The day was bright and fair, and many a stag
Came bounding o'er the rocks from crag to crag;
The antelope looked down from dizzy height,
And ravens screamed in their airy flight.
In this sequestered spot I saw a maid,
Seated in the deep, cool-forest shade;
A peasant girl she seemed, of tender years,
But her cheek was pallid and bedewed with tears
Her eye was wild and restless as a gleam
Of starlight on a turbid, mountain stream.
Her brow was strongly marked with anxious care,
And near her stood a boy with flaxen hair;
His golden ringlets floating in the breeze,
That from the vale came sighing through the trees,

Bearing upon its light wing many a sigh
Of fainting flowers beneath a sunny sky.
How sad it is, thought I, that one so young
Should weep; but as I wondered thus she sung:

TERESA'S SONG.

"Oh! happy dreams of infancy,
How dear your memory is to me;
Why lingered not those joyous hours?
When but a child in quest of flowers
I plucked the wildest rose, and say
Was I not pure and wild as they?
But ah! 'tis past, they've fleeted by,
And nought is left but infamy.
Tell if ye can, ye limpid streams,
That now so wildly drink the beams
Of the warm sunshine, as ye go,
What fate awaits you? Ah! no, no!
We simple peasants, like these brooks,
Find in our paths a thousand nooks;
But the proud, the opulent, the gay,
Are mightier streams, yet like us, they
Through darker, deeper channels go,
All bright above, all black below."

But soon a cloud had gathered o'er the mount,
And higher rose the gushing crystal fount,
As if to pierce its sable, mystic shroud,
And drink the sunshine through the threat'ning cloud.
But dense and fleeting mists swept o'er the plain,
And now in torrents falls the dashing rain;
From shattered crag to crag forked lightnings leap,
And tempests howl in the forest deep.
Peal after peal of thunder shook the ground,
Till yawning caverns echoed back the sound.
Alarmed, the mother clasped in fond embrace
Her rosy boy, and down the mount retraced

A rugged path, that near a chasm led,
Where dark below a foaming torrent sped.
How anxiously I watched her gliding form
Among the rocks and trees; but soon the storm
Had thickened into night, save when a flash
Of lurid lightning clave some mountain ash.
May Heaven preserve, cried I, that lovely pair,
But, as I spoke, a shriek of wild despair,
A cry of mingled horror burst without,
Amid the raging storm's tumultuous shout.
I hastened to the spot, but ah! too late!
No human power could change the dreadful fate.
High on a towering crag Teresa stood,
Swayed to and fro as roll'd the impetuous flood.
"My child! my boy! she cried, O stop the stream!
What! lost? It cannot be, 'tis but a dream.
Just now on yonder ledge of rocks we stood—
But where is he?—I faint!—my child!—my God!"
Her trembling arms in air she wildly threw,
Then plunged into the flood and sank—adieu.

VIEW OF THE MIND RELEASED FROM MATTER.

There is a thought that springs from truths innate,
That culture cannot form, nor mind create;
That genius never drew from fancy's mould,
A sense of latent powers that must unfold;
That will expand, when freed from matter crude,
To roam the vast domain of nature's God.
To mind thus free what may not time reveal!
For error cannot now the truth conceal.
Infinity she grasps through time's duration,
And solves the deep enigmas of creation.
Amazed, she soars on high, while 'neath her whirls
The whole stupendous frame of clustering worlds.
What ecstacy of soul! what strains of love!
Now burst in hymns of praise to God above,

From earth's redeemed; while many a twinkling throng
Of starry worlds augment the tide of song.
But now she hovers; resting on those beams
Of crystal light, that bridge affliction's streams;
Those tides of human tears, that pit of woe,
That vortex of despair in which they flow,
Sweeping, as their floods tumultuous roll,
Like withered leaves, the hopes of many a soul.
The earth she sees engulphed in moral night,
Nor can her pitying tears obstruct the sight.
Darkly it swings around its central sun,
While red with human gore its rivers run.
Its lofty domes, its minarets, its towers,
Rocked to and fro, as roll contending powers.
E'en pestilence, with foul, infectious breath,
Now stalks abroad, a parasite of death.
Oppression's hand hath bound in servile chains,
The brothers, ah! of those who hold their reins,
And with iron hand hath crushed their sacred shrines,
And robbed e'en hell of half its black designs.
Sighing she turns to seek in Eden's bowers,
Those founts of joy that spring from beds of flowers,
Laughing as their crystal arms entwine
The ripening fruit that clusters on the vine,
And sprinkling with golden spray like floods of light,
Flowers that bloom forever fresh and bright.

THOUGHTS ON CREATION.

Geologists surmise,
Nay, prove it to a fraction,
That this fair earth was at her birth
In a state of liquefaction;
But that nature and time wrought many a change
And drew forth objects new and strange.

The motion on her axis,
Produced conglomeration;
And soon a crust of rock and dust,
Was formed for vegetation.
A dent in this shell the ocean found,
And left quite bare the fertile ground.

The seasons went and came,
But left no fossil time;
Though herbs and trees, and flowers and bees,
And mountains that towered sublime,
Appeared on the face of the infant earth,
And to many a fish did the sea give birth.

Meantime, while nature toiled,
Great rivers changed their beds;
And where the sea was wont to be,
Tall mountains reared their heads.
Reptiles and beasts had all been formed,
And the air with birds and insects swarmed.

Yet all was not complete;
The lord of this creation
Was not yet made to wield the spade,
And nurture vegetation;
But at length there sprang from nature's hand
The crowning work, a perfect man.

Thus, science contradicts
The words of inspiration;
For Moses says, within six days
God finished all creation;
The heavens, with all their clustering stars,
The earth, its animals and flowers.

That, on the seventh day,
From all his works he rested;
And that one, of seven, might taste of heaven,
He hallowed it and blest it;
As proof that these were days, not years,
The evening and the morn appears.

Yet should one dare to question
The primeval earth's fluidity,
Geologists would sneer and hiss,
And call it sheer stupidity:
These scientific men of letters
Regard themselves as Moses' betters.

LOVE'S CHAIN.

Oh, why should poets dream so sadly?
Hath poesy no other strain?
Or why, misanthropes, rave so madly,
Can hatred break love's golden chain?

Linked to the brightest hopes we cherish,
It vibrates through eternal years;
But broken, every ray must perish
Amid the gloom of skeptic fears.

From things of nature's first creation,
To orders of a higher mould;
From eyes that beam with animation,
And hearts that throb with powers untold;

From world to luminous world extending,
Unbroken lies love's golden chain;
From sphere to loftier sphere ascending,
Till heaven ends the glittering train.

Dimly it skirts hell's dark dominions,
And glimmers on the verge of night;
And now upborne on seraph's pinions,
It melts in heaven's purest light.

TWILIGHT SHADOWS.

Twilight shadows thick were flying,
Like the leaves of autumn sighing,
Sighing as they fall;
Sprites with bat-like wings distended,
Brushed the lamps that hung depended
From night's dusky wall.

Winds, that all the day had rustled
Through the leafy groves, now bustled
Blustering o'er the plains.
Midnight gloom was creeping o'er me,
As the lamp burned dim before me,
Fitfully it waned.

Mournfully the windows clattered,
While without the rain-drops pattered,
Pattering evermore;
Coals upon the grate were glowing,
But with wild, strange light were throwing
Shadows on the floor.

One by one I saw them dying,
Crumbling and in ashes lying,
Tinkling as they fell;
So, thought I, if all we cherish,
Like these fading embers, perish,
What can break Fate's spell?

Thus, if every pure emotion
Sink in passion's boundless ocean,
Fathomless and drear,
How shall every holy feeling
Melt in christian light, revealing
Cordials for each fear?

Softly o'er my brow were playing
Breezes, while a voice seemed saying
Jesus is the way;

Morning shall dispel thy sadness,
As the birds, with songs of gladness,
Welcome in the day.

So shall faith unbar hope's prison
When the sun of truth is risen,
Setting conscience free;
Mind shall soar on buoyant pinions,
Scanning nature's vast dominions,
Through eternity.

A FABLE.

"In olden time," tradition says,
"When Charity was young,
A squad of philanthropic flies,
Of every caste and tongue,
Assembled on the bright green glade,
With circumspect intention,
Beneath a palm tree's spreading shade,
In general convention.
A dignitary filled the chair,
With parchment, scrip and scribe,
And many a delegate was there,
From every buzzing tribe.
A worthy sage, with numerous eyes,
And legs of great dimension,
Arose, and in the following wise,
Addressed the said convention.
"Most excellent sir, and worthies all,'
The speaker thus began,
"Our tyrants, ever since the fall
That so perverted man,
That threw all nature out of gear,
Have tried their subtlest arts,
To see how they could best ensnare
The victim of their sports.

Our flesh and blood too long have been
A staple of their food,
And now 'tis time that we begin
To seek each other's good;
To rescue from the iron heel
Of tyranny our brothers,
To make our vile oppressors feel
That we are good as others.
For this most holy cause we're met,
In this secluded place,
To take some measures requisite
To guard our injured race.
These ugly, sprawling monsters weave
Their webs in every hole,
Where they suspect or half believe
A fly is like to crawl;
Then in some corner lie in wait,
Till one comes peeping in,
When, oh! 'tis horrid to relate,
The bloody monsters spin
Their tangled webs around him fast,
Regardless of his groans;
Then with a fiendish grin at last,
They pick his quivering bones.
Arise ye patriots, break your chains,
And say we will be free!
A vict'ry shall reward our pains;
To arms 'tis fate's decree!"
The stamping of countless feet declar'd
That willing hearts were found,
While a wondrous buzzing fill'd the air
For many rods around.

Speaker. "They say they have a natural right
To trap the thievish fly,
That justice, always yields to might:
(*A voice.*) "The villains lie."

Speaker. "They say we're all such pilfering things,
That mankind think us asses,
Because we dip our filthy wings,"
(*A voice.*) "In their molasses."

Speaker. "They say the Fates did not design
That we should e'er be free,
That they have organs more refined,
And whiter blood than we.
They think us low and worthless curs,
Not worth an altercation:
Brothers, my blood with anger stirs,
And fury's indignation.
Their boasts are all a pack of lies,
And most consummate knavery;
With death, we will not compromise,
Nor covenant with slavery.
Therefore, I offer, noble sirs,
A list of resolutions,
With which my heart in full concurs,
But wait your wise conclusions:"

"PREAMBLE.

"Inasmuch as liberty is not an especial but common right,
Not an inheritance, but a universal birth-right,—
Neither a creature of chance, nor confer'd by fate
Since from man to the beetle, and from the cricket to the mite,
All living things 'neath the sun, and the twinkling eyes of night,
Are made of the same free elements increate.
Therefore, resolved, that the fly shall be free
To roam where he pleases, o'er land and sea;
To sport on the beams of the common sun,
Or on the lake's bright mirror'd bosom to run.
Second, resolved, that each flower and tree,
Was made for the spider, as well as the bee;—
That insects should feed on the green leaves of wood,
And not slay each other, for pleasure or food.

Thirdly and lastly, resolved, that we force
Our blood-thirsty tyrants to this wise resource;
To spend the bright summer on some cool, green tree,
And through the cold winter, lie torpid like we."

Once more the pattering of countless feet
And general acclamation,
Declared all plans were now complete,
And met with approbation.

At this, a troop of dragon-flies,
With loud vociferation,
Arose, and looking wondrous wise,
Denounced all agitation.
"We may not hope to change," said they,
"What nature hath decreed,
That some were formed for slavery,
Is evidenced indeed."

Another gang, with galaxies
Of eyes like constellations,
Stook up and said: "'tis better, sirs,
To stop these agitations.
They'll only lead to civil strife,
And more insidious trappings,
By which we'll lose more precious life,
Than years of such kidnapping.
Besides, 'tis not the better class,
Whose natural rights are questioned,
But only a low, ignoble race,
Who were for this predestin'd.
However much we may abhor
This barbarous institution,
We shudder at the thought of war,
And dread of dissolution.
We, therefore, cannot recommend
So hazardous a position;
Our boast of equal rights would end
At last in tame submission.

The weak should always yield to might,
The simple to the wise,
The spider, therefore, deems it right
To trap defenseless flies.
Let those whom nature's hand hath fitted
To serve this humble end,
Be not by fiery zealots pitted
To impiously contend
Against ther fate, in bold defiance
Of nature and her laws;
Worthies refrain from all alliance
With so unjust a cause.
Philanthropists should never aim,
By hostile demonstration,
To add fresh fuel to a flame,
In view of amelioration.
The end can never sanctify
Unholy means employed,
The law embraces man and fly,
And naught can make it void.
We, therefore, totally deprecate
All forms of intervention;
No allied powers can baffle fate,
Or thwart her fix'd intention.
Once more, we would reiterate
Our dragon friends' suggestion,
Let no one dare to agitate
Again this dangerous question.
May gentle peace, while yonder sun
Brings life and warmth with day,
Shine o'er our paths, where'er we run,
And rule our destiny."

Thus spake this cow'ring, servile crew,
'Gainst freedom's holy cause;
And then exultingly withdrew,
'Mid rapturous applause.
Resistless roll'd this mighty flood
Of suasive eloquence,

While from the assembled multitude,
Arose the meek response:
May gentle peace, while yonder sun,
Brings life and warmth with day,
Shine o'er our paths, where'er we run,
And rule our destiny.
'Twas plain the wind had tuned her pipes.
To quite a different air;
And they who would not dance to stripes,
Must follow the tune, 'twas clear.
E'en liberty's most ardent friends,
Seem'd favorably impressed,
And at last, to gain some private end,
Most cordially acquiesced.

"The public weal demands," said they,
"Some honorable concession:
Let's give at least to tyranny
A peaceable possession.
Our only sacrifice will be
A weak and worthless tribe,
And by this compromise, you see,
Her boundaries we'll prescribe.
We hate these mad enthusiasts,
Who urge emancipation,
Without respect to grade or caste:
Away with agitation.
Its tendency has ever been,
The captive's bonds to tighten.
By precept we may hope to win,—
Example may enlighten.
Let each discordant note be tuned,
And let this strife be ended;
Time oft hath healed a deeper wound,—
A wider breach hath mended.
Let every web that spiders spin,
To trap their harmless neighbor,
Be shunned as their besetting sin,
And drive these knaves to labor."

A FRAGMENT.

There is a time, when yet the mind is new,
That thoughts half-fledged go forth on feeble wing,
And poised in ether, much bewildered, view
Through fancy's glass, the gliding forms that spring
From unseen hands, to float awhile in air,
Then like the melting mists at early dawn,
Give place to brighter forms of beauty rare,
That ages past from mystery have drawn.
Oh, faithful time! what progeny is thine!
The universe appeared at thy decree;
But who made thee, thou Artisan divine?
Self-made, thou art, from all eternity.
Presumptuous thoughts, abortions of the mind,
Of sickly birth, and creatures of a day.
How vain, to scan what God himself designed,
And call his perfect work Time's progeny.
Blind Fate! did'st thou, through ever-during dark,
Grope o'er the elements that formed this world,
And strike from chaos first the electric spark,
That lit up space where mad confusion whirled?
Crude matter sublimed, and rolling nebulæ,
Which time hath since reduced to radiant suns,
And from the foam, hath formed a galaxy,
That through high heaven's expanse unbroken runs.

REFLECTIONS IN YOUTH.

One summer's morn, as I strolled along,
With heart as free as the lark's gay song,
Plucking the wild sweet flowers, that grew
Where the maples their soft, deep shadows threw
I thought as I kissed from their glossy leaves
The crystal dew, how much there breathes
In nature of true piety,
Of love, and deep humility.

Through every fabric that Nature weaves
From the simple fern, with its drooping leaves,
To the giant oak that defies the blast,
(Yet meekly bends as the gales sweep past,)
From the clinging vine, that darkly crawls
'Mong ruined towers and broken walls,
That sigh as the night winds whisper of old—
Of deeds that the darkness hath not yet told;
Of impious man, who so sadly fell,
And made of this bright fair earth a hell.
No! not of the earth, 'tis the soul within
That makes for itself a world of sin,
The world without is a joyous one,
Busy and bright, 'neath a glorious sun.
From age remote, o'er a boundless waste,
Through the path of time this thread is traced;
Weaving the stars in a robe of light,
To clothe in beauty the silent night;
A chord of love and sympathy,
That vibrates through eternity.
Of such, the angel harps were strung,
When heaven's celestial choirs sung,
All glory, honor, and power be given,
To Him who reigns in earth and heaven.

THE VOYAGE OF LIFE—A SONG.

How rights the ship, when the world goes merrily,
   When sweet success crowns every wish;
Bright beams the sun, and the birds sing cheerily,
   When showers of plenty fill our dish.

How rights the ship, as her sails catch greedily
   Each prosperous wind that kindly blows,
Gaily sings the crew, when she glides on speedily,
   O'er life's deep sea so sweet in repose.

Night holds his watch 'neath a cloudless canopy,—
  With hanging lamps o'er the bright sea's crest,
Till young morning spreads, like a golden panoply,
  A flood of day o'er its glassy breast.

Sparkling like dew-drops distilled on sweet violets,
  Life's sea of light unruffled lies;
Away darts the ship o'er the silvery breast of it,
  Her white sails spread to the breeze, she flies.

Morning hath op'd those golden eyes of hers,
  But scarce one glance o'er the world hath shone,
When far to the west a gathering cloud appears,
  Gleaning the darkness that *night* had strown.

How tosses the ship when the world goes crabbedly,
  When storms of deep affliction rise!
Loud shrieks the blast as the waves roll rapidly,
  Till hope amid the tumult dies.

LINES WRITTEN ON THE FIRST OF APRIL, 1852.

If nature sanctions all the rules
  That govern wind and weather,
Then, by her we are all made fools,
  And April fools together.

For when Aurora raised the vail
  That shades old Sol's complexion,
A cloudless sky his coming hailed,
  Nor raised one slight objection.

The birds rejoiced to see the eye
  Of morning beam so gladly;
But ere the day had fleeted by,
  They, too, were fooled most sadly.

The prince of that mysterious power
  That keeps the ocean stewing,
Despatched a sprite at midnight hour,
  To set a storm a-brewing.

And sure enough, it came blust'ring on
  From snow-crowned Alleghany;
And though the morning brightly dawned,
  The day was cold and rainy.

So round the cradle often beams
  Bright rays of hope and gladness;
But oh, how changed are childhood's dreams,
  When age brings scenes of sadness.

A prosperous sun may set at noon,
  And leave the future hazy,
A fickle freak of fortune soon
  May drive a mortal crazy.

A LEGEND.

In Jersey there lived, as I have been told,
  When science was yet in its shell,
A worthy old Dutchman, who offered much gold
  To any wise man who could tell

How to drive from his cellar a troublesome witch,
  Who nightly disturbed his repose,
By leading him forth o'er thorn-hedge and ditch,
  By a ring made fast in his nose.

"So droubled am I," said our hero one day,
  "Tat I'd giff de pest hoss in me parn,
To any old wizard tat may dravel tis vay,
  For to trive tis old hag from me varm.

"My cals tey run vild, my cows tey run try,
No putter my voman can make;
My pees leave de hives, my gattles dey dies,
No gomfort at all can I dake.'

One evening when all had retired to bed,
And left the old man in his chair,
He sighed as the darkness grew thicker, and said,
"Ich wold garn ins bet ga won ich darf."

But the old mansion shook with a November gale,
Dread spectres were stalking without,
And howl'd through each crevice the horrible tale
That Mynheer was thinking about.

Dense wreaths of tobacco smoke curled round his head
While the old kitchen clock, that for years
Had measured each moment of time as it sped
Tick'd louder to banish his fears.

But the darkness grew thicker, the candle burnt blue,
A sulphurous smell filled the room,
While the tumult without waxed fiercer, as grew
The clock face more pale in the gloom.

While Van Hochtail thus mused (for that was his name)
The clock in the corner tolled one;
The candle went out, when a fit seized his frame
And he thought, sure the devil is come.

The door was thrown open, a figure rushed in,
A bellowing sound—then a crash;
All consciousness fled, while away on the wind
The Dutchman was borne in a flash.

The whole of that night, in the form of a horse,
He scoured the country around,
With a witch on his back, as a matter of course,
And not until morning he found

Himself in his chair, his hat in his hand,
  His pipe and his wig on the floor;
The storm had passed off, the morning was clear
  And the clock tick'd on as before.

THE HARPER.

RESPECTFULLY DEDICATED TO MESSRS. HALL AND ARTMAN
BY FRANCES J. CROSBY.

Oh, speak not harshly to the humble poor,
Nor chide the wanderer that with trembling hand
Taps at your door, and in a feeble voice,
Choked with emotion, asks a simple crust,
Which human sympathy could not deny.
Ye little know the wrongs that heart hath borne;
The bitter anguish that hath rudely crushed
Its best affections. Nature is but weak;
And though it long may patiently endure,
May struggle hard to bear its toilsome lot,
Yet there are moments when the aching breast,
Robb'd of its dearest hopes and brightest joys,
Feels like itself a burden, and would fain
Breathe its last sigh, and sleep its last long sleep.
The golden sun had set, and the blue sky,
Yet beautiful with rich crimson tints,
That softly lingered on its azure breast,
Seemed wooing nature to a sweet repose.
Calm and serene the evening star looked forth,
As if to chant His praise who gave her birth;
All, all was lovely; 'twas the hallowed hour
When memory whispers of long-absent ones,
And bears us back to days and years gone by.
A weary man, whose form was bent with age,
Whose silver locks were floating on the breeze,
That seemed to pity as it passed him by,
Had turned, dejected, from the busy throng,
And with a look which might have moved a heart
Of adamant, was wending his lone way

Towards his humble cottage. All day long
Through crowded streets his wild harp he had borne.
And o'er and o'er its rustic airs had played,
To those who heeded not, till, sick at heart,
When the dim shadows of the twilight came,
He gathered up his scanty pittance, and
Covering his face with his shriveled hand,
He wept, not for himself, but for his child.
Within a drear and comfortless abode,
On a rude couch, a gentle girl reclined;
Her cheek was pale as marble, and her eye
Turned ever and anon, with restless glance,
Toward the open casement. Hark! 'tis he!
She faintly murmured, while a placid smile
O'erspread her pallid features. Yes; 'tis he;
My father! And the old man slowly bent
O'er that loved form, and pressed his lips to hers.
There was a change, a sad and fearful change,
Since he had left her at the early morn;
And he felt that the icy hand of death
Was at her heart. 'T was more than he could bear.
My child, he said, the staff of my old age,
How can I lose thee? Thou wert all to me;
And who will comfort me when thou art gone?
God will protect thee, (was the quick response,)
Father! she paused for breath, then suddenly,
As if a light had burst upon her soul,—
Father, ere from the world and thee I part,
There is a secret I would fain disclose.
Dost thou remember Rodolph? At that name
She slightly trembled, but her voice grew calm
As she proceeded: Near our happy cot, my childhood home,
There was a shady nook, o'erhung with woodbines and the evergreen,
And there at eve, with Rodolph by my side,
While the light zephyrs with their silken wings,
Fanned the sweet flowers that slept beneath our feet,
I listened to the gentle words he breathed.
He sought my hand—my heart had long been his;

But my mother from thine arms was torn,
And laid beneath the cold and silent tomb.
I felt 'twere wrong to leave thee thus alone.
Yet, Rodolph was unchanged; and when the storms
Of adverse fortune drove us from our home,
To seek a shelter in a foreign clime,
I saw the tear-drop gather in his eye;
He clasped my hand convulsively in his,
And whispered, "Ella, thou shalt yet be mine."
Three long and weary years since then have passed,
And he perchance ere this hath wooed and won
A lovelier maiden. Oh, how I have prayed
And struggled to forget him, but in vain.
She ceased. The old man with attentive ear
Had listened to the long suspected cause
Of that deep sorrow, which too well he knew
Had nipp'd the rose-bud in its tender bloom,
And doomed his idol to an early grave.
Oh, what a sacrifice, he groaned aloud;
God bless thee, Ella; I have ill repaid
A love so holy and so pure as thine.
'Twas then a traveler on his jaded steed
Paused at that dwelling, and in breathless haste
Flew up the narrow staircase; hope and fear
Alternate whispering to his anxious heart.
The old man's last words fell upon his ear:
It is enough, he cried; thank heaven she lives!
And springing forward, in his trembling arms
He clasped that dying girl, now but the wreck
Of what he once had deemed so beautiful.
It was too late. One long and lingering gaze
From those deep eyes of mild ethereal blue,
And with her head pillowed upon his breast,
And his dear name upon her quivering lip,
Her gentle spirit passed from earth away,
With scarce a sigh to tell that she had gone.

AUTUMN.

BY MISS MARGARET BELCHES,

*Of the Indiana Institution for the Blind.**

I come, I come, o'er valley and hill,
Casting a shade o'er the sparkling rill,
Stripping the leaves from each quivering bough,
Strewing my pathway as onward I go.

The tree of the forest, the grass of the plain,
Submissively bow to my despotic reign ;
The flow'rets that bloom in the garden and heath,
All wither and droop at the touch of my breath.

I come not as spring with its gifts profuse,
Decking the earth with its gorgeous hues;
Scattering blossoms like glittering gems,
More precious than those of earth's diadems.

The hum of the insect, the song of the bird,
No more in the glades of the forest are heard;
Though silent I tread, yet my footprints are seen
In the withering herbage wherever I've been.

I come not as spring, with its long sunny hours,
Decking the earth with its verdure and flowers;
I come to forewarn the mortal who clings
To the perishing phantom of temporal things.

I come to admonish the children of clay,
To turn from a world of death and decay;
To seek for a portion more lasting and sure,
In the land of the blest, the just, and the pure.

* It may be interesting to the reader, to know that this authoress dictated her poems to a deaf and dumb sister, her usual amanuensis, by means of the manual alphabet.

Where the smile of the Lord is his people's delight;
Where the soul is untouched by a canker or blight;
Where the heart's best affections forever shall bloom,
Beyond the dark valley of death and the tomb.

THE DYING SISTER.

BY MARGARET BELCHER.

Sister! I'm going home; a voice of love,
  In dreams was gently murmured in my ear,
Like angel whispers, echo'd from above,
  It bade me haste from all that binds me here;
    Sweet, as of plaintive music soft and low—
    Sister, oh let me go!

They stood around my bed a shining band,
  And on their heavenly pinions far away
They bore me swiftly to a radiant land—
  To realms of endless bliss and cloudless day;
    There flowers of fadeless beauty sweetly blow—
    Sister, oh let me go!

Bright was the starry pathway that we trod,
  Surpassing fair the scenes that met our eyes;
Countless the hosts before the throne of God,
  In that fair world of peace beyond the skies;
    And music filled the air in ceaseless flow—
    Sister, oh let me go!

I saw them, too, the loved, the lost of earth,
  The cherished ones who watched our infant years,
Who smiled upon us in our hours of mirth,
  Whose soothing words oft checked our rising tears;
    They smiled on me as none now smile below—
    Sister, oh let me go!

Our sister, too, was there with radiant brow,
  She of the sunny smile and dove-like eye,
The beautiful on earth, far lovelier now,
  Arrayed in light and immortality;
    She whispered come, in heavenly accents low—
    Sister, oh let me go!

And he was there, the wanderer from the fold,
  For whom so oft in agony we prayed;
But on his brow no stain of earthly mould,
  Not as on earth, in sin's dark vestures 'rayed;
    His shining robes were white as spotless snow—
    Sister, oh let me go!

Death's seal is set upon this fevered brow,
  O'er these dim eyes the gathering shadows come;
Heaven's zephyrs seem to play around me now,
  And woo me to my far-off distant home;
    None view such scenes and longer dwell below—
    Sister farewell, I go!

THE FOREST TREE.

BY MARGARET BELCHES.

Tree of the forest, gigantic and old,
What ages unreck'd of have over thee rolled;
Oh, could'st thou but tell us each varying scene
That long since has passed 'neath thy branches of green.

Thou hast seen the glad summer in beauty approach,
And the woods wake in smiles at her magical touch,
When the soft wind swept over the delicate flowers,
Fresh laden with sweets from the tropical bowers.

Thou hast shivered and tossed in the whirlwind's blast,
And seen thy companions uptorn as it pass'd;
And still thou art rearing thy old rugged form,
To smile on the summer and frown on the storm.

The king of the forest, long, long hast thou stood,
The pride of the desert and vast solitude,
Ere the step of the white man the wilderness stirred,
Or his sharp ringing axe in the forest was heard.

In days long gone by, how often perchance,
Hast thou looked on the Indians' wild, native dance;
Or marked the deep scowl of his red, gleaming eye,
As he glared on his victim, and doomed him to die.

Thou hast seen the pale captive, and heard his wild shriek,
Which told of the anguish that words might not speak,
As he saw through the darkness the red, glaring fire,
And knew while he gazed 'twas his funeral pyre.

But away with those scenes of darkness and blood,
Sweet sounds are now heard in thy once solitude;
The laughter of childhood in innocent glee,
Blends sweet with the husbandman's song on the lea.

Perchance thou hast seen on bright summer eves,
When the zephyr was stirring thy dark, glossy leaves,
A maiden steal forth with a timorous eye,
And a blush on her cheek, for her lover was nigh.

And there she has listened to love's magic tone,
Believing his heart was as true as her own;
But, alas! she was seeking an undying love,
Which only is found in the regions above.

The wayworn traveler hails with delight
The mantling shade as you rise on his sight
And sinks to repose on the green mossy bed,
Which oft in his childhood has pillowed his head.

How solemn to think of the thousands of earth,
That are sleeping in death since first thou had'st birth;
And still thou art waving, majestic and free,
The monarch of ages, the old Forest Tree.

THE VOICE OF THE SEA.*

BY MARGARET BELCHES.

What art thou, voice, on the wild winds borne—
Heard 'bove the shriek of the furious storm—
Sweeping along o'er the angry surge,
Like the strange, wild notes of a funeral dirge?
Art thou a spirit foreboding woe,
Come from the fathomless depths below?
For the laugh is hushed, and each cheek grows pale,
As the seaman lists to thy mournful wail.
Art thou come to tell of some desolate shore,
Where the wild waves dash and the breakers roar—
Of the whirlpool nigh, with its chambers dark—
The tomb of many a gallant bark?
Or, perchance, from the ocean's gem-lit caves,
Thou wert weary of sport 'neath the feathery waves,
Midst the unknown tombs where the sea nymphs fair,
Their vigils keep o'er the sleepers there;
Where the mermaid wreathes her golden curls
With crimson coral and rarest pearls;
Where the naiads' sweet, low melodies
Resound through the amber palaces.
But why art thou come from homes like these,
To float 'mid the tempest—child of the seas—
When the sable hue of the night is spread,
Like a funeral pall, o'er the voyager's head—

* We are informed by navigators that strange cries, resembling the human voice, have frequently been heard far out at sea, the causes of which have never been satisfactorily explained.

Where no ray of brightness greets the sight,
Save the curling waves' phosphoric light,
That fearfully on the billows loom,
Like spectral forms amid the gloom?
Oh, were our hearts but freed from sin,
We would fear thee not 'mid the tempest's din—
We would welcome thee as an angel voice,
At the gates of the Heavenly Paradise.

THOUGHTS ON NIAGARA.

BY MICHAEL M'GUIRE.

I stood where swift Niagara pours its flood
Into the darksome caverns where it falls,
And heard its voice, as voice of God, proclaim
The power of Him, who let it on its course
Commence, with the green earth's first creation;
And I was where the atmosphere shed tears,
As giving back the drops the waters wept,
On reaching that great sepulchre of floods,—
Or bringing from above the bow of God,
To plant its beauties in the pearly spray.

And as I stood and heard, *though seeing nought*,
Sad thoughts took deep possession of my mind,
And rude imagination venturing forth,
Did toil to pencil, though in vain, that scene,
Which, in its every feature, spoke of God.
Oh, voice of nature! full of strength and awe;—
Unceasing sermon, where Omnipotence
Is at once the theme and illustration.
O thou pervading sound! o'erwhelming all
With vast conceptions of might infinite!
Hallow my inspirations, and subdue
Whatever in me jars with holy thought.
Let thy loud tones speak to my inmost soul,
And teach it ever to acknowledge God.

Full of thyself, great flood, how vain the task
To tell thy might, or adequately know
How vast thou art,—so very small are we!
If such the thoughts are which thy voice stirs up,
Then what the awe that would entrance the mind
At viewing thy dread strength, thy power sublime!
Or beauty that o'ertops the highest range
Of boldest fancy, whose most lofty flight
Would fall beneath thee far, and much abashed.
Oh place most sacred! full of awe and God.
Where every sound, and all that's seen, combine
To teach our minds to humbly trust in Him,
Whose fiat called, and who sustains the world.
O spot! if any spot on earth can be
A temple, where Jehovah is felt most,
Raise my dejection, and enable me
To speak as may befit thee and myself;
And teach me to address, in proper terms,
Him, for whose honor thou wast form'd to flow,
And talk forever of his power supreme.
O Thou, that givest all that we possess,
Whose might is infinite, and goodness, too,
Bend to my voice thy always ready ear,
And hearing grant, O grant my earnest prayer,
One which hypocrisy hath ne'er abused,
Nor has been by the drowsy formalist.
The verdant earth which thou hast made,
The sky through which the blazing sun doth ride,
And the moon with her large train make progress
These are thy works, which well assert thy migh'
And goodness, and addressing us, doth speak
Wherever culture rules or nature reigns.
Yet, sight of sky, of sea, or of the earth,
Of wild plant, or of cultivated flower,
Of quiet lake that sleeps in loveliness,
Wound in a belt of perfect solitude,—
Of streams that flow contented in their course,
And leave a legacy of flowers behind,—
Is not to me vouchsafed,—nor may I look

Upon the cataract's unfetter'd rage,
That wildly hurries it to the abyss,
Which, like a gap in nature, waits the flood
Which, ever rolling, leaves it waiting still.
Of this, imagination tells alone!
Is forced to copy, oh, how faint transcribe,
Where all its paintings must be in itself,
Nature's designer, and her artist, too.
For me, the world is black, and filled with gloom;
Huge darkness sits recumbent on the air,
Oppressing it with universal night,
And making melancholy joys supplant,
Till cheerfulness removes from where gloom reigns,
Leaving the mind a prey to thoughts unblest.

And here, where Thou art ever felt to be,
Where nature loudly owns Thee as her God,
Whose praise is sounded by the cataract,
Hearken to me, and my petition hear,
As from each recess of my struggling soul,
The sighs of sickly hope, assembling fast,
Meet in a perfect flood of fervent prayer,—
Which all express'd is this,—Lord, give me sight
And that so long unheard, is unheard still.

THE VOICE OF THE FALLING LEAVES

BY FRANCES BROWN.

A friendless Minstrel walk'd alone,
  Where the autumn twilight lay
Cold on the woods, and leaves were strewn
  By thousands in his way:
He thought of the promise-breathing spring,
  And of summer's rosy eves;
And he said: "Alas! for the withering,
  And the time of falling leaves!"

The music of bird and breeze had passed,
  From the woodlands, hush'd and dim—
But there came an answering voice at last,
  From the dying leaves to him:
And it said: "Oh! thou of the sleepless thought,
  In thy musings sad and lone,
Weep not the close of our tearless lot,
  But rather mourn thine own;—

"For the greenness of early spring was ours,
  And the summer's palmy prime
And the glowing tints that deck'd the bowers
  In the glorious harvest-time!
And have we not seen the roses die?—
  For their splendors might not stay;
And the summer birds are gone—then why
  Should not leaves, too, pass away?

"Yet the flowers may fade, and the leaves may fall,
  And the glory of woods depart;
But mourn in thy sorrow, more than all,
  The withering of the heart;
And the soul's young brightness dimm'd so soon,
  'Twas a glory early o'er;
For Time hath taken that blessed boon—
  That Time can ne'er restore.

"And mourn for life's perish'd hopes, that died
  While the spring was flowery still;
For the stainless love which the grave hath hid,
  Though it could not change nor chill;
For the weary eyes that have look'd for light
  Which never met their gaze;
And for all who have lived through storm and blight,
  But saw no summer days."

The winds in their lonely power awoke,
  As the night came darkly on—
And the voice which in twilight stillness spoke,
  With that twilight hour was gone;

"And oh!" said the minstrel, "strange, in sooth,
  Are the spells which Fancy weaves,
For now she has given a voice of truth,
  To the fading, falling leaves!"

BLACKLOCK'S PICTURE OF HIMSELF.

While in my matchless graces wrapt I stand,
And touch each feature with a trembling hand,
Deign, lovely self! with art and nature's pride,
To mix the colors, and the pencil guide.

Self is the grand pursuit of half mankind;
How vast a crowd by self, like me are blind!
By self the fop in magic colors shown,
Though scorned by every eye, delights his own;
When age and wrinkles seize the conquering maid,
Self, not the glass, reflects the flattering shade.
Then, wonder-working self, begin the lay;
Thy charms to others, as to me, display.

Straight is my person, but of little size;
Lean are my cheeks, and hollow are my eyes;
My youthful down is, like my talents, rare;
Politely distant stands each single hair.
My voice, too rough to charm a lady's ear;
So smooth a child may listen without fear;
Not form'd in cadence soft and warbling lays,
To soothe the fair through pleasure's wanton ways.

My form so fine, so regular, so new,
My port so manly, and so fresh my hue,
Oft as I meet the crowd, they laughing say,
"See, see Memento Mori cross the way."
The ravish'd Proserpine, at last, we know,
Grew fondly jealous of her sable beau;
But, thanks to nature, none from me need fly.
One heart the devil could wound—so cannot I.

Yet though my person fearless may be seen,
There is some danger in my graceful mien:
For, as some vessel, tossed by wind and tide,
Bounds o'er the waves, and rocks from side to side;
In just vibration thus I always move:
This who can view, and not be forced to love!
Hail! charming self! by whose prosperous aid,
My form in all its glory stands display'd:
Be present, still; with inspiration kind,
Let the same faithful colors paint the mind.

Like all mankind, with vanity I'm blessed,
Conserves of wit I never yet possessed.
To strong desires my heart an easy prey,
Oft feels their force, but never owns their sway.
This hour, perhaps, as death I hate my foe;
The next I wonder why I should do so.
Though poor, the rich I view with careless eye;
Scorn a vain oath, and hate a serious lie.
I ne'er for satire, torture common sense;
Nor show my wit at God's nor man's expense.
Harmless I live, unknowing and unknown;
Wish well to all, and yet do good to none.
Unmerited contempt I hate to bear;
Yet on my faults, like others, am severe.
Dishonest flames my bosom never fire:
The bad I pity, and the good admire:
Fond of the muse, to her devote my days,
And scribble, not for pudding, but for praise.

These careless lines if any virgin hears,
Perhaps in pity to my joyless years,
She may consent a generous flame to own;
And I no longer sigh the nights alone.
But, should the fair, affected, vain or nice,
Scream with the fears inspired by frogs or mice;
Cry, "Save us, Heaven! a spectre, not a man!"
Her hartshorn snatch, or interpose her fan:

If I my tender overture repeat,
O! may my vows her kind reception meet;
May she new graces on my form bestow,
And with tall honors dignify my brow.

EPITAPH, ON A FAVORITE LAP-DOG

I never barked when out of season;
I never bit without a reason;
I ne'er insulted weaker brother;
Nor wronged by force nor fraud another.
Though brutes are placed a rank below,
Happy for man, could he say so.

THE YOUNG.

BY FRANCES BROWN.

The world may believe in the wisdom time teaches,
  And trust in its truth as the anchor of age,
But many and cold is the winter that reaches
  Not only the head, but the heart of the sage.
There are lights on the first steps of life that awaken,
  Oh, never again on the far journey flung,
But true to the wisdom our years have forsaken,
  And bright in their wrecks are the schemes of the young.

As hearth-light illumes the dark eve of December,
  Affliction may beam through the winter of years,
But will not the miser in silence remember
  Some brow that still bound with his roses appears!
Alas! for the dust and the change may pass over
  The step and the tone to our memory that clung—
But time hath no shadow that bright track to cover,
  And life hath no love like the love of the young.

Remains there a mine unexplored but believed in,
Where lies the lost gold of our days at the goal—
Hath friendship a glance that she ne'er was deceived in,
Oh! they fall from us early, those stars of the soul!
Have we trusted the light, have we toil'd for the treasure,
Though dimness and doubt o'er the searcher's path hung—
And oh, could we pour to Time's truth the full measure
Of trust that is found in the faith of the young!

Thou dreamer of age, there were themes of proud story,
And song that rose on thee like stars from the sea,
Old Time hath no scythe for the might of their glory—
But how hath that glory departed from thee!
Thy soul yields no more to the spell of their splendor,
The tones it sent forth when the lyre was new strung—
There are echoes still there for the brave and the tender,
But none such as gush from the hearts of the young.

Or say, have they pass'd from the paths of thy journey,
The miss'd among thousands, the mourn'd-for apart—
From the toil, from the tumult of life dost thou turn thee,
At times to revisit the tombs of the heart?
Green, green, in the leaf-fall of years will they greet thee,
If fill'd by the flowers in thy home-shade that sprung—
And blessed are the lessons of love that will meet thee
From mem'ries laid up in the graves of the young.

Bright spring of the spirit, so soon passing from it,
Thou know'st no return, and we ask thee not back—
For who that hath reach'd e'en the snows of the summit,
Would wish to retrace all the thorns of his track?
And thorns, it may be, 'mid the verdure have found us—
Deep, deep have they pierced, though the pang be unsung.
But oh, for the dew of that day-spring around us
Once more, as it falls on the paths of the young!

THE GOD OF THE WORLD.

BY FRANCES BROWN.

The gray of the desert's dawn
  Had tinged that mighty mound
That stands as the tomb of Babylon,
  On her ancient river's bound—
For the land hath kept no trace beside
Of the old Chaldean's power and pride

Upon that lonely height,
  To mark the morning climb
The skies of his native solitude,
The genius of the desert stood,
  And saw the conqueror Time
Approach on pinions swift and dim,
But ever welcome was he to him.

For his journey left no track
  On the long untrodden sand—
No human hopes or homes were there,
No blooming face or flowing hair,
  To fear his withering hand;
And the genius greeted him who made
So wide the bounds of his scepter's shade.

They spoke of their ancient swav,
  Of the temples rich and vast
That mouldered in their sight away;
  And the scorn of ages passed
O'er the desert-dweller's lip and brow,
As he said—"What gods do they worship now!"

The father of the years
  Looked up to the rising sun,
And said—"In the bounds his path surrounds,
  There reigns no god but one:
All faith beside hath grown faint and cold,
The only god in the world is gold.

"'Tis gold in the city proud,
 'Tis gold in the hamlet low,
To it they kneel with the bridal vail,
 And the mourner's garb of woe—
And childhood's joy, and youth's bright hair,
And the peace of age are offered there.

"I stood on Nimrod's tower,
 When it rose to meet the stars,
And the boundless pride and the empire wide
 Of the world's first conquerors,
Brought tribute to the gods of old—
But they ne'er were served like that mighty gold!

"They praise the christian's God,
 And they build him temples fair;
The prayer is made, and the creed is said—
 But gold is honored there;
For they bear from the holy place no sign
 That tells of a worship more divine.

"Still are the temples raised
 To the God of light and song,
For many scorn, and some are borne
 By the tides of life along,
Who oft in their weariness look back
To the light they left in that chosen track.

"In groves and crowded marts,
 I have sought love's shrines in vain,
Yet it may be that in silent hearts
 Their ruins still remain—
But scorch'd by fire, and stain'd with tears,
And buried deep in the dust of years."

"And has the world grown old
 In vain?" said the shadowy sage,
"And come at length to the age of gold,
 But not to the golden age?

Is this the fruit of her latter days,
From the gather'd love of centuries,
And piled up wisdom of the past,
To bow to her very dust at last?"

THE ECLIPSE.*

BY FRANCES BROWN.

Watchers are on the earth ; and o'er the sky
Strange darkness gathers, like a funeral pall,
Shrouding the summer day, while stars, that lie
Far in the depth of heaven, rekindle all
Their faded fires. But where is now the sun,
That arose so glorious on the Alps to-day?
Methinks his journey short and early done.
Not thus his wont to leave fair Italy
Not thus so near the skirts of rosy June!
Why is the midnight come before the noon?

Night, but not silence, for old Pavia speaks,
As with the voice of unforgotten years,
When victory was her's. What now awakes
Such music in the fallen land of fears?
Is it some ancient echo in her heart,
Surviving Roman power and Gothic gold?
Or, glorious dream, that might not all depart—
The memory of brave battles won of old—
That wakes the pealing of that joyous cheer,
Which the far mountains answer deeply clear?

* During the eclipse of the sun which occurred in the end of July, 1844, the citizens of Pavia assembled in multitudes, in the principal square, for the purpose of witnessing the phenomenon; and in the midst of the deepest darkness, when the moon and stars were plainly visible, the whole concourse burst into one simultaneous shout.

Or, hath the gathered city's mighty voice
  The queen of night amid her trophies hailed,
As conqueror of the sun? Could she rejoice
  To see the splendor of his presence vailed,
Who walked the heavens in unshared majesty,
  Since Time was born, the brightest and the first
Of thousand gods:— still glorious on his way,
  As when through ancient night his chariot burst,
And swept the circuit of those cloudless skies,
That yet heard only starry harmonies?

Not so rejoiced the Grecian legions, led
  By great Iskander to the Persian shore;
No so Ceoropia's host. But days of dread
  Are past—the twilight of the world is o'er,
With all its shadows. Pavia, from thy walls
  We hear the spirit of our brighter days
Proclaim to Alpine huts and Roman halls,
  The morn that met the sage or prophet's gaze,
Through the far dimness of that long eclipse,
Whose mighty darkness sealed great Galileo's lips.

AUTUMN.

BY FRANCES BROWN.

Oh, welcome to the corn-clad slope,
  And to the laden tree,
Thou promised autumn; for the hope
  Of nations turned to thee,
Through all the hours of splendor past,
  With summer's bright career;
And we see thee on thy throne at last,
  Crowned monarch of the year!

Thou comest with the gorgeous flowers
  That make the roses dim,
With morning mists and sunny hours,
  And wild bird's harvest hymn;

Thou comest with the might of floods,
  The glow of moonlit skies,
And the glory flung on fading woods,
  Of thousand mingled dyes!

But never seem'd thy steps so bright
  On Europe's ancient shore,
Since faded from the poet's sight,
  That golden age of yore;
For early harvest-home hath poured
  Its gladness on the hearth,
And the joy that lights the princely board
  Hath reached the peasant's hearth.

O Thou, whose silent bounty flows
  To bless the sower's art,
With gifts that ever claim from us
  The harvests of the heart—
If thus thy goodness crowns the year,
  What shall the glory be,
When all thy harvest, whitening here,
  Is gathered home to thee!

FAREWELL TO THE FLOWERS.

BY FRANCES BROWN.

Farewell! farewell! bright children of the sun,
  Whose beauty rose around our path where'er
We wander'd forth since vernal days begun—
  The glory and the garland of the year.
Ye came, the children of the spring's bright promise—
  Ye crown'd the summer in her path of light;
And now when autumn's wealth is passing from us,
  We gaze upon your parting boon, as bright
And dearer far than summer's richest hue—
    Sweet flowers, adieu!

You will return again; the early beams
 Of spring will wake ye from your wintry sleep,
By the still fountains and the shining streams,
 That through the green and leafy woodlands sweep;
Ye will return again, to cheer the bosoms
 Of the deep valleys, by old woods o'erhung,
With the fresh fragrance of your opening blossoms,
 To be the joy and treasure of the young—
With birds from the far lands, and sunny hours,
 Ye will return, sweet flowers.

But when will they return, our flowers that fell
 From life's blanch'd garland when its bloom was new
And left but the dim memories that dwell
 In silent hearts and homes? The summer's dew,
And summer's sun, with all their balm and brightness,
 May fall on deserts or on graves in vain;
But to the locks grown dim with early whiteness,
 What spring can give the sable back again,
Or to the early wither'd heart restore
 Its perish'd bloom once more?

In vain, in vain—years come and years depart—
 Time hath its changes, and the world its tears;
And we grow old in frame, and gray in heart—
 Seeking the grave through many hopes and fears
But still the ancient earth renews around us
 Her faded flowers, though life renews no more
The bright but early broken ties that bound us,
 The garlands that our blighted summers wore:
Birds to the trees, and blossoms to the bowers
 Return—but not life's flowers!

Thus sang the bard, when autumn's latest gold
 Hung on the woods, and summer's latest bloom
Was fading fast, as winter, stern and cold,
 Came from his northern home of clouds and gloom.

But from the dying flowers a voice seem'd breathing
  Of higher hopes; it whisper'd sweet and low—
"When spring again her sunny smile is wreathing,
  We will return to thee—but thou must go
To seek life's blighted blossoms on that shore
    Where flowers can fade no more!"

THE LAST OF THE JAGELLONS.

BY FRANCES BROWN.

"Oh, minstrel, wake thy harp once more,
  For winter's twilight falls,
And coldly dim it darkens o'er
  My lonely heart and halls:
But memories of my early home
  Around me gather fast—
For still with twilight shadows come
  The shadows of the past.

"Then wake thy lyre, my faithful bard,
  And breathe again for me
The songs that in my land was heard,
  While yet that land was free
The lays of old romantic times,
  When hearts and swords were true—
They will recall the dazzling dreams
  That youth and childhood knew."

Twas thus the noble matron spake
  To one whose tuneful strains
Could win her exiled spirit back
  To Poland's pleasant plains;
But how did memory's wizard-wand
  Far distant scenes portray,
As thus the minstrel of the land
  Awoke her lyre and lay:

The shout hath ceased in Volla's field,
But still its echoes ring
With the last thunder-burst that hail'd
Sarmatia's chosen king.
For young Jagellon now ascends
His father's ancient throne;
Yet still the chosen monarch stands
Uncrown'd—but not alone!

"A lovely form is by his side,
A hand is clasp'd in his,
That well might be a monarch's bride,
Even in an hour like this;
For never fairer form was seen
In saint's or poet's dreams,
Nor ever shone a nobler mein
In Poland's princely dames.

"Oh, many a princely dame is there,
And many a noble knight—
The flower of Poland's famed and fair—
The glory of her might.
But there is pride in every face,
And wrath in every tone,
As on that fair young brow, their gaze
Of gather'd scorn is thrown.

"There came an ancient senator,
With firm and stately tread,
And to the silent monarch there
In courtly phrase he said:
'The love that cannot grace a throne
A king should cast aside—
Then let Jagellon reign alone,
Or choose a royal bride.'

"The monarch yet more closely clasp'd
That small and snowy hand;
Then like a knightly warrior grasp'd
His own unrivall'd brand;

And from his dark eye flash'd the pride
  Of all his martial line,
As—'By my father's sword,' he cried,
  'Such choice shall ne'er be mine:

"'My land hath seen her ancient crown
  Bestow'd for many an age,
While other nations have bow'd down
  To kingly heritage;
And now the crown she freely gave,
  I render back as free;
For, if unshared by her I love,
  It shines no more for me.'

'He said—but from the throng arose,
  Ere yet his speech was done,
A wilder, louder cheer than those
  That told of conquests won—
When far in many a famous field,
  Through long, victorious years,
O'er Tartar bow and Paynim shield,
  He led the Polish spears.

"And thus they said, 'The flower whose worth
  Inspired a soul so great
With love like this, whate'er her birth,
  Should be a monarch's mate;
And as thy tameless heart was found
  To love and honor true—
Oh, early tried and far renowned,
  Be true to Poland, too!'"

The minstrel ceased, and with a sigh,
  That noble matron said—
"Alas, for Europe's chivalry—
  How hath its glory fled!
Perchance in sylvan grove or glen,
  Such faithful love is known,
But when will earth behold again
  Its truth so near a throne!"

THE SPECTRE OF THE HEARTH.

BY FRANCES BROWN.

Old Europe boasts of the broad low lands
She won from the western main;
But the wasting wave and the whelming sands
Are winning them back again:
Long and fierce is the war they wage
And the conquest groweth from age to age.

The song of the billows' sounding march,
Is heard where the anthem rose;
O'er sculptured column and stately arch
The dreary sand-hill grows,
And fills the waste of the sterile shore,
Where corn was bent by the breeze of yore.

No trace doth the bare, gray summit keep
Of buried spire or dome;
But still, 'tis said, where the drifted heap
Lies high o'er a peasant's home,
The place of the hearth may yet be known
To wanderers forth in the twilight lone.

For there, when stars through the deep'ning gray,
Shine far over wave and height,
Or their crests give back the ruddy ray
Of the hamlet-fires of night,
A spectre-woman pours her woe
O'er the cold and the quench'd of long ago.

Old is the tale—aye, old and strange
As the peasant's lore of dreams;
Yet how hath it kept through fear and change
That changeless truth, which seems,
In the power of its undecaying proof,
A golden thread in the rustic woof!

Are there not hearts—the worn, the wise—
  That ever in vain return
To some spot where their old love-memory lies,
  Though they only come to mourn
The dust and the debris piled between
Their souls and the rest they might have seen!

The sands! oh, the severing sands upflung
  By the world's wide sea of fears!
And the heart, in its toiling silence stung
  By the solitude of years!
And the lights that shine on its lonely ways,
At times, through the twilight-fall of days!

The winters wane, and the ruins grow
  With the wrecks of wave and mind;
But, oh! were the dust less deep below,
  And the stars above more kind,
How many a dream by the hearth might rest,
That now returns but a spectre guest.

THE LONELY MOTHER.

BY FRANCES BROWN.

My home is not what it hath been,
When the leaves of other years were green,
Though its hearth is bright and its chambers fair,
And the summer beams fall lightly there;
But they fall no more on the clear young eye,
  And the lip of pleasant song,
And the gleaming night that wont to lie
  On the curls so dark and long.

Oh, pleasant is the voice of youth,
For it tells of the heart's confiding truth
And keeps that free and fearless tone,
That ne'er to our after years is known:
I hear it rise in each hamlet-cot,
O'er evening prayer and page;
But woe for the hearth that heareth nought
But the dreary tones of age.

The glow is gone from our winter blaze,
And the light hath pass'd from our summer days;
And our dwelling hath no household now
But the sad of heart and the gray of brow.
For the young lies low 'neath the church-yard tree,
Where the grass grows green and wild;
And thy mother's heart is sad for thee,—
My lost, mine only child!

But a wakening music seems to flow
On me from the years of long ago,
As thy babe's first words come sweet and clear
Like a voice from thy childhood to mine ear
And her smile beams back on my soul again,
Thy beauty's early morn,
Ere thine eye grew dim with tears or pain,
Or thy lovely locks were shorn.

Alas! for the widow'd eyes that trace
Their early-lost in that orphan face;
What after-light will his memory mark,
Like the dove that in spring-time sought her ark
For long in that far and better land
Were her spirit's treasures laid;
And she might not stay from its golden strand
For the love of hearts that fade.

But woe for her on whose path may shine
The light of no mother's love but mine;
Oh, well if that lonely path lead on
To the land where her mother's steps have gone—

The land where the aged find their youth,
  And the young no whit'ning hair:
Oh! safe, my child, from both time and death—
  Let us hope to meet thee there.

THE FRIEND OF OUR DARKER DAYS.

BY FRANCES BROWN.

'Twas said, when the world was fresh and young,
  That the friends of earth were few;
And shrines have blazed, and harps have rung,
  For the hearts whose love was true!
And say, when the furrowing tracks of time
  Lie deep on the old earth's brow,
The faith so prized in her early prime—
  Shall we hope to find it now?

It may be found, like the aloe's bloom
  In the depth of western woods,
To which a hundred springs may come,
  Yet wake not its starry buds;
But if, through the mists of wintry skies,
  It shine on life's weary ways—
What star in the summer heavens will rise
  Like that friend of our darker days?

We know there are hands and smiles to greet
  Our steps on the summit fair;
But lone are the climber's weary feet,
  Where the steep lies bleak and bare.
For some have gain'd far heights and streams,
  To their sight with morning crown'd;
But the sunrise shed on their hearts' first dreams,
  And its light, they never found!

Yet, O for the bright isles seen afar,
  When our sails were first unfurl'd,
And the glance that once was the guiding star
  Of our green unwithered world!
And, O for the voice that spake in love,
  Ere we heard the cold world's praise;
And one gourd in our promised noon, to prove
  Like the friends of our darker days!

Alas! we have missed pure gems that lay
  Where the rock seemed stern and cold;
And our search hath found but the hidden clay,
  Where we dreamt of pure bright gold.
And dark is the night of changing years
  That falls on the trust of youth,
Till the thorns grow up and the tangled tares
  In the stronghold of its truth.

The shrines of our household gods, perchance
  We have seen their brightness wane;
And the love which the heart can give but once,
  It may be given in vain;
But still from the graves of better hopes—
  From the depths of memory's maze,
One blessing springs to the heart and lips,
  For the friend of our darker days.

WE ARE GROWING OLD.

BY FRANCES BROWN.

We are growing old—how the thought will rise
  When a glance is backward cast
On some long-remembered spot that lies
  In the silence of the past:
It may be the shrine of our early vows,
  Or the tomb of early tears;
But it seems like a far-off isle to us,
  In the stormy sea of years.

Oh! wide and wild are the waves that part
  Our steps from its greenness now·
And we miss the joy of many a heart,
  And the light of many a brow;
For deep o'er many a stately bark
  Have the whelming billows rolled,
That steered with us from that early mark—
  Oh! friends, we are growing old!

Old in the dimness and the dust
  Of our daily toils and cares,
Old in the wrecks of love and trust
  Which our burdened memory bears.
Each form may wear to the passing gaze,
  The bloom of life's freshness yet,
And beams may brighten our latter days,
  Which the morning never met.

But oh! the changes we have seen
  In the far and winding way—
The graves in our path that have grown green
  And the locks that have grown gray!
The winters still on our own may spare
  The sable or the gold;
But we saw their snows upon brighter hair—
  And, friends, we are growing old!

We have gain'd the world's cold wisdom now
  We have learn'd to pause and fear;
But where are the living founts, whose flow
  Was a joy of heart to hear?
We have won the wealth of many a clime,
  And the lore of many a page;
But where is the hope that saw in Time
  But its boundless heritage?

Will it come again when the violet wakes,
  And the woods their youth renew?
We have stood in the light of sunny brakes,
  Where the bloom was deep and blue;

And our souls might joy in the spring-time then,
  But the joy was faint and cold;
For it ne'er could give us the youth again
  Of hearts that are growing old.

SONGS OF OUR LAND.

BY FRANCES BROWN.

Songs of our land, ye are with us forever;
  The power and the splendor of thrones pass away
But yours is the might of some far-flowing river,
  Through summer's bright roses or autumn's decay.
Ye treasure each voice of the swift-passing ages,
  And truth, which Time writeth on leaves or on sand
Ye bring us the bright thoughts of poets and sages,
  And keep them among us, old songs of our land!

The bards may go down to the place of their slumbers,
  The lyre of the chamber be hushed in the grave;
But far in the future the power of their numbers
  Shall kindle the hearts of our faithful and brave.
It will waken an echo in souls deep and lonely,
  Like voices of reeds by the summer breeze fann'd;
It will call up a spirit for freedom, when only
  Her breathings are heard in the songs of our land!

For they keep a record of those, the true-hearted,
  Who fell with the cause they had vowed to maintain;
They show us bright shadows of glory departed,
  Of love that grew cold, and the hope that was vain.
The page may be lost, and the pen long forsaken,
  And weeds may grow wild o'er the brave heart and hand
But ye are still left, when all else hath been taken,
  Like streams in the desert, sweet songs of our land

Songs of our land, ye have followed the stranger,
  With power over ocean and desert afar;
Ye have gone with our wand'rers thro' distance and danger
  And gladden'd their path like a home-guiding star.
With the breath of our mountains in summers long vanish'd,
  And visions that passed like a wave from the sand,
With hope for their country and joy for her banish'd,
  Ye come to us ever, sweet songs of our land!

The spring-time may come with the song of her glory,
  To bid the green heart of the forest rejoice;
But the pine of the mountain, though blasted and hoary,
  And the rock in the desert, can send forth a voice.
It is thus in their triumph for deep desolations;
  While ocean waves roll, or the mountains shall stand
Still, hearts that are bravest and best of the nations
  Shall glory and live in the songs of their land!

www.ingramcontent.com/pod-product-compliance
Lightning Source LLC
LaVergne TN
LVHW020120110826
845151LV00001B/216

* 9 7 8 1 4 2 5 5 4 1 3 3 0 *